PENGU

ELECTRA

SOPHOCLES was born at Colonus, just outside Athens, around 496 BC, and lived for ninety years. His long life spanned the rise and decline of the Athenian Empire; he was a friend of Pericles, and, though not an active politician, he held several public offices, both military and civil. The leader of a literary circle and friend of Herodotus, Sophocles was interested in poetic theory as well as practice, and he wrote a prose treatise entitled *On the Chorus*. He seems to have been content to spend all his life at Athens and is said to have refused several invitations to royal courts.

Sophocles first won a prize for tragic drama in 468, defeating the veteran Aeschylus. He wrote over a hundred plays for the Athenian theatre and is said to have come first in twenty-four contests. Only seven of his tragedies are now extant, these being *Women of Trachis*, *Ajax*, *Antigone*, *Oedipus the King*, *Electra*, *Philoctetes* and the posthumous *Oedipus at Colonus*. A substantial part of *The Trackers*, a satyr-play, was recovered from papyri in Egypt in modern times. Fragments of other plays remain, showing that Sophocles drew on a wide range of themes; he also introduced the innovation of a third actor in his tragedies. He died in 406/5 BC.

DAVID RAEBURN was educated at Charterhouse and Christ Church, Oxford. He followed a career as a Classics teacher and as the headmaster of two schools. On retiring from the headship of Whitgift School in 1991, he returned to Oxford, where he taught Greek and Latin to undergraduates for the Classics faculty and later mainly at New College. His particular interest is in Greek tragedy and its performance aspects. He is known for his many productions with school and university students, mostly in the original but also in translations, including his own. Uniquely he has directed in all three of the century-old Greek Play traditions at Oxford, Cambridge and Bradfield College in Berkshire.

PAT EASTERLING was Regius Professor of Greek in Cambridge from 1994 until her retirement in 2001; before that she taught in Manchester, Cambridge and London (UCL). Her main field of research is Greek literature, particularly tragedy; she also has a special interest in the survival of ancient texts and the history of performance. Her most recent book is *Greek and Roman Actors: Aspects of an Ancient Profession* (2002), which she co-edited with Edith Hall. She is currently writing a commentary on Sophocles' *Oedipus at Colonus* for the Cambridge Greek and Latin Classics series, of which she is a general editor.

# SOPHOCLES

# Electra and Other Plays

## Women of Trachis
## Ajax
## Electra
## Philoctetes

*Translated and edited by* DAVID RAEBURN
*With an Introduction by* PAT EASTERLING

PENGUIN BOOKS

PENGUIN CLASSICS

Published by the Penguin Group
Penguin Books Ltd, 80 Strand, London WC2R ORL, England
Penguin Group (USA) Inc., 375 Hudson Street, New York, New York 10014, USA
Penguin Group (Canada), 90 Eglinton Avenue East, Suite 700, Toronto, Ontario, Canada M4P 2Y3
(a division of Pearson Penguin Canada Inc.)
Penguin Ireland, 25 St Stephen's Green, Dublin 2, Ireland (a division of Penguin Books Ltd)
Penguin Group (Australia), 250 Camberwell Road, Camberwell, Victoria 3124, Australia
(a division of Pearson Australia Group Pty Ltd)
Penguin Books India Pvt Ltd, 11 Community Centre, Panchsheel Park, New Delhi – 110 017, India
Penguin Group (NZ), 67 Apollo Drive, Rosedale, North Shore 0632, New Zealand
(a division of Pearson New Zealand Ltd)
Penguin Books (South Africa) (Pty) Ltd, 24 Sturdee Avenue, Rosebank, Johannesburg 2196, South Africa

Penguin Books Ltd, Registered Offices: 80 Strand, London WC2R ORL, England

www.penguin.com

This edition first published in Penguin Classics 2008

026

Translation, Prefaces and Notes copyright © David Raeburn, 2008
General Introduction, Chronology and Further Reading copyright © Pat Easterling, 2008
All rights reserved

The moral right of the translator and editor has been asserted

Set in 10.25/12.25pt PostScript Adobe Sabon
Typeset by Rowland Phototypesetting Ltd, Bury St Edmunds, Suffolk
Printed and bound in Great Britain by Clays Ltd, Elcograf S.p.A.

ISBN: 978-0-140-44978-5

Performance Rights:
All rights whatsoever in these plays are strictly reserved, and application for
performance, etc., should be made before rehearsals commence to:
Penguin Books Ltd, 80 Strand, London WC2R ORL

www.greenpenguin.co.uk

MIX
Paper | Supporting
responsible forestry
FSC® C018179

Penguin Books is committed to a sustainable
future for our business, our readers and our planet.
This book is made from Forest Stewardship
Council™ certified paper.

# Contents

# Preface

The first translations of Sophocles' seven extant tragedies to be published in Penguin Classics were by E. F. Watling, whose clear, flowing and very actable *Three Theban Plays* (1947) was followed by *Electra and Other Plays* (1953). The former was succeeded by the version of Robert Fagles (1984), complemented by Bernard Knox's introductions and notes, which were much more substantial than those in the earlier volume. This book is the second attempt to introduce the other four tragedies of Sophocles to the readers of this series.

During the last fifty years, public interest in the classical world generally and Greek tragedy in particular has grown apace. Translations and 'acting versions' of the plays have proliferated. The Archive of Modern Performance of Greek and Roman Drama at Oxford showed on its database no fewer than 1,715 professional or amateur productions of Sophocles' plays or their adaptations in various countries between 1953 and 2006, a period which has also seen the publication of several excellent new commentaries on individual tragedies and formidable critical writing on all. This volume represents a distillation of what I have learned from studying the texts in the original Greek, teaching most of them to students, reading some of the criticism and, importantly, directing three of the four plays in live performance. Although these texts can be usefully regarded and explored as socio-historical documents for the light they throw on the practices and values of ancient Athenian society, I see them, before all else, as works of art and masterpieces of world drama. It is principally in that light that I have tried to present them in my

translations and the supporting material. Indeed, I have given
my introductions to the separate plays the title of 'Preface',
in imitation of Harley Granville Barker, whose illuminating
*Prefaces to Shakespeare* (published between 1927 and 1947)
owed no more to his scholarship than to his experience in
directing Shakespeare's plays and his sense of the way they
'worked' in the theatre.

I have many to thank for their help in this challenging enterprise. I am grateful above all to Professor Pat Easterling, a world
authority on Sophocles and Greek tragedy generally, for her
comments on my prefaces and notes as they progressed, and for
the great compliment she paid me in agreeing to write the General
Introduction to this book. James Morwood gave me the benefit
of his knowledgeable and sympathetic reactions to both the translations and the other work. My wife, Mary Faith, not only
encouraged me in the project, but carefully read my early hand-
written drafts and identified many points for improvement in
expression and choice of imagery. I also owe much to my editor,
Peter Carson, for his valuable notes on points of detail in the
translation.

For my understanding of the text, I started, like all serious
students of Sophocles, from the great editions (recently republished) of the nineteenth-century scholar Sir Richard Jebb, whose
insights into the poet's language have been unsurpassed. For
detailed nuances I often profited from the commentaries of
J. Kamerbeek. On broader issues of interpretation, as well as
problems of text and language, I owe most to the edition of
*Trachiniae* by P. E. Easterling, and to those of W. B. Stanford
and A. F. Garvie on *Ajax*. Among the various critical works I
consulted, I found none to compare with R. P. Winnington-
Ingram's *Sophocles – An Interpretation* for its profound insights
based on a meticulous command of detail.

Finally, I have specially to acknowledge the indispensable
help given me by my former secretary, Pat Dawson-Taylor, who
typed out my manuscript drafts and then processed the innumer-
able changes that were needed as the work moved forward to
completion.

The book is dedicated to the many students in schools and

universities with whom I have read Greek tragedies in the original or who have taken part in my productions of these wonderful, time-enduring plays.

D.A.R.

# Chronology

Year BC
c.525/4 Birth of Aeschylus

508 Democracy established at Athens

c.496/5 Birth of Sophocles

490 Darius' invasion of Greece; Battle of Marathon
480 Xerxes' invasion of Greece; Battle of Salamis

472 Aeschylus, *Persians*
468 Sophocles' first drama prize

c.462 Radical democracy at Athens
460–445 Athens at war with Sparta and Persia

458 Aeschylus, *Oresteia*
456/5 Death of Aeschylus in Sicily
455 Euripides' first competition
443–442 Sophocles holds office as treasurer of Delian League
441–440 Sophocles serves as general

443 Pericles established as leading politician at Athens
440 Samian revolt from Athens
431 Peloponnesian War begins

430 Great Plague at Athens
429 Death of Pericles

428 Euripides, *Hippolytus*

421 Temporary peace
between Athens and Sparta
415–413 Sicilian expedition,
ending in disaster

413 Sophocles serves as
magistrate to deal with
crisis after Sicilian defeat

411 Oligarchic coup at
Athens
410 Restoration of democracy
at Athens

409 *Philoctetes*
406 Death of Euripides in
Macedonia
406/5 Death of Sophocles

405 Final defeat of Athens
404 Surrender of Athens,
installation of 'The Thirty'
backed by Sparta
403 Restoration of democracy

401 *Oedipus at Colonus*
produced posthumously

# General Introduction

Sophocles has been an unchallenged classic since his lifetime (496/5–406/5 BC) – one of very few great writers of whom this can be said. Seven tragedies out of his much larger output have survived complete; this small sample has had a profound influence on the history of drama and of Western cultural identity, and each play continues to have a distinctive life of its own, achieving its impact by many different means: through translation, adaptation, transmutation into different genres and – increasingly in modern times – through performance. Before we ask what gives these plays their extraordinary ability to have fresh meaning for new generations of readers and audiences, in times and places far different from Athens in the fifth century BC, it is worth starting with the beginning of Sophocles' story and setting him in the context of theatrical culture at Athens.

## SOPHOCLES IN CONTEXT

Sophocles was born into a well-to-do Athenian family of the Colonus district, at a time when the tradition of dramatic competitions was well established but still developing. This had rapidly become an important and very sophisticated feature of the city's life, and a great deal of time, effort and expense was devoted to performances at the major festival of Dionysus (the City Dionysia) in late March each year. The festival was an elaborately organized event lasting for several days, at which audiences could expect to see a series of competitions. There were contests between three sets of plays, each set composed of three tragedies and a satyr-play; between five comedies; and between two sets of ten dithyrambs, lyric performances by choruses of men and boys, each representing one of the tribes into which the citizen body was divided. All the plays had singing and dancing choruses, since 'drama' and 'music' were overlapping concepts. When Sophocles first competed in 468, his older contemporary Aeschylus had been active for around thirty years and had already made a decisive impact on tragedy as composer and performer; Sophocles at once showed his own formidable powers by winning first prize, though Aeschylus, placed second on this occasion, still had some famous victories to come.

In order to be allowed to compete at the festival, an aspiring dramatist needed to have achieved some reputation for dramatic talent, and it would be good to know where Sophocles had been given his early training and had found opportunities to try it out. One would like to think he belonged to a family with particular skills or interests in performance, but if there were older relatives already involved in composing and performing in plays, we know nothing of them. The only potentially significant thing we are told about Sophocles' early years is that 'naked and anointed with oil' he led with his lyre the group – presumably a boys' chorus – that danced and sang a paean at the celebrations after the Battle of Salamis in 480. This anecdote may have been preserved (or even invented) to make a link with the tradition that Sophocles himself took the part of Thamyras, and played the lyre, in his play about the great musician of legend who made the tragic mistake of competing with the Muses. For this early period, very little indeed can be reconstructed about the way in which a creative individual came to develop the extraordinary range of skills he needed in order to qualify as a tragic poet and compete at the festivals. The objective was not only to be able to compose four new verse plays, each with its elaborate patterns of song and dance (including energetic and playful lyrics for the chorus in their roles as satyrs in the final play), but also to direct the production and, in most cases, to take a series of leading roles himself. Somehow, by his late twenties Sophocles had mastered all these skills and was able to convince a demanding audience and the competition judges.

He went on composing plays for the next sixty or so years, last competing in 406, not long before his death. We have 123 known titles, but there could have been a few more that escaped the surviving records. The ancient sources tell a story of unalloyed success, crediting him with more victories than any of his contemporaries. These include eighteen first prizes (i.e. for seventy-two plays) at the City Dionysia and an uncertain number more at the lesser festival, the Lenaea, which from the 440s–430s onwards included tragic contests in its programme, but with sets of two plays rather than four. Sophocles may have lacked the kind of vocal powers needed by masked actors in large open-air theatres, and he fairly soon gave up acting in his own plays, but he seems to have found talented performers to work with him. As tragedy became ever more popular and spread to other venues, including festivals in the local districts of Attica and in other cities, the demand for highly trained actors evidently grew, and as early as 449 a prize was instituted for the best actor in each tragic competition. It would not be long before actors became independently organized professionals, but at this stage the most influential groups in the theatrical world of Athens were no doubt the dynasties of dramatists and performers such as the one founded by Aeschylus, whose son Euphorion and nephew Philocles were both famous as tragic poets, while his other son Euaeon was a noted actor (the family tradition continued, in fact, for three further generations). Sophocles' son Iophon and grandson Sophocles were active in the dramatic competitions, too, a pattern matched by several other families.

Sophocles must have been a charismatic personality: he seems to have been as well known for his prominence in Athenian public life and for his charm and wit as for his theatrical distinction, and by his later years he was something of a national treasure.[1] He held a number of offices, including serving as general along with Pericles in the Samian War, and he was prominent in some

of the city's cults, particularly in the establishment of the cult of
Asclepius, the healing god, at Athens around 420. So far as we
know, he stayed wedded to his home city: he does not seem to
have accepted invitations to travel to the courts of patrons, or to
compose plays for them – as Aeschylus did for Hiero, Tyrant of
Syracuse, or Euripides for King Archelaus of Macedon – and he
was often idealized along with Pericles, in antiquity and later, as
representing Athens at its most nobly impressive. This idealiz-
ation also underlay a tendency among the critics of antiquity to
contrast Sophocles favourably with the grand (and as he came to
seem) archaic Aeschylus on the one hand, and the newfangled
and undignified Euripides on the other, as 'the most perfect' of
the tragedians. It is a tidy simplification, owing a good deal to
Aristophanes' *Frogs*, in which the 'good-humoured' Sophocles
(82) is presented as serenely detached from the contest between
the other two for the seat of honour in Hades (786–94). Of
course, the reduction of Greek tragic poets, of whom there were
many, to the 'big three' is a vast simplification of the historical
situation, but it became canonical and decisively affected their
chances of survival.

The more attention we pay to the lost plays, the more varied
Sophocles' range appears, and against this background the
remark in chapter 33 of *On the Sublime* (a treatise of the Roman
period, traditionally attributed to Longinus) that Sophocles, like
Pindar, was one of the great poets whose work sometimes fell
miserably flat may seem less puzzling. The least admired experi-
ments no doubt fell out of the repertoire early, but there were
highly successful plays in their own time and after (*Niobe, Thyestes, Tereus, Andromeda*) which may have been less to the taste
of later centuries; ultimately, the most important criteria for
really long-term survival were adaptability to different times and
places and supposed suitability for educational purposes. Early
Christian and Byzantine schools followed the example of their
pagan predecessors in making their pupils study the poetry of
the past as a way of acquiring Greek culture, and portions of
Homer, some tragedies, plays by Aristophanes, and works by

Pindar and Hesiod kept their place in the curriculum, a remarkable fact considering that such authors could have been dismissed as downright dangerous for a Christian education.

Of the seven plays of Sophocles that have survived in the continuous tradition, all must have been well known and in demand over a long period; we still have the (much-reduced) remains of what commentators wrote about them from the Hellenistic period to late antiquity. From these notes, particularly on *Ajax*, the play most often read, studied and quoted through the Byzantine period, the Renaissance and beyond,[2] we can trace how the plays were interpreted for students, with great attention paid to what was ethically instructive and appealed to humane values, especially sentiments expressed in memorably pointed verse.

## PLAYS SURVIVING AND LOST

For an author who made so strong an impression on the audiences of his time, the chronological evidence, dependent on the chance survival of inscriptions or relevant notes by ancient scholars, is disappointingly slim. Those sixty years when Sophocles was a leading figure in the dramatic competitions yield only a couple of secure dates to which we can attach names of plays: 468 for his first victory with the lost *Triptolemus* and three other unknown titles, and 409, when he was victorious with *Philoctetes* (again, no doubt, part of a set of four); his *Oedipus at Colonus* was posthumously staged by his grandson in 401. This leaves the surviving *Ajax, Antigone, Women of Trachis, Oedipus the King* and *Electra* without firm dates; many scholars would put them roughly in this order, with none of them staged earlier than the 450s, and *Electra* perhaps only a few years before *Philoctetes*, but this leaves plenty of scope for radical disagreement, and among the plays in this volume David Raeburn has chosen to deal first with *Women of Trachis*. The last two, *Electra* and *Philoctetes*, show signs of formal experiment with the choral parts, perhaps in response to more general changes in performance style: both make much use of lyric exchanges

between actors and chorus, and *Philoctetes* has only one act-
dividing choral ode. With so little really hard information, it is
impossible to tell a confident story of Sophocles' overall 'development', and we can only guess, from trying to evaluate the fragments of the lost plays, how closely the seven that we have reflect
the original oeuvre. But at least it is worth trying to identify some
of the main qualities that they all share.

One thing that stands out sharply is Sophocles' strong interest in
the theatrical effect of a single, free-standing play, detached from
the complex thematic threads of Aeschylus' favoured pattern, a
trilogy following the fortunes of a single family over generations,
or even a tetralogy, if the satyr-play drew on stories associated
with the main tragic characters. It may not actually have been
Sophocles' innovation to make the normal unit a single play
enclosing the whole dramatic happening within the short space
of about 1,500 lines (Aeschylus, after all, had put on three uncon-
nected plays along with *Persians* in 472), but what evidently
mattered most to him was to achieve an effect of powerful concentration. His plot-lines are almost ruthless in their selective
handling of particular myths, and although there are often long
debates, in which ideas are developed with great rhetorical brio,
and detailed narratives, in which past events, and events happening elsewhere, are brought vividly into the action, there is usually
a remarkable intensity of focus. This gives plenty of cues to actors
for the shaping of their lines, in language that at the same time
contrives to open up depths and ambiguities of motivation.

The plays typically start at, or just before, 'zero hour', as in
*Antigone*, where Creon has already forbidden the burial of Poly-
neices, or in *Oedipus the King*, where the plague at Thebes has
reached the point of crisis, and Oedipus is waiting for news from
Delphi. In *Women of Trachis*, the critical moment of danger for
Heracles, foretold by the oracle, has just arrived; in *Ajax*, the
hero has already been driven mad and killed the cattle, mistaking
them for his intended victims, his comrades; in *Electra*, Orestes
is already back in Argos intent on vengeance; in *Philoctetes*,
Odysseus and Neoptolemus have already landed on Lemnos, to

fetch Philoctetes back to Troy. The effect is to create an immediate sense of urgency and, often, of inevitability. Events seem to be
taking their inexorable course, but in a pattern that paradoxically
puts the emphasis on the choices that the individuals caught in
these extreme situations are forced to face.

In all the plays that survive, there is a very strong concern to
engage audiences with the characters' inner thoughts and feelings: this is more subtle than a preoccupation with 'character
portrayal' for its own sake, and is achieved through small details
of language, or through gaps left for the actor or reader to fill.
We can take our cue sometimes from the questions posed by the
speakers of the text: Neoptolemus' repeated 'What can I do?' in
*Philoctetes* points up the moral problem that faces him in using
trickery to deceive a comrade, and at the same time encourages
the audience to wonder about his motives and his feelings
towards both Philoctetes and Odysseus. When the chorus leader
in *Women of Trachis* asks the departing Deïanira, 'Going without
a word? You surely know your silence argues your accuser's case'
(813–14), there is no reply from her, but it is a good question
for the audience at that moment, when they must fear that she is
on her way to suicide.

In Sophocles, as in most surviving Greek tragedy, there are scenes
of extensive argument, with urgent articulation of the social,
political and moral issues that underlie the conflicts driving the
plots. But despite giving so much emphasis to the issues, and
using the types of rhetoric familiar from the democratic assembly
and the law courts, the plays do not offer solutions: exposing
and exploring the uncomfortable questions seem to be much
more important than answering them. *Electra* and *Philoctetes*
are particularly stark examples of dialectical plays in which irre-
concilable positions are argued with great finesse, but the history
of interpretation and reception suggests that there is no consensus
on the 'right' evaluation of what happens. The matricide in
*Electra* continues to be fiercely debated after two-and-a-half
millennia, as does the double ending of *Philoctetes*, forcing us to
decide which we are to take more seriously, Philoctetes' refusal

to return to Troy and help the comrades who have abandoned him, or the 'solution' imposed by Heracles, giving voice to the divine will that requires him to obey.

The presence of the gods and their involvement in human affairs are always taken as given in the plays, which is not surprising in view of the resilience of Greek polytheistic culture and the fact that gods were everywhere both in the lives of cities and in the earlier poetic tradition. But they are treated with remarkable obliqueness, not made to offer intelligible explanations for the way things happen or the way people behave. Athena's role in *Ajax*, for example, has been very variously explained: here is the city goddess of Athens presenting the maddened Ajax (one of the revered tribal heroes of the Athenian audience) for Odysseus to gloat over, and identifying him as an offender against the gods (127–30), but later we are told that her anger against Ajax for his past acts of disrespect will last one day only (756–7), which makes the situation far harder to evaluate. When Odysseus persuades Agamemnon to allow the dead Ajax an honorific burial, there are clear intimations that this looks forward to his cult at Athens.[3] So is the goddess truly hostile, or has she saved Ajax from irretrievable disaster, so that his posthumous power will work for her city? Neither question turns out to be helpful; just as with oracles that impinge enigmatically on human decision-making, the focus is always on what the human beings do with the divine messages, not on the motivation of their sources.

A similar argument applies to fate, which characters often look to as a way of explaining their predicament. There is nothing to be gained from seeing these tragic figures as marionettes manipulated by some cosmic power, and even in plays which make such insistent use of oracles mapping out the future as *Oedipus the King* or *Women of Trachis*, it remains true, as Rush Rehm puts it, that 'human limits are the basis of what freedom we have.'[4] Similarly the idea of a family curse, prominent in the Theban plays and hovering in the background in *Electra*, is not used as an essential key to the understanding of the action, although it can serve as an image for compulsions which individuals feel are driving them or which observers detect in their behaviour.[5] Necessity, after all, however figured, is a valuable component in many stories and dramatic plots, and Sophocles makes creative use of it. One example is the way some of his endings seem designed to link the events just witnessed in the tragedy to the realities of the community's religious and civic experience through stage action, especially song and movement evocative of shared ritual, as in the processions at the end of both *Women of Trachis* and *Ajax*, which seem to foreshadow the honouring of the dead heroes in cult. But these are glancing references at the ends of plays, where there is a place for reminding the audience of their own time and institutions in a particularly pointed way.

More pervasive throughout is the implicit bridging of past and present, which makes the Sophoclean imaginary world so freely accessible to readers and audiences of different times and places. In keeping with contemporary tragic practice, Sophocles set his stories in the (mainly Greek) past as it was known from the great body of inherited oral poetry and storytelling that had enabled tragedy to establish itself so rapidly as an authoritative genre.[6] The plays are full of glimpses of the landscape inhabited by the subjects of the stories, intimately known to the people in the audience by its natural features, its buildings, cults and traditions, whether at first hand or through familiar poetry. It is through this linking of past and present, with the characters from long ago set in a sharply realized 'now', that some of the richest effects are achieved. In *Women of Trachis* there is vivid evocation of the area around Thermopylae dominated by the heights of Mt Oeta, and the sacred precinct on the island of Euboea across the strait, where Heracles is trapped in the poisoned robe; *Electra* opens with the old slave pointing out to Orestes the famous landmarks of Argos, including 'Mycenae, rich in gold' and the palace of Orestes' forebears 'rich in blood' (9–10); in *Philoctetes* the hero's farewell to the desolate island suggests both an identifiable landscape and an image of his lonely suffering.

In all these cases, the choice of language is crucial: often it is through a Homeric echo or an unusual lyric expression that a passage gains its distinctiveness and is able to work in symbolic and literal terms at the same time. Sometimes it is a contemporary political or intellectual resonance that creates the sense of 'relevance', but the point is neither to create antiquarian pastiche nor to shock with anachronistic juxtaposition. The effect of this understated but pervasive use of multiple associations is to bring the action urgently close while still holding it at some sort of bearable distance: the plots themselves deal with extremes of horror, anguish, sorrow and pain, but the plays are not revolting, and their paradoxical impact is best described as one of tragic pleasure.[7]

# WOMEN OF TRACHIS, AJAX, ELECTRA, PHILOCTETES

The four plays in this volume are sometimes characterized for convenience as the 'non-Theban' plays, which is at best an unhelpful way to think about them. Looking for more constructive ways of grouping them may help to illustrate Sophocles' range and, at the same time, to bring out their complex relation to other plays in the tragic corpus (though if we had more tragedies surviving, the links would certainly be more complex still). The importance of interaction between dramatists who worked in close rivalry and often, no doubt, in artistic comradeship cannot be overemphasized, especially as they could rely on audiences attuned to watching, comparing and evaluating their work at the same annual festivals. It is our misfortune, so many centuries later, to see them in artificial isolation.

## Women of Trachis

This is the only play of the four collected here whose plot does not deal with the aftermath of the Trojan War and – unlike the Oedipus plays and Antigone – it does not relate to the Theban epics either, but draws on some of the many traditions about the monster-killer Heracles, long celebrated in poetry as the most

xxii                    GENERAL INTRODUCTION

spectacularly heroic warrior, on the grandest and sometimes the most destructive scale, of all the Greeks remembered in legend and cult.[8] It tells of events leading to Heracles' agonizing death, according to a pattern that has seemed to many scholars to play a variation on the famous central event of Aeschylus' *Agamemnon*: Clytemnestra's murder of her husband on his triumphant return from Troy. If this is correct, we at least have a date, 458 BC, when the *Oresteia* was staged, before which the play cannot have been composed, but that leaves a period of approximately thirty years during which it could plausibly have been put on. Unlike *Agamemnon*, this is a play without a significant city setting, and the death of Heracles, evidently momentous for its panhellenic meaning, carries none of the political implications of the killing of the King of Argos: Deïanira and Heracles have been living in exile in Trachis (though Heracles has been on his travels most of the time), and the chorus consists of inexperienced young girls of the locality, not elderly men with a strong sense of their city's history and identity.

Like *Ajax*, *Women of Trachis* deals with the death of a great man, but whereas in *Ajax* it is the suffering public figure who gets the best lines, the first three-quarters of this play view events through the perceptions and motivation of his wife Deïanira, revealing her anxiety for her absent husband, then her pity for his captives, including the princess Iole, whose city he has destroyed and whom he now brings home as his trophy. Deïanira's despair when she learns that she is to be ousted by Iole prompts her to make the secret plan – painstakingly shared with the chorus and audience – which turns into the most disastrous possible mistake. Deïanira understands the power of passion, over herself as well as her husband, but she lets her longing to recapture Heracles overwhelm her judgement. Only too late does she recognize that the 'love-charm' given her by the dying centaur Nessus really carries poison from Heracles' arrows, when the welcoming gift she has prepared, a ceremonial robe smeared with the imagined charm, clings destructively to his body, melting in the heat of the fire as he burns animal victims in a great sacrifice. This is a short play, but its structure makes Heracles' dying an agonizingly slow-motion sequence: first Deïanira has to listen to their son's outraged narrative of his suffering, which precipitates her suicide, and only then is Heracles carried in, not dead, but aroused to spasms of pain, mingled with furious rage when he learns that it was his wife who sent the poisoned robe.

When Heracles finally understands that he is dying, the word that clinches his understanding is *Nessus*, just as Oedipus' memory is suddenly stirred by the mention of the place 'where three roads meet' and he fears for the first time that he may be the killer of King Laius.[9] Heracles now knows how he should have understood Zeus' oracle of long ago, and gives orders that he is to be carried to the mountain top and his still-living body burned on a pyre. There seems to be some significant, though unexplained, meaning in these final dispensations, linked, no doubt, for contemporary audiences with the fact that there was a prominent cult of Heracles on the top of Mt Oeta. But his brutal instructions to his son Hyllus and his failure to show any sorrow for his wife have often struck readers and critics as untypical of their notion of 'the Sophoclean hero'. It is better to admit that we have a very limited knowledge of what was typical of Sophocles' whole tragic range and to take each play on its own terms. Heracles was in any case an extraordinary hero, about whom multiple and not always consistent stories were told (in Euripides' *Heracles* the theme is the divinely inspired homicidal madness that made him the killer of his wife Megara and her children; he was also a rollicking figure in comedy and satyr-play). One tradition that certainly became well known in the latter part of the fifth century was the notion that he was not merely destined for status as a cult hero, but taken up to heaven from the top of Mt Oeta to join the Olympians,[10] and his command to Hyllus that he should marry Iole (1221–8), which for Hyllus is outrageously horrifying, might have had a different significance for audiences who knew the pair as the revered ancestors of Heracles' descendants. But the play ends in sorrow and bafflement, with Hyllus denouncing the gods for their cruelty towards Heracles: '. . . the hearts of the callous gods / Feel nothing in all these sorry events. / They beget their sons and are called our fathers, / Yet look down calmly on our great pain' (1266-9). If the final words of the play, ending 'And all this story is great Zeus' are to be spoken, as many scholars believe, by the chorus and not by Hyllus, there may be a final glancing hint that the audience's view could be different from his.

The play pays close attention to the chain of causation and to the way in which Heracles' own actions are implicated in all the horror that he has to suffer, set ironically against the universal expectation that, as a son of Zeus, he will be given special protection by his father: after all, he has already survived more ordeals than anyone else in the world. The irony is deepened by the fact that oracles at Zeus' ancient shrine of Dodona had given Heracles what looked like reliable outlines of his future, but the ambiguity of the evidence (as in *Oedipus the King*), and the violence of the poison that consumes him, make the decoding of the truth excruciatingly difficult for the characters caught up in the action.

If there are features of *Women of Trachis* that link it with *Oedipus the King* and *Ajax*, its enactment of extreme physical pain can be compared with a similar scene in *Philoctetes*. But closer still is Euripides' *Hippolytus* (staged in 428 BC) with its similar interlocking structure, its motif of overpowering sexual passion, and its monstrous and highly symbolic beast, the bull from the sea, which parallels the monsters – the river god Achelous, the Hydra, Nessus – prominent in *Women of Trachis*. There is a culminating scene of dying agony in both plays, and each must have derived some of its intense theatrical power from the fact that two major contrasting, but interconnected, roles were played by the same lead actor, Deïanira and Heracles in *Women of Trachis*, Phaedra and Theseus in *Hippolytus*.[11] The implication of these parallels is that *Women of Trachis* is not a Sophoclean oddity, as critics at one time were tempted to think, but a play in the mainstream of his creative output, and if his *Phaedra* had survived in more than a few fragments, there might be further evidence in support of this approach.

## Ajax

In terms of the choice of story, *Ajax* falls well within one of the dominant types of tragic plot material: traditions about the aftermath of the Trojan War, in this case Odysseus' victory in the famous contest for the arms of Achilles, which drove Ajax into a homicidal rage against his comrades, averted in the most drastic manner by his mad killing of cattle, and leading finally to his suicide. The episode was well known from the post-Homeric epic poems that filled out the story of Troy, particularly the *Little Iliad*;[12] it had also been dramatized by Aeschylus in a trilogy, which began with the contest itself (*Judgement of the Arms*); continued with the suicide, as reported by a messenger (*Thracian Women*); and ended with what happened after Ajax's death, when his brother Teucer and son Eurysaces returned to Salamis, and Teucer was sent into exile by his father as a punishment for coming back without Ajax (*Women of Salamis*). For some, perhaps many, of Sophocles' first spectators, these wider resonances of the story, and its links through Ajax's family with Attic traditions, would have provided a context or background for their reception of his play. The action is set in the Greek camp on the beachhead at Troy, but the chorus of Salaminian sailors bring the Attic landscape vividly into the imaginary world when they sing of their longing '. . . to sail home and to pass the headland . . . That washes the shore beneath / Sunium's lofty heights' (1216–21).

In *Ajax* the events are extraordinarily condensed, opening with a sinister little scene staged by Athena, who displays the mad Ajax for the benefit of her protégé Odysseus. This use of a divine figure to set up – and comment on – the action is unique among Sophocles' surviving plays, but may well have had a parallel of some sort in (for example) his lost *Niobe*, in a scene where Apollo seems to be giving instructions to Artemis to shoot Niobe's daughters; its possibilities are explored in typically creative ways by Euripides in such plays as *Trojan Women* and *Heracles*. Athena introduces a moral perspective by treating Ajax as an object lesson for Odysseus ('You see, Odysseus, the gods can be so strong!' (118)), but Odysseus challenges her invitation to exult over a humiliated enemy ('. . . But, enemy though he be, / I'm bound to pity him none the less, poor man!' (121–2)), and the sight of Ajax on stage amid the slaughtered cattle arouses horror, pity and increasing alarm on the part of his dependants, as it becomes clear that what he had been trying to do was to murder his comrades. His own reaction is intense shame that he has so grotesquely missed his intended target, shame which inexorably leads to his suicide. For his concubine Tecmessa and his sailors, the inexorability is less clear than for the audience, and even they may begin to wonder if he has changed his mind when he talks of burying his sword: 'I'll find a place untrodden by human foot / And dig a hole to bury this sword of mine, / This hatefullest of weapons, where none can see it' (657–9). There is intense dramatic focus on what Ajax 'really' intends – is he deliberately deceiving his friends, or are they misunderstanding his words, and while still intending suicide, has he grasped something about his situation that he did not know before? But his unapologetic soliloquy before he falls on his sword (so effected in the stage action, evidently, that the audience believe they witness it (see p. 274, n. 61) leaves these questions unresolved, and the rest of the play grapples with the problem of how the corpse of the unrepentant Ajax should be treated: with honour, or with the ultimate disgrace of exposure.

As in *Antigone*, the issue is deeply political and must have had easily recognizable relevance to contemporary situations.[13] The tense debates and angry insults that follow, between Teucer as Ajax's champion and the hostile Menelaus and Agamemnon, are ultimately bypassed by the intervention of Odysseus, and a dignified funeral procession takes the place of what might have been a desperate and furtive attempt to rescue the dead Ajax. The stage presence of his corpse has unexpectedly taken on something of the hallowed nature of a hero's burial place, and the final procession is best understood as prefiguring both the fame in antiquity of Ajax's tomb at the Hellespont and – more pointedly – his status as one of the ten tribal heroes at Athens, with a festival, the Aianteia, celebrated at Salamis to commemorate the great naval victory in 480 BC, and a well-established cult, too, of his son Eurysaces.[14] This does not mean that Ajax has been 'justified', or the problematic nature of what he has done wiped away: the story remains one of a great fighting man whose career ends in disaster. But it gains meaning from the imagining of what it feels like to be such a man – in madness and in sanity – or one of his nearest and dearest in this dire emergency, and by his being given one of the most profound speeches in Sophocles (646–92), on the working of time and change in human experience. This is closely echoed, and its significance reaffirmed, in a much later play, *Oedipus at Colonus*, when the aged Oedipus passes on to Theseus the similar lessons he has learned (607–28). Much depends on the ease with which the play can move between local, contemporary preoccupations at Athens and a 'timeless' evocation of the poetic world of epic and earlier tragedy, intensified by the recurrent association between Ajax and the Hector of the *Iliad*, particularly in the scene of Ajax with Tecmessa and their child, with its poignant but also enigmatic echo of Hector and Andromache with Astyanax on the walls of Troy in Book 6 and in the reminder (at 658–65 and 817–18) that the sword of Ajax, the play's most significant stage property, was a gift to him from Hector after a famous duel.

## Electra

Like *Ajax*, *Electra* relates to a familiar Aeschylean treatment of the story it dramatizes,[15] and as in *Ajax* a single episode becomes the focus of intense concentration – in this case Orestes' return, years after the killing of his father, to take vengeance with his sister's help on his mother and Aegisthus. Aeschylus' handling of this event in *Libation Bearers*, the second play of the *Oresteia* (458 BC), was clearly a benchmark that no later dramatist could ignore; several decades later, probably some time between 420 and 410, both Sophocles and Euripides made explicit use of it to offer new, and for contemporaries no doubt strikingly modern, explorations of the well-known plot, each replacing Orestes by Electra as the part to be played by the protagonist. Which of the two new *Electra* plays came first is not known; they certainly relate closely to one another, in ways that suggest that their audiences appreciated such interplay between different treatments of the same model and different responses to the same issues. More important than the question of relative dating is the interplay itself; a couple of examples will illustrate some of the many levels on which it operates.

One of the most famous stage pictures from *Libation Bearers* is the scene early in the play where Electra and the women of the chorus (who carry drink-offerings sent by Clytemnestra to the tomb of Agamemnon) discuss the proper prayers to accompany these libations. Guided by the women, Electra prays, as she pours the offerings, for vengeance on her father's murderers, rather than the appeasement that her mother had hoped for, and the scene culminates in her discovery of a lock of hair left at the tomb by Orestes, which is soon followed by her reunion with Orestes himself. Both Sophocles and Euripides make the recognition happen much later in the action and in more problematic circumstances, but each play has Electra with an urn at a significant point in the action. In Euripides it is a humble water-pot which she carries on her head like a slave-girl – a token of the poverty she lives in with her peasant husband, and perhaps of the distance between her world and that of earlier tragic heroines. In Sophocles it is the bronze funerary urn supposedly holding Orestes' ashes, the visible sign of the deception that dominates the play, and in its emptiness the symbol of all that Electra has lost.

The seeds sown by *Libation Bearers* can be seen bearing fruit in another example, particularly important for Sophocles' version of the story. Two passages in Aeschylus' play use the idea of chariot-racing in relation to Orestes: the first at 794–9, when the chorus, praying for success in the act of vengeance, compares Orestes to a young horse drawing a chariot (794–9),[16] and the second, even more tellingly, when – after he has killed his mother and feels madness coming upon him – he describes himself as like a charioteer being driven off course (1021–3). There are important moments in Euripides' *Electra* when Orestes is thought of as a victor in the games, crowned with garlands, in grim contrast to the horrible reality of the killings, but in Sophocles the image gives shape to the whole play. Right from the start, Orestes talks like a charioteer: he sees the old slave who has brought him back to Mycenae as a loyal thoroughbred, still full of mettle (24–8), and his plan of revenge (47–58) is built on the idea of his death in a racing accident at the Pythian games. The old man later tells the story with virtuoso elaboration in a heart-rending speech at 680–763, making Electra as well as Clytemnestra a victim of the deception, which is still at work when Aegisthus comes to gloat over Orestes' supposed death (1442–4).

At the same time, the image of the chariot race makes an essential link with the chain of evils, and of revenge for evils, inherited by the family of Agamemnon: 'When Pelops in past ages / Won the race with his chariot, / What never-ending sorrow / Struck this land! / When Myrtilus, his helper, / Was drowned beneath the ocean / Tossed headlong from his chariot, / . . . Since that day, / This palace has been haunted / By suffering and anguish' (504–15). The story goes back to the time of Agamemnon's grandfather Pelops, who was doubly deceitful, outdistancing Oenomaus by bribing his charioteer Myrtilus to tamper with the axle-pins and later drowning the charioteer, which in some versions earned him and his family a lasting curse.[17] There were many grim episodes in the history of the house of Pelops to choose from, particularly the conflict between Atreus and Thyestes in the next generation, and the Myrtilus story gets no mention in *Libation Bearers* or Euripides' *Electra*, but for Sophocles in this play the race seems to have been the dominant image for rivalry, deceit, and glory turning into disaster. For many readers, such dark associations are balanced by the portrayal of Electra as the most morally sensitive, eloquent and sympathetic figure in the play; like Antigone or Ajax, it is she who gets the best poetry, suffers most keenly, and expresses the play's most intense insights. Even so, there is something spine-chilling in the way she stage-manages the killing of Clytemnestra and torments Aegisthus with the final act of deception: the presentation of Clytemnestra's corpse masquerading as that of the dead Orestes.

*Electra* is perhaps the paradigm case of a brilliantly designed drama which evenly balances the issues of conflicting loyalties, using every possible means of engaging the audience in the contradictory emotions of revenge. The play's concentration on the stark issue of the rights and wrongs of kin-killing is intensified by its elimination of the politics of the city – the house and not the city is at the imaginative centre of the action – and by the fact that the divine level of causation remains completely enigmatic. *Electra* does not ignore Apollo's oracle, and characters within the play pray to him at significant moments, but his involvement in the action is neither examined nor challenged. Even less than Zeus in *Women of Trachis*, or Athena in *Ajax*, is Apollo in this play allowed to function as an interpreter, which may be one reason why Electra has been so open to different readings and stagings in later times, many of them overtly political.[18]

## *Philoctetes*

There are many ways in which this play, securely dated to 409 BC, recalls *Electra*, not only in formal features such as its handling of the choral element, but in the use of deception as the main dynamic of the action, in the urgency of the moral debate that this prompts and in the absence for most of the play of anything but the most distant divine causation. But then there is a surprise ending, when the deified Heracles takes on the role of 'god from the machine' and overturns the agreement just made between Neoptolemus and Philoctetes (that Philoctetes will not after all go back to Troy to help the Greeks, after they had abandoned him so shamefully years ago, and Neoptolemus will take him home, though at the cost of his remaining unhealed). This has often been seen as Sophocles late in his career taking cues from Euripides, who uses the device to reorder the direction of action which seems to have strayed too far from any version of the story as traditionally told (as in *Helen* or *Orestes*), but it is not out of the question that Sophocles had used the deus ex machina elsewhere, and the double ending he achieves by using it here turns out to be a powerful way of leaving interpretation open, engaging audiences or readers in the dilemmas with which the characters have been trying to deal all through the play.

Contemporaries must have set this treatment of Philoctetes in the context of other versions they had seen in the theatre, all drawing on the epic stories that gave the tragedians their main source material. Both Aeschylus and Euripides had dramatized the story of the wounded Philoctetes' exile on Lemnos and the Greeks' attempt to induce him back to Troy, and (although the dates are unknown) Sophocles himself wrote a play about Philoctetes at Troy – the healing of his diseased foot, his killing of Paris – as did another of his fellow-dramatists, Achaeus, much admired in his own time and later. So far as we can tell, the main new moves made by Sophocles in this play were to turn Lemnos into a desert island, despite its well-known history as an inhabited place from the *Iliad* onwards, and to introduce Neoptolemus, son of Achilles, as a member of the mission to fetch Philoctetes. (In the epic tradition, only Diomedes figured; Aeschylus replaced him with Odysseus, and Euripides sent both.)

It was a bold step to make Lemnos deserted, but it gave Sophocles a dominant image for the play: the wild surroundings, with only wild creatures for company and sustenance, are a kind of analogue for Philoctetes himself, cut off from all the ordinary benefits of life in a community. He has survived, despite the continuing horror of his disease – it had been the stench from his wounded foot and his cries of agony nine years before that had made his comrades abandon him – and his only resources have been a cave for shelter and wild prey to eat, shot with the great bow given by Heracles to his heroic father. Philoctetes' sense of betrayal by his comrades is so great that any suggestion of his rejoining or helping them looks bound to fail.

By introducing a young and untried son of a famous father with the task of taking part in an elaborate trick on Philoctetes, Sophocles gives the story a new focus, making Neoptolemus' attitude to the deception central to the action, his longing for glory balanced, but at last outweighed, by his pity for the suffering Philoctetes. The effect is to throw the interaction between Neoptolemus and the two older men into relief: when he tries to carry out his orders from Odysseus ('. . . [y]ou can be as rude as you like / About *me*. I shan't take it amiss' (65–6)) and deceive Philoctetes into thinking he is being taken home, it is never quite clear how much of what he says about himself and Odysseus is truly meant and how much is lies inspired by his eagerness to succeed. Each reader or spectator must try to imagine the feelings and motives behind Neoptolemus' words, and, just as his sincerity is always at issue, so is the working of Odysseus' supplementary plan, when he sends a crew member disguised as a passing trader to move the action along. The latter's false story, functioning rather like a play within a play, exquisitely complicates the situation. He quotes a prophecy that Philoctetes must be brought back by persuasion, and reports Odysseus saying he will try, but will use force if persuasion fails; the spectator must wonder whether this is a true report of the prophecy and therefore crucial for the action, or yet another trick, and in any case wonder at what kind of effect the message is having on Neoptolemus' sense of what he is doing.[19]

The artfulness of such scenes recalls the use of deception and intrigue in *Electra*, and in both plays a highly self-referential technique seems to be at work, drawing attention to the fictiveness of drama itself, reminding the audience that they are in the present as they watch 'past' events unfold, but none the less challenging them to empathize with the characters and engage with their dilemmas. In *Philoctetes*, composed so soon after the oligarchic coup at Athens in 411, it is easy to see the play's intense scrutiny of ends and means, and its arguments about values, weighing communal utility against compassion for individuals, as echoing contemporary political debates at a time of great collective unease and disillusionment, but the remote setting makes the action emblematic rather than pointedly topical. The desert-island scenery, and the fact that the chorus is made up of Neoptolemus' loyal crew rather than local citizens, lift the play out of a too immediately recognizable context and make it one that can be used to reach out to the needs of audiences of different times and places.

The problems posed by the ending have been endlessly debated: should Philoctetes yield to persuasion after all the wrongs he has suffered; is the cause of the Greeks at Troy worth fighting for anyway; do the heroic values represented by Heracles mean anything in a politically corrupt society? Much depends on the effect of the scene in which Philoctetes suffers paroxysms of pain (730–826) and on the fact that healing is promised for him at Troy: if this healing can serve as an image for integration and reconciliation, is it something to wish for, even in an imperfect world?[20] This must have been one of the thoughts that prompted Seamus Heaney to adopt *The Cure at Troy* for the title of his translation/adaptation inspired by the events in Northern Ireland – a distinguished example of the continuing appeal of Sophocles' plays for modern writers.

David Raeburn's translations owe much to his own deep practical interest in Greek plays, particularly tragedy, as scripts for performance as well as texts on the page. His long experience as a teacher and director has helped him achieve his ambitious goal: to make a precise rendering of the Greek that will capture the variety of its rhythms and help anyone who reads it, or hears it performed, to sense the intensity, economy and artistry of Sophocles' compositions.

# NOTES

1. In Book 1 of the *Republic* (329b–d), Plato makes the aged Cephalus recall a conversation with Sophocles when he was an old man, about his relief at being liberated from the tyranny of sexual passion, in terms that evoke both his authority and his quotability. Fragments of the memoirs of Ion of Chios, Sophocles' friend and fellow-dramatist, paint a similar picture.
2. *Electra* and *Oedipus the King* were the next most commonly studied plays in the Byzantine period.

3. See A. Henrichs, 'The Tomb of Aias and the Prospect of Hero Cult in Sophokles', *Classical Antiquity* 12 (1993), pp. 165–80; J. Hesk, *Sophocles: Ajax* (London 2003), pp. 17–24.

4. In *Radical Theatre: Greek Tragedy and the Modern World* (London 2003), pp. 69, 86.

5. As at *Antigone* 583–603, 853–71; *Oedipus at Colonus* 1383–96, 1432–4.

6. For the background, see Richard Buxton, *Imaginary Greece* (Cambridge 1994).

7. See A. D. Nuttall, *Why Does Tragedy Give Pleasure?* (Oxford 1996).

8. See, for example, the entry 'Heracles' in J. March, *Dictionary of Classical Mythology* (London 1998).

9. *Oedipus the King* 715–30.

10. For more details see P. E. Easterling, *Sophocles: Trachiniae* (Cambridge 1982), pp. 15–19.

11. A further possible link is the vignette of Iole's story at *Hippolytus* 545–54, part of a meditation on the destructive power of love.

12. The story is glancingly referred to in the *Odyssey* (11.541–65). See A. F. Garvie, *Sophocles: Ajax* (Warminster 1998), pp. 1–6 for this and other sources.

13. Critics have often tried to link Ajax with famous contemporary figures such as Cimon or Themistocles, but see Hesk (note 3), pp. 20–21.

14. See E. Kearns, *The Heroes of Attica* (London 1989), pp. 80–82, 141–2, 164.

15. The story was of course much older: in the *Odyssey*, the story of Orestes as avenger of his father is mentioned repeatedly, beginning at 1.29–31.

16. Perhaps also to a charioteer, but the text is uncertain.

17. See, for example, Euripides, *Orestes* 988–1011.

18. For some striking examples, see E. Hall and F. Macintosh, *Greek Tragedy and the British Theatre 1660–1914* (Oxford 2005), chap. 6; S. Goldhill, *Who Needs Greek?* (Cambridge 2002), chap. 3.

19. For a fuller discussion of this scene, see *The Cambridge Companion to Greek Tragedy* (Cambridge 1997), pp. 169–71.

20. See S. Schein, *Sophokles: Philoktetes* (Newburyport, MA 2003), pp. 112–17 for a sympathetic analysis of the ending.

# Further Reading

## TEXTS

The standard texts in Greek are the Oxford Classical Text edited by H. Lloyd-Jones and N. G. Wilson (1990; rev. edn 1992) and the Teubner edition by R. D. Dawe (third edn, Stuttgart and Leipzig 1996).

## COMMENTARIES

There are commentaries on all seven surviving tragedies by R. C. Jebb, with text and translation (Cambridge 1883–1900), reprinted with new introductions (London 2004), and by J. C. Kamerbeek (commentary only; Leiden 1959–84).

### Ajax

W. B. Stanford (London 1963)
A. F. Garvie, with translation (Warminster 1998)

### Electra

J. H. Kells (Cambridge 1973)
J. March, with translation (Warminster 2001)
P. J. Finglass (Cambridge 2007)

### Philoctetes

T. B. L. Webster (Cambridge 1970)
R. G. Ussher, with translation (Warminster 1990)

Women of Trachis (Trachiniae)

P. E. Easterling (Cambridge 1982)
M. Davies (Oxford 1991)

## OTHER TRANSLATIONS

### Prose

H. Lloyd-Jones, Sophocles, Loeb Classical Library, 2 vols (Cambridge, MA 1994); a third volume (1996) is devoted to the fragments of lost plays

### Verse

R. Fagles and B. Knox, Sophocles: The Three Theban Plays (London 1984)
D. Grene and R. Lattimore (eds), Sophocles I and II (Chicago 1988)
M. Ewans, G. Ley and G. McCart, Sophocles: Four Dramas of Maturity, and Sophocles: Three Dramas of Old Age (London 1999, 2000)

## GREEK THEATRE AND SOCIETY

A. W. Pickard-Cambridge, The Dramatic Festivals of Athens (second edn, rev. J. Gould and D. M. Lewis, Oxford 1988)
J. J. Winkler and F. I. Zeitlin (eds), Nothing to Do with Dionysos? (Princeton 1989)
R. Scodel (ed.), Theater and Society in the Classical World (Ann Arbor 1991)
A. Sommerstein, S. Halliwell, J. Henderson and B. Zimmermann (eds), Tragedy, Comedy and the Polis (Bari 1993)
J. R. Green, Theatre in Ancient Greek Society (London 1994)
E. Csapo and W. J. Slater, The Context of Ancient Drama (Ann Arbor 1995)
R. Green and E. Handley, Images of the Greek Theatre (London 1995)

S. Goldhill and R. Osborne (eds), *Performance Culture and Athenian Democracy* (Cambridge 1999)

D. Wiles, *Greek Theatre Performance* (Cambridge 2000)

P. Wilson, *The Athenian Institution of the Khoregia: The Chorus, The City and the Stage* (Cambridge 2000)

P. Easterling and E. Hall (eds), *Greek and Roman Actors: Aspects of an Ancient Profession* (Cambridge 2002)

R. Parker, *Polytheism and Society at Athens* (Oxford 2005), chap. 7

# GREEK TRAGEDY IN CONTEXT

S. Goldhill, *Reading Greek Tragedy* (Cambridge 1986)

M. Heath, *The Poetics of Greek Tragedy* (London 1987)

J-P. Vernant and P. Vidal-Naquet, *Myth and Tragedy in Ancient Greece*, Cambridge, MA 1988)

E. Hall, *Inventing the Barbarian: Greek Self-definition through Tragedy* (Oxford 1989)

R. Padel, *In and Out of the Mind: Greek Images of the Tragic Self* (Princeton 1992)

B. Williams, *Shame and Necessity* (Berkeley and Los Angeles 1993)

R. Buxton, *Imaginary Greece: The Contexts of Mythology* (Cambridge 1994)

R. Seaford, *Reciprocity and Ritual* (Oxford 1994)

M. Silk (ed.), *Tragedy and the Tragic* (Oxford 1996)

P. E. Easterling (ed.), *The Cambridge Companion to Greek Tragedy* (Cambridge 1997)

C. Pelling (ed.), *Greek Tragedy and the Historian* (Oxford 1997)

D. Wiles, *Tragedy in Athens: Performance Space and Theatrical Meaning* (Cambridge 1997)

B. Goward, *Telling Tragedy: Narrative Technique in Aeschylus, Sophocles and Euripides* (London 1999)

N. J. Lowe, *The Classical Plot and the Invention of Western Narrative* (Cambridge 2000)

H. P. Foley, *Female Acts in Greek Tragedy* (Princeton 2001)

R. Rehm, *The Play of Space: Spatial Transformation in Greek Tragedy* (Princeton 2002)

C. Sourvinou-Inwood, *Tragedy and Athenian Religion* (Lanham, MD 2003)

O. Taplin, *Greek Tragedy in Action* (second edn, London 2003)

J. Gregory (ed.), *A Companion to Greek Tragedy* (Oxford 2005)

E. Hall, *The Theatrical Cast of Athens: Interactions between Ancient Greek Drama and Society* (Oxford 2006)

G. Ley, *The Theatricality of Greek Tragedy: Playing Space and Chorus* (Chicago 2007)

# RECEPTION

P. E. Easterling (ed.), *The Cambridge Companion to Greek Tragedy* (Cambridge 1997), chaps 9–12

R. Rehm, *Radical Theatre: Greek Tragedy and the Modern World* (London 2003)

R. Garland, *Surviving Greek Tragedy* (London 2004)

E. Hall and F. Macintosh, *Greek Tragedy and the British Theatre 1660–1914* (Oxford 2005)

—— and A. Wrigley, *Dionysus since '69* (Oxford 2004)

S. Goldhill, *How to Stage Greek Tragedy Today* (Chicago 2007)

# SOPHOCLES

B. M. W. Knox, *The Heroic Temper: Studies in Sophoclean Tragedy* (Berkeley and Los Angeles 1964)

R. P. Winnington-Ingram, *Sophocles: An Interpretation* (Cambridge 1980)

R. G. A. Buxton, *Sophocles = Greece & Rome New Surveys in the Classics* (16 second edn, Oxford 1995)

C. Segal, *Sophocles' Tragic World* (Cambridge, MA 1995)

J. Griffin (ed.), *Sophocles Revisited: Essays Presented to Sir Hugh Lloyd-Jones* (Oxford 1999)

# THE FOUR PLAYS IN THIS VOLUME

There are detailed bibliographies on the plays in the following:

## Ajax

J. Hesk, *Sophocles: Ajax*, Duckworth Companions to Greek and Roman Tragedy (London 2003)

P. Wilson, *Introduction* to reprint of Jebb's commentary on the play (London 2004), pp. 31–47

## Electra

J. March, *Introduction* to reprint of Jebb's commentary on the play (London 2004), pp. 31–56

M. Lloyd, *Sophocles: Electra*, Duckworth Companions to Greek and Roman Tragedy (London 2005)

## Philoctetes

S. Schein, *Sophocles: Philoketes*, translation with notes and interpretative essay, Focus Classical Library (Newburyport, MA 2003)

F. Budelmann, *Introduction* to reprint of Jebb's commentary on the play (London 2004), pp. 31–49

H. Roisman, *Sophocles: Philoctetes*, Duckworth Companions to Greek and Roman Tragedy (London 2005)

## Women of Trachis

B. Goward, *Introduction* to reprint of Jebb's commentary on the play (London 2004), pp. 31–48

B. Levett, *Sophocles: Women of Trachis*, Duckworth Companions to Greek and Roman Tragedy (London 2005)

# MODERN POETIC ADAPTATIONS

Ezra Pound, *Sophocles: Women of Trachis* (London 1956, 1969)
Seamus Heaney, *The Cure at Troy: A Version of Sophocles's Philoctetes* (London 1990)
Martin Crimp, *Cruel and Tender: After Sophocles' Trachiniae* (London 2004)

# A Note on the Translation

This volume aims primarily to introduce four masterpieces of European drama to first-time readers interested in classical literature and drama. Others, perhaps, may enjoy returning to old friends in a new version. I also hope that it will prove interesting and useful to students reading these plays in translation as part of a course in Classics, classical civilization, drama or theatre studies. Finally, my own interest and experience in the direction of Greek tragedies on stage has led me to strive for a version that will be clear and speakable enough to perform, while remaining as faithful as possible to the meaning and spirit of the ancient Greek text.

Sophocles is not an easy dramatist to pin down, either in his overall thinking or in the detail of his language. His diction is a subtle blend of natural and artificial, concrete and abstract, literal and metaphorical, and there are crucial differences in style between the main scenes for the solo actors and the lyric songs of the chorus. Whatever the difficulties of tone and expression, though, he composed his plays in verse, and there was never any doubt in my mind that I should try to translate him into English verse and to take account of the three different kinds of Greek verse he used: iambic, lyric and anapaestic.

With nineteenth-century translators of Greek tragedy, it was the norm for the original 'iambic trimeters' (six feet) of the solo characters' speeches and dialogue to be rendered in the five-foot iambic line used by Chaucer, Shakespeare, Milton and countless others. This convention, with the adoption of a deliberately archaic style, was carried into the twentieth century in the translations of Gilbert Murray, which brought Greek tragedy in English

to a wider readership than ever before and achieved a number of
productions on the professional stage. Modern translators have
usually preferred a more relaxed verse form and less artificial
diction; I have followed this later tradition. Most of the lines in
my version work to a pattern of five stresses, similar to the verse
plays of T. S. Eliot. I have made more use of light (unstressed)
syllables in the confrontational, nearer-colloquial sequences;
straight iambic pentameters tend to occur in the more obviously
poetic or reflective speeches. In the formal stichomythic (line-for-
line) exchanges, I have sometimes employed a four-stress line to
quicken the pace. This kind of flexibility, I felt, would lead to a
livelier and more compelling text to read or to act.

In translating the choral odes, I have departed from the practice
of most modern translators into English and aimed at as close a
replication as was possible of the ancient Greek metrical structure. In the original, these poems, designed to be sung to pipe
music and accompanied by choreographed movement and gesture, were composed in elaborately varied and complex verse
patterns. The melody of the songs is irretrievably lost and would
probably sound extremely strange to our ears. However, an
analysis of the verse produces a musical 'score' in *rhythmical*
terms, which can still be heard and responded to as both exciting
in itself and appropriate to the dramatic context. An important
aspect of the play's music can thus be said to survive and, I
believe, to be accessible to ourselves, even in translation. I have
therefore attempted to interpret this by composing an 'isometric'
version, in which the original patterns of long and short syllables
that define the rhythm in the original Greek are echoed in English
by corresponding patterns of heavy and light syllables.

This needs a little more elaboration. Where possible, I tried
to find groups of English words which fell naturally into the
rhythmical phrases of the Greek choral text. Sometimes, however, Sophocles contrived special effects (reflected, probably, in
his choreography) which can only be demonstrated in English
through the use of accents to mark the pulse or fall of the foot
in the dance. Particular examples of this occur in the sequences
of heavy syllables at *Electra* 482–5 (= 498–501) and in the
irregular 'dochmiac' phrases in *Electra* 1384ff. In these lines,

syllables *not* marked with an accent should be left unstressed in delivery, if the more intricate rhythms of the odes are to be recaptured in the mind's ear of the reader or in live performance.

The passages in the intermediary anapaestic metre are translated into a similar rhythmical pattern, but without the strict syllabic correspondence that I have aimed to preserve in the lyric stanzas. To draw attention to the three different poetic modes, the anapaestic passages are slightly indented in the printed text as compared to the normal dialogue, and the sung lyrics indented by as much again.

Throughout my challenging task I have been conscious of the view described by the seventeenth-century writer James Howell: 'Some hold translations not unlike to be / The wrong side of a Turkey tapestry.' Of the many particular difficulties for a translator of Sophocles, I would highlight two. The first is the problem of rendering ethical and cognitive concepts. Such Greek words as are commonly treated as denoting 'good' or 'bad', 'wise' or 'foolish', have a wide range of meanings, as do their English counterparts, and these need to be interpreted in their particular contexts. The same word cannot be clearly and convincingly translated in the same way every time that it occurs. Another difficulty, of a different kind, is that Greek tragedy is rich in cries of lamentation which cannot be put into English without banality or bathos. Here I have usually resorted to the expedient of transliterating the original Greek sounds, expressive in themselves, in preference to a feeble substitute. Occasionally, as in the case of Philoctetes' cries of pain, I have simply used a stage direction and left it to the actor or the reader's aural imagination.

The plays in this book have been printed in what *might* be their chronological order of composition. This has to be conjectural, as the only one of the four that can be dated with any certainty is *Philoctetes*, first produced in 409 BC, when Sophocles was in his eighties. *Electra* is also thought to be late, but it could be ten or more years earlier. *Women of Trachis* and *Ajax* have been attributed by scholars to the middle period of the poet's output and could belong to the earlier 440s. I have allowed priority to the former on grounds explained in the prefaces to those two plays.

The line numbering follows or comes very close to that of the published Greek text as it has been reconstructed by modern scholars on the basis of manuscripts dating from the tenth to the fifteenth centuries AD and ultimately derived from editions of the plays compiled by scholars at Alexandria in the third century BC. Modern editions vary in many details. While I have usually worked from the standard Oxford text of H. Lloyd-Jones and N. G. Wilson (1990; rev. edn 1992), I have followed other readings or emendations where I preferred them. We can never reconstruct Sophocles' original scripts with complete confidence, but it is clear that the Alexandrian texts included short interpolations made by ancient actors performing in revivals. Here again scholars disagree over what is authentic or not, and I have exercised my own judgement in excluding lines which I felt to be spurious and, in most cases, supplying a translation of these in the notes.

On the spelling of proper names I have preferred to follow the traditional Latin forms of the Greek names – for example, Ajax rather than Aias, Electra for Elektra, Neoptolemus for Neoptolemos, Oeta for Oite. For versification purposes, I have assumed what used to be their conventional pronunciations – for example, Philóctétes, not Philóctetes. Today there appears to be no standard or 'correct' way of pronouncing the ancient Greek names, but the Glossary lists the names in the plays with their assumed pronunciation and offers a guide to the 'old' pronunciation of the vowel sounds and consonants in English.

Rather more important are the prefaces and notes to each of the four plays. For the modern reader, notes may be useful in explaining matters of details which would have been familiar ground to the original audience. My notes also include a commentary on the 'movements' of each drama as it develops, together with points of special interest on the plays' staging in the ancient Greek theatre. In the prefaces I have attempted to go a little further and explore the creative processes behind the composition of the plays. For this purpose, each discussion falls into five sections. The first gives the essential features of the story that Sophocles inherited from the epic poets or earlier tragic treatments, and would have been generally familiar to his audience. Almost all surviving Greek tragedies were based on this mythology, and it was the poet's task to bring the story alive in the theatre through the formal medium outlined in the Appendix. Within a certain broad outline he was free to contrive the mechanics and details of the plot and to present the different characters in his own way, making innovations to the tradition for his own artistic purposes. The second sections of the prefaces therefore give a synopsis of the story as Sophocles himself developed it in the action (*drama* in Greek) of his play.

In ancient times, the tragic poet was also considered to be a teacher, not only of the actors and chorus whom he himself directed, but also of his audience. It should never be forgotten that these tragedies were first performed in the context of a major civic and religious festival. Besides aiming to move, excite and entertain, he would use his drama to draw out the truths about human beings and their relationships to society or to the unseen world, which he himself saw his story as exemplifying. These truths might be local and contemporary, or they could be universal. Generalization, along with an extraordinary eye for the particular, was fundamental to the ancient Greek mentality. The third sections of my prefaces therefore attempt to explore the governing ideas that animate Sophocles' treatment of his story and to suggest what he might have intended it to mean to his contemporaries, and, by implication, what – like the very greatest poets and playwrights – he might have to teach us about ourselves.

I also hope to persuade my readers that these tragedies are not only great literature but magnificent works of theatre, and to imagine themselves as members of an audience, picturing the plays, to some degree, as an Athenian spectator might have done in antiquity. The Appendix also describes the physical milieu and human resources that the poet had at his disposal, and the prefaces include brief sections on staging and casting – an instructive, if sometimes speculative, line to pursue. The prefaces' fifth and last sections discuss some of the ways in which Sophocles used his medium to express his interpretation of the traditional story convincingly and excitingly in theatrical terms. In his case, the form and conventions of Greek tragedy were no straitjacket.

One can only marvel at the skill with which, in each one of his plays, he united the different elements to create a 'structure of feeling' in the calculated succession of emotional responses that he wanted his audience to experience.

In my notes and prefaces I have commented on a few questions relating to the plays' original staging and use of theatrical space where I have thought it helpful to express a view. Such questions, however, remain largely matters of conjecture, and I have generally preferred to explore Sophocles' control over his plots, the development of his characters (where that is appropriate), his deployment of tragic form and (occasionally) his use of spectacle. Even in these respects I have not attempted a comprehensive analysis of his dramatic technique, but have concentrated on what struck me as salient features of it in each of the plays. In so doing, I hope to have identified some of the factors that must have made his tragedies powerful in his own time and that still make them eminently readable and performable today.

# WOMEN OF TRACHIS

# Preface to Women of Trachis

## THE TRADITION

Sophocles' audience would have been very familiar with the many stories of the strong man Heracles, the son of Zeus and Alcmena, persecuted throughout his life by Zeus' wife, Hera, and subjected to his famous labours by Eurystheus, king of Tiryns. In these and other exploits, he was seen as the great liberator of Greece from various beasts and monsters. Tradition told how Heracles died by wearing a poisoned robe sent to him by his wife Deïanira, whom he had originally won in a fight with the river god Acheloüs. Sophocles also drew on an epic poem, *The Capture of Oechalia*, in which Heracles enslaved Iole, the daughter of King Eurytus, and brought her home as his concubine. In historic times, Heracles was accorded status as a hero who (uniquely) went on to become a god. There were numerous cults of him in Attica, and the myth of his cremation on a pyre at the top of Mt Oeta in Thessaly may have been created to explain the existence of an early cult there also. There was another tradition current in Sophocles' time that Heracles was transported to join the gods on Olympus, and it is very possible that this apotheosis was associated with the story of the pyre on Mt Oeta.

# SYNOPSIS

Heracles has left home on his final journey, and Deïanira, now
approaching middle age, anxiously awaits his return. News is
brought by a messenger of the sack of Oechalia by Heracles, who
has sent ahead a group of captive women. The captives, who
include the beautiful princess Iole, arrive. The herald Lichas
who leads them at first disguises the truth that Iole is Heracles'
concubine, but is later persuaded to admit the facts. Deïanira,
determined to regain Heracles' love, sends him a present she
believes will act as a love-charm: a robe anointed with the preserved blood of the centaur Nessus, whom Heracles had killed
many years before with an arrow tipped with the venom of the
Hydra of Lerna. When Heracles dons the robe, it sticks to his
flesh with horrifying results. On learning from her son Hyllus
that she has destroyed her husband, Deïanira herself commits
suicide. The dying Heracles finally returns home in agony and
gives Hyllus instructions to cremate his body on Mt Oeta and to
marry Iole.

# INTERPRETATION

*Women of Trachis* is the least well known and possibly the most
puzzling of Sophocles' extant tragedies. It appears to fall into
two unequal, apparently disjointed parts: the first and much
longer part with Deïanira as the central character, and the second,
which concentrates on Heracles' agony in the throes of death.
There is a further strange disparity between the domestic, civilized milieu associated with Deïanira, the faithful wife who seeks
to regain her erring husband's love, and the primitive, violent
fairy-tale world of beasts and monsters that Heracles inhabits.
Another difficulty is that there is no external evidence for dating
the play in the sequence of Sophocles' oeuvre.[1] Modern criticism,
however, has done a great deal to demonstrate the unity of the
piece and to make it a great deal more accessible to the modern
reader or theatre audience.[2]

In the first place, it is clear that the drama shows primitive emotions impinging on civilized society. The river-god Acheloüs and the centaur Nessus are explicitly associated with the power of sexual passion, which has such a disruptive influence on the marriage of Heracles and Deïanira. This motif lies at the play's very centre and is an important aspect of its unity.

Furthermore, there is no point in debating whether Deïanira or Heracles is the leading character in the tragedy. In the ancient theatre, the two roles were performed by the same actor, and the play takes its title from neither but from the Chorus, presumably because the two characters are to be seen equally as integral to a single tragic movement. Structurally, the plot follows the 'return home' pattern of a king or hero.[3] Although Heracles himself does not come on until the last quarter of the play, his return is being anticipated and spoken about almost from the outset; his actions and behaviour are very much in the forefront as the drama proceeds. Among the other characters, Hyllus and Lichas are important in relation to both Heracles and Deïanira, and there is a crucial visual link in the play's sole prop: the casket containing the poisoned robe, which leads to the death of both characters played by the lead actor.

No less significant are the themes that bind the fates of Heracles and Deïanira together. First, as we have already noted, is the power of sexual love, *erôs*, which motivates the actions of them both. Twice the Chorus refers to the presiding agency of the 'Cyprian goddess', Aphrodite, who is not portrayed on stage but who is powerfully present in the background of the play's imagery. Moreover, the 'sickness' language associated with sexual passion at several points links it with the poisoned robe. A second idea at the heart of the play is that of mutability in a natural cycle of change in human life. This theme is articulated in the imagery and rhythmical patterning of the Chorus' entrance song (see note 9) and reflected as much in the reversals of mood and expectation as in the tragedy's actual events. Lastly there is the theme of partial and complete knowledge, of learning the truth in the end. This first comes to the fore when Deïanira, after being deceived by Lichas into believing that Iole is someone of no importance, discovers that she in fact has a young and

attractive rival for Heracles' affections. Her next dreadful discovery occurs when she realizes that the 'love-charm' of the
anointed robe may be a trick of Nessus (deceit again) to avenge
his own death on Heracles – partial knowledge made complete
when she hears Hyllus' terrible description of what happened
when Heracles actually put the robe on. The final recognition is
that of Heracles himself when he perceives the meaning of the
oracles about the end of his labours and changes from his mood
of agonized rage and vindictive indignation to a resigned and
much calmer acceptance of his destiny. His death can thus be
seen not as an unwelcome appendage to Deïanira's tragedy, but
as an integral progression from it: his wife can only respond to
the knowledge she has acquired by killing herself, while he,
though facing death, is able to confront it with heroic courage.

It seems very possible, if not certain, that the traditional view
of Deïanira (her name means 'husband-killer') represented her as
deliberately killing Heracles; she was the human agent of Hera's
hatred in punishing him for bringing home Iole as his concubine.[4]
That would make her like Clytemnestra, who kills her husband
Agamemnon, as the embodiment of justice for the sacrifice of
their daughter Iphigenia, on his return from Troy in Aeschylus'
Oresteia. If that is right, Sophocles' portrayal of Heracles' wife
as a gentle, compassionate and diffident character is a crucial
innovation. Her situation is a great deal more tragic if she kills
her husband unintentionally, with the aim of recovering his love.
Sophocles may also have been the first poet to have linked the
centaur Nessus with the death of Heracles[5] and to have introduced the detail of the arrow steeped in the Hydra's venom[6] as
the basis of the supposed love-charm which Deïanira sends to
her husband. This certainly adds to the sympathy we feel for her,
as she can also be seen as the unwitting instrument of the centaur's revenge.[7] In any event, she emerges as one of the most
attractive of Greek tragedy's heroines – no villainess, but a faithful and devoted wife, married to a husband who is constantly
absent, and never free from fear and apprehension on his behalf.

Heracles, by contrast, is anything but sympathetic, even if he
is 'the greatest man in the world' (177). His insensitivity is evident
before he appears in the introduction of Iole into his house and

in his brutal treatment of the wretched Lichas, who has brought
him the poisoned robe.[8] When he is onstage, the line (1133) in
which he regrets that Deïanira has taken her death out of his
own hands by suicide is perhaps the most dreadful moment in
the play. In some ways he is as much of a beast as the monsters
he has destroyed. And yet there is a kind of magnificence in
Deïanira's imagined picture (607-9) and Hyllus' description of
Heracles standing in the splendid golden robe as he prepares to
sacrifice to Zeus at Cenaeum. There is enough greatness established to arouse some compassion for the shattered column of a
man whom we see and hear 'sobbing . . . like a girl' (1071-2) in
his frightful pain. The great moment of recognition when Hyllus
mentions Nessus and Heracles sees the meaning of the paradoxical or ambiguous oracles about himself is deeply moving.
After that, despite his self-centred (though very Greek) insistence
on Hyllus marrying Iole (see note 83), we are bound to admire
the way in which he takes control of all the arrangements for his
passing and the heroic courage of his closing lines, before he is
carried off to die in the pyre on Mt Oeta.

Scholars have been divided on whether Sophocles expected
his audience to watch the closing scene with the perspective of
Heracles' eventual apotheosis implicitly in the background. Some
have argued that if the poet had intended this point to be borne
in mind, he would have made it more explicit, or else that the
portrayal of Heracles is too repellent for him to be imagined as
becoming a god. The prevailing view now seems to be that
apotheosis was so embedded in all the traditions and cult practices to do with Heracles that it could not possibly be left
altogether out of account. Indeed, there would be no point in the
constant references to Mt Oeta and the drama's conclusion in
the march to the pyre unless the apotheosis were implied. As for
Heracles' vices, these, like those of other Sophoclean heroes, are
to be accepted along with his virtues as two sides of the same
coin. His courage and resolution cannot be separated from his
selfishness and pride; heroic greatness is not to be submerged
beneath civilized refinement. If we ask why apotheosis is never
mentioned, the artistic reason is not far to seek: it enhances
Heracles' heroism in the face of the pyre, and so the irony of the

situation, if he is himself ignorant of the fact (although the audience knows it) that this will lead him not to Hades but to
Olympus.

Where, then, does this horrific but strangely beautiful play lead
us? The divine perspective has lifted the drama well above the
level of human domestic tragedy. The concluding lines of the
Chorus summarize the suffering they have witnessed and add,
'And all this story is great Zeus.' Aphrodite is not the only deity
presiding over the action. The name of Zeus is invoked again
and again in the text, and his will is expressed in the oracles and
written tablets of prophecy which the plot shows being fulfilled.
In the end, Zeus was not blind and indifferent to his own son (cf.
140). All this suggests an outlook that human life, in all its
instability, may be cruelly hard and unpredictable, but there is
still an underlying meaning and purpose to it. The gods have
knowledge where mortals are ignorant. That message is what
makes *Women of Trachis* so peculiarly powerful. The play is not
merely saying, 'Even the greatest men can be brought down by the
power of sex.' It also grapples philosophically with the mystery of
human suffering.

# CASTING

The first actor must have played both Deïanira and Heracles in
a doubling almost inconceivable in the modern theatre, which
could well have emphasized the continuity and progression
between the earlier and later parts of the drama. The second
actor probably took the roles of Hyllus and Lichas; the third
combined the Nurse, the Messenger and the Old Man. Mutes
required were: Iole (no doubt distinctively masked) among the
group of captive women, soldiers guarding them, Deïanira's
attendant and men bearing Heracles' litter.

# STAGING

There are no technical problems in this play. The stage-building
would have represented the house associated with Deïanira. One
of the *eisodoi* (see Appendix) could have served for almost all
entrances from elsewhere, the other, perhaps, being reserved for
the solemn exit to Mt Oeta at the very end. Opportunities for
spectacle were there in the choral dances, the entry and grouping
of the captives, and the processions on and off with the dying
Heracles on his litter. The moment when Heracles reveals his
body with the poisoned robe clinging to him would have been
the visual high point in the long closing scene.

# DRAMATIC TECHNIQUE

*Women of Trachis* and *Ajax* are regarded as the earlier two
among the four plays of Sophocles in this volume, but neither
can be exactly dated. The former is printed first, as it seems the
closest in technique to the extant plays of Sophocles' predecessor,
Aeschylus. The drama of that earlier poet, though outstandingly
powerful, does not hang in the main on what is actually *done*
onstage. The carefully contrived dynamic thrust depends above
all else on what is *said*. This may include some description of
past events, but words are also conceived and employed as having
*power* to control the fate of the persons or communities with
which the plot is concerned, either favourably or adversely. Thus
prayers for good or expressions of hope are 'performative utterances' felt to carry the drama forward in a positive kind of way,
while curses or expressions of fear are assumed to have a contrary
effect. Sometimes language can be used ambiguously or contain
resonances of which the character speaking may or may not be
aware, but which the audience (or some of it) has the knowledge
to pick up. This last phenomenon is known as dramatic (or
tragic) irony and often regarded as an artistic device that lends a
kind of spice to the drama. Irony, however, runs more deeply
than that, if words are seen as a form of *action*, including action

of which the characters performing it may not be fully in control and which implies the existence of forces, personified by the gods or fate, mysteriously operating in the background and contributing to the drama's momentum towards a conclusion, whether sad, joyful or strangely enigmatic.

Thus in Aeschylus' *Agamemnon* (with which *Women of Trachis* has certain things in common) the issue of Agamemnon's homecoming to be murdered by his wife Clytemnestra is shaped not by showing the queen plotting with her lover Aegisthus, but by ominous words spoken by the Chorus and solo-speaking characters, which inspire an overwhelming sense that when Agamemnon returns to Argos victorious after the sack of Troy, he is completely doomed. The Chorus and principals favourable to Agamemnon keep trying to say the right, well-omened thing, but their train of thought and utterance always leads them to a dismal conclusion, while the malevolent Clytemnestra indulges in a sinister kind of wordplay, like a witch's spell, full of double meanings, to hammer verbal nails into Agamemnon's coffin.

Sophocles dramatizes the return of Heracles in a similar way. In the play's very first words, Deïanira begins by quoting an 'old saying': 'Call no man happy until he is dead.' Now one might explain this opening quite simply, by saying that Deïanira is using a commonplace maxim in order to contradict it. She goes on to tell the audience that she knows already before *she* dies (as in fact happens in the play) that her own life is *un*happy. But the chief issue in the play as it unfolds is to be the death of Heracles. Did *he* die happy or unhappy? The *visual* climax of the play is excruciatingly frightful: we see the dying, but still alive, Heracles tortured by the most appalling physical agony, displaying the wounds on his mangled body, which is being eaten away by the 'shirt of Nessus'. But Heracles' final speech (1262) speaks of a *joyful* ending to his travail. He means the release that death will bring him, but his words also convey the resonance of the apotheosis in the Athenian cult of the hero. As note 3 on the text points out, this specific conclusion may also be implicit in the resonances of Deïanira's initial quotation.

Deïanira is not, of course, malevolent to her husband like Clytemnestra. Indeed, in this respect, Sophocles seems to have departed from tradition (see p. 6). However, her constant expressions of fear and her modifications of positive statements by qualifying 'if' or 'unless' clauses⁹ may be seen, in themselves, as words of bad omen. Moreover, if we know, as the ancient audience would have done, what will happen to Heracles when he puts on the poisoned robe, Deïanira's words about a gift 'in *fitting* response' to the ones that Heracles sent (494) are a fine example of the sort of unconscious irony which Aeschylus liked to put into the mouths of his characters – as is Lichas' promise at 623 to deliver the robe to Heracles and 'tell him about your vow, to *clinch* the matter'.

In a similar way, what happens in this play is determined by the oracles and prophecies, which keep recurring, though always in a slightly different form – a ploy that has the effect of enhancing the mystery and maintaining suspense. Sophocles makes play with oracles in almost all his extant dramas, and their ambiguous or paradoxical quality is part of the magical power of words that also lies at the root of dramatic irony.

Not all of the language in Sophocles is ominous or ambivalent. Nevertheless, it is remarkable how much of what *happens* in *Women of Trachis* is not enacted onstage, but described in long narrative speeches. The 'messenger speech' convention was, of course, part of the Greek tragedy recipe from its very outset, but the most striking formal characteristic of this play is that Deïanira, Lichas, Hyllus and the Nurse are all given graphic stories to tell in 'messenger mode'. All of these speeches, except for Lichas' narrative at 248–90 (which is strangely confused in its arrangement and entails a major suppression of the truth), either anticipate or describe the disasters to which the drama is leading, and so can legitimately be regarded as parts of the play's *action*.

Paradoxically, the one character actually called a messenger has a comparatively short speech. His function as a foil and counterweight to Lichas is as important as his news-bearing role. In general, there is much less in the way of stichomythic exchange in this play than in the rest of Sophocles' extant output. This makes the exchanges we *do* get all the more exciting: the altercation between the Messenger and Lichas (with Deïanira in

between, turning from one to the other as they volley their shots),
and the two important verbal tussles between the dying Heracles
and his son Hyllus in the closing scenes.

Although the Chorus bears the title of this play, it is nothing
like so prominent as in Aeschylus' surviving plays.[10] The women
still play a significant part in the drama's dynamic. The imagery
of their beautiful songs highlights the general themes of *erós* /
Aphrodite, the mutability of human life and oracles as an expression of its ordered pattern. They are also used to identify
with Deïanira's joys and hopes or (more often) her sorrows and
fears. In so doing they contribute much to the play's continuity
through Sophocles' choral technique of backward and forward
reference. In their sympathy with Deïanira, the Trachiniae are
characterized as *young* women, unaffected so far by the stresses
of marriage and parenthood. This is important for the one
moment when they become involved in the action in a practical
way, rather than responding to it as witnesses. When Deïanira,
with her characteristic diffidence, asks them if they think it foolish
of her to send Heracles the anointed robe before she has tested
the ointment out, they advise her to act regardless, with the naive
comment that 'you'll never know [whether it's safe] unless you
try.' And so Deïanira hands over the casket to Lichas, with
disastrous consequences.

The point just mentioned about continuity needs reinforc-
ing. Far from composing a 'broken-backed' play, something
Sophocles has been accused of in the past, his technique keeps
the drama moving forward, within its formal conventions, with
the inexorable logic of a musical composition. The notes to the
play aim to show how this is done, particularly in the use of
'dovetailed' entrances as an alternative to introducing new
arrivals by formal announcements. No less important, of course,
are the sudden changes and reversals of mood, which illustrate
the suddenness of change in human life.

Finally, I have suggested in my discussion of the play's
interpretation that Sophocles' public entered the theatre with
expectations of a vengeful Deïanira, and that the different characterization of Heracles' wife in this play may well be innovative.
It is also highly likely that the audience assumed that Heracles

was going to his deification at the end, even if this was only
suggested by an association of ideas. This 'discrepant awareness'
on the audience's part is not simply an incidental point of technique. As in other Sophocles plays, it is a crucial factor in his
peculiar brand of irony, integral to the way in which his drama
works in the theatre and the kind of pleasure it will have inspired
in its original audience. With a minimum of supplementary information, it can inspire a similar pleasure in a spectator or reader
today.

## NOTES

1.  Any date between 457 and 430 is possible.
2.  I am particularly indebted here to the important work of Pat
    Easterling and to articles by Jenny March, Philip Holt, Robert
    L. Fowler and Barbara Goward.
3.  Two obvious examples are Homer's *Odyssey* and *Agamemnon*,
    the first play of Aeschylus' Orestean trilogy.
4.  Homer (*Iliad* 18.117–19) refers to Heracles being 'subdued by
    fate and the cruel wrath of Hera'. The Hesiodic *Catalogue of
    Women* (sixth century BC) mentions Deïanira's anointing of
    a robe, which she gave to Lichas. Iole was known from *The
    Capture of Oechalia*.
5.  This story also occurs in a dithyramb by the lyric poet Bacchylides
    (fifth century BC), but it is not possible to establish whether he
    derived it from Sophocles or vice versa.
6.  Representations in art show Heracles killing Nessus, who had
    tried to rape Deïanira, with his club or a sword.
7.  It also gives Sophocles the opportunity for the tragic paradox of
    'the dead killing the living', of which he was so fond (see note
    77). Heracles himself becomes the victim of the monsters (the
    Hydra and Nessus) whom he has rid the world of by his heroic
    prowess.
8.  Not to mention his imputed murder of Iphitus in Lichas' narrative
    (269–73), which we have no reason to doubt on this particular
    point.
9.  For example, at 27, 228, 243 and especially 586–7.
10. Except in *Prometheus Bound*, which many scholars today believe
    to be the work of another hand.

# Characters

DEÏANIRA, *wife of Heracles*

NURSE

HYLLUS, *son of Deïanira and Heracles*

CHORUS *of women of Trachis*

MESSENGER

LICHAS, *a herald*

OLD MAN

IOLE, *daughter of King Eurytus*

CAPTIVE WOMEN, GUARDS, ATTENDANT, BEARERS

## SCENE 1²

[*Enter* DEÏANIRA *from the palace.*]
DEÏANIRA:
An old saying goes: 'You can never know for sure
Whether a mortal's life has been good or bad
Until his death.'³ You can in my case. I know
Too well, this side of the grave, how hard and unlucky          5
My life has been. When I lived in Pleuron,
In my father Oeneus' house, I dreaded the thought
Of marriage more than any girl in the land.
My hand was sought by the river god Acheloüs,
Who took three shapes when he asked my father to make          10
Me his: first, he revealed himself as a bull,
Then as a serpent with shimmering⁴ coils, and last
As a monster in human form with the horns of an ox
And rivulets streaming over his tangled beard.
Waiting in terror, I kept on praying to die          15
Before I yielded to such a lover's embrace.

At last, to my huge relief and joy, he arrived –
Heracles, Zeus' and Alcmena's glorious son.
He closed in combat with the river god          20
And set me free. How the battle was fought
I could not tell, as I do not know. Some brave,

Intrepid spectator might be able to say.
For me, I sat apart, benumbed with terror,
25  Shuddering to think of the pain my beauty could win.
But Zeus, the god of battles, brought about
A happy ending – if happy it was. I became
Heracles' bride, but still I'm haunted by one fear
After another, in endless fretting for him.
30  Night follows night, and worry succeeds to worry.
We did have children, but Heracles rarely saw them,
Like a farmer who only visits a distant field
At seed-time and harvest. That was my husband's life,
35  Coming and going from home in endless servitude.
        [*Enter* NURSE *from palace.*]⁵
And now when he has surmounted all these labours,
I feel more frightened than ever I did before.
The killing of lphitus⁶ meant we had to uproot
40  Ourselves and live as guests with the king of Trachis.
But where my husband is not a soul can tell.
I only know the bitter pains that his absence
Inflicts on *me*. He's in some danger now,
I am almost certain. Fifteen months have gone by
45  And still no news. He *must* be in terrible danger.
That tablet he left for me when he went away –
How often I pray to the gods it bodes no harm!
NURSE:
Deïanira, mistress, I've often watched you
50  Sobbing and shedding tears in long lament
For Heracles' never-ending absence abroad.
I'm only a slave, but may I presume to advise you?
Why aren't you sending one of your many sons
55  To search him out? Hyllus would be the best,
If he's at all concerned for auspicious news
Of his father's welfare. Look now, here he is,
Racing towards the house just when we need him.
So if you believe that my advice is sound,
60  You can take advantage of his arrival too.
        [*Enter* HYLLUS *by a side entrance.*]

DEÏANIRA:
My dearest boy! Listen, it doesn't take breeding
To talk good sense. This woman's only a slave,
But you wouldn't think it, to judge by her words just now.
HYLLUS:
What has she said? Please tell me, Mother.
DEÏANIRA:
You haven't inquired about your father. He's been                    65
Abroad for such a time. It does you shame.
HYLLUS:
I know where he is, if report can be trusted.
DEÏANIRA:
Exactly where have you heard, my boy?
HYLLUS:
For all of the past twelve months they say
He has worked as a slave for a Lydian woman.[7]                      70
DEÏANIRA:
Heracles work as a slave? No, no!
HYLLUS:
At least he's released from *that*, I hear.
DEÏANIRA:
Where is he now, alive or dead?
HYLLUS:
He's in Euboea,[8] marching an army
Against King Eurytus' city, Oechalia –                               75
Or just about to invade.
DEÏANIRA:
Euboea! My son, you know he left me
An oracle about that very place?
HYLLUS:
I don't know, Mother. What did it say?
DEÏANIRA:
That 'either Heracles would end his days,
Or else this exploit would be followed by                            80
A life of happiness for ever after.'
His fate lies in the balance, my dear son.
So won't you go to help? His life and safety

85  Mean *our* safety, or we're lost with him.
    HYLLUS:
    Mother, of course I'll go. If I'd only known
    About this prophecy, I'd have been there long since.
    I trusted my father's usual luck, and never
    Allowed myself to fret or be over-anxious
90  On his behalf. But now I've heard those words,
    I'll spare no effort to learn the truth behind them.
    DEÏANIRA:
    Be off, then, son. However late you arrive,
    News of success is always a source of gain.

          [*Exit* HYLLUS, *by a side entrance;* DEÏANIRA *and* NURSE *go
          back into the palace.*]


# CHORAL ENTRANCE SONG[9]


          [*Enter* CHORUS *of young Trachinian women.*]
    CHORUS:
          O Sún whom Night, spóiled of her shímmering
              stárs,                                    [*Strophe* 1]
95        Brings forth and puts to sleep in a cradle of flame,[10]
          Helios, Helios, help us!
          Cry aloud your answer, tell me
          Where is the son of Alcmena,
          Heracles, thou lord of the burning ray?
100       To eastward near the Pontus' straits?
          Or westward, straddling continents?[11]
          Speak out, O Sun, all-seeing master!

          I héard it said, Deïaníra, the príze         [*Antistrophe* 1]
          He fought for, weeps and waits in her longing desire,
105       Cries like a bird in bereavement,
          Always longing, always weeping,
          Never closing her eyelids
          Fast in sleep; but feeding a fear that recalls
          Her man who's gone, she watches, anxious,
110       Racked upon her lonely bed,
          Distraught with grief and grim foreboding.

See, on the breadths of the ocean                    [*Strophe* 2]
Roller on roller advancing,
Driven by blasts of the tireless
Winds from the south or the north.                                115
So Héracles tósses on life's
Stórmy seas. Nów he's submerged,
Nów upraised; nów in a trough,
Nów on the crést. Yet sóme divíne
Spirit prevents his toppling down,                                120
Down to the house of Hades.[12]


[DEÏANIRA *re-enters from the palace.*][13]
Lady, I love and respect you,                        [*Antistrophe* 2]
Yet must I fault you for grieving.
Do not despair in your sorrow,
Hold to your hopes for the good.                                  125
King Zeús, the ordaíner supreme,
Rúled that life cánnot remain
Freé from all páin and distress.[14]
No, in a cycle of joy and pain,
Fortune revolves from day to day,                                 130
Órbiting líke the Gréat Bear.


The shimmering night yields to dawn,                 [*Epode*]
Man's disasters pass away;
A flash, and golden wealth is lost.
It soon becomes our neighbour's turn                              135
For dáys of jóy or leán tímes.
So nów I bíd you, lády, keép this ín your héart
And líft your hópes hígh. For whó behéld Zeús
So blínd, cóld, hárd towárds his ówn sóns?[15]                    140


# SCENE 2[16]

DEÏANIRA:
You're here, I suppose, because you've heard about
My unhappy plight. I hope you never know
For yourselves the pain I feel deep down inside me.

Young plants are grown in sheltered places, untroubled
145  By sun's strong heat, the rain or stormy winds.
A girl's like a sapling, happy and carefree,
Until her girlhood's ended and she's now
A wife. We start to lie awake at night
150  And fret about our husbands or our children.
You'll learn then from your own changed way of life
The kind of misery that is torturing me.

Well, I've had many reasons for distress,
But here is something absolutely new.
155  When Heracles went from here on his last journey,
He left behind an ancient tablet,[17] inscribed
With mystic letters. He'd never mentioned it
Before, when he'd gone off on one of his labours.
160  His thoughts were on success, never on death.
This time he spoke as though his end had come.
He gave instructions, first for what he'd settled
On me as his wife, and then on how he willed
His estate should be divided among his children.
165  He specified a time and said to me,
'When I have been abroad for fifteen months,
The moment will have come when I shall either
Have to die, or else survive to live
A life that's free from pain for ever after.'
170  This, he declared, Fate had ordained should mark
The last of Heracles' labours. So Dodona's
Ancient oak had spoken, through the mouth
Of the twin priestesses[18] at Zeus' oracle.

The moment's now. Those words are coming true.
175  That's why, dear friends, when I'm asleep at night,
The nightmare startles me out of bed in terror.
To stay bereft of the greatest man in the world!
CHORUS LEADER:
No more ill-omened words![19] I see a man coming,
His head crowned with a wreath. He bears good news.
  [*Enter* MESSENGER.]

MESSENGER:
My lady Deïanira, allow me to be                              180
The first to give you tidings and calm your fears.
Heracles is alive, victorious, bearing
The battle spoils' first fruits to the gods of Malis.

DEÏANIRA:
Amazing news, old sir! Please tell me again.

MESSENGER:
I say your glorious husband will soon be coming              185
Home to your house, in all the might of victory.

DEÏANIRA:
How and where on earth did you find this out?

MESSENGER:
In a field where the oxen graze in summer, Lichas
The herald's addressing a crowd. As soon as I heard him,
I darted away, in order, of course, to bring                 190
The news to you first and so ensure my reward.

DEÏANIRA:
Why isn't he here himself with his joyful tidings?

MESSENGER:
Madam, it's hardly easy. The whole population
Of Malis is thronging round and interrogating him.
He can't move an inch. They all have their own questions     195
To ask and won't let him go till they've had their answers.
So, willy-nilly, he's trapped. But it won't be long
Before he arrives and you can see him yourself.

DEÏANIRA:
O Zeus, god of the sacred meadow on Oeta's                   200
Heights![20] At last, at last you have brought us joy!
Raise the cry, you women within the house,
And you who stand without. This comforting news
Is a rising sun I never thought to see!

CHORUS:
        Now sing a sóng of jóy![21]                          205
        Now let the héarth resóund
        *Álalalaí!*
        The hoúse awaíts the bríde and groóm. So lét the chóir
        Of mén crý stróng for óur Deféndér,

210     Apólló, árcher gód.
        And wíth them, ó maídens, ráise
        Víctory's páean, the tríumph hýmn,
        And shôut his síster's náme alóud,
        Délian Ártemis, tórch goddess, shôoter of déer.
215     Práise the nýmphs of Málís!
        I sóar to héaven, enthrálled to héar
        The jóyful, skírling pípe,[22] O máster óf my sóul.
        Oh sée, hôw it transpórts mé –
        *Euhóí!* –
        My ívy crówn, which whírls me róund
220     In frénzied Bácchus' wíld dánce!
        [*The* CHORUS *dances round, as* LICHAS *and some soldiers
        enter with a group of captive women, including* IOLE.]
        *Ió, ió, Paián!*
        Lóok, oh lóok, my lády déar,
        The néws is trúe, the shíp's come ín,
        Befóre your éyes in fúll víew!
DEÏANIRA:
225     Yes, yes, dear women. I have watched it all.
        I see the whole procession. Herald, at last
        You've come, and I wish you joy – if your news is joyful.
LICHAS:
        My coming here's auspicious. So is your welcome.
230     The occasion merits it, madam. When fortune's fair,
        Fair greetings are the order of the day.
DEÏANIRA:
        You are the best of friends! First questions first.
        Is Heracles coming home to me alive?
LICHAS:
        Yes, surely. When *I* left him, he was alive
235     And strong as ever, in the best of health.
DEÏANIRA:
        And where was that? In Greece or farther abroad?
LICHAS:
        You know Euboea. There on Cape Cenaeum
        Your lord is consecrating ground to Zeus,
        For altars and for tribute-bearing soil.[23]

DEÏANIRA:
Fulfilling a vow, or on some oracle's orders?
LICHAS:
He made a vow when he planned to take and uproot          240
The country of these women you see before you.
DEÏANIRA:
Who are these women? Who's their master? Tell me.
Their plight, if I'm not deceived, is worth some pity.
LICHAS:
When Heracles sacked Oechalia, these were the ones
He chose for his household slaves or temple servants.      245
DEÏANIRA:
Was it to take that city he stayed away
Those countless days, so unforeseeably long?
LICHAS:[24]
No, most of the time he was detained in Lydia.
He wasn't a free man – so he says himself –
As he'd been sold as a slave. (Madam, no need            250
To take offence, where Zeus is clearly at work.)
Yes, he was Omphale's slave and freely admits
He served the Lydian queen for one whole year.
He was so incensed at suffering this disgrace
That he bound himself with a solemn oath to act:          255
'I swear I'll make a slave of the man who caused me
All this shame – along with his wife and children!'
His words weren't spoken in vain. Once purified,
He formed a private army and marched against
The city of Eurytus, who he claimed was the person        260
Solely to blame for his recent humiliation.

Why so? When he was staying at Eurytus' house
As a guest and family friend, his host had treated
Him to a load of malicious and foolish insults.
'Your arrows may be unerring,' he'd jeered, 'but you're still   265
A less good archer than my own sons.' He then
Exclaimed, 'Eurystheus' slave! You're being broken
By all those labours.' Last, when Heracles got himself
Drunk at a banquet, he'd thrown him out of the house.

270   Your husband took his revenge when Eurytus' young son
Iphitus later came to the hill of Tiryns,
Following in the tracks of some straying horses.
The youth was looking distractedly over the plain,
When Heracles pushed him over the citadel walls.

275   This incident made Olympian Zeus, the royal
Father of all, extremely angry. He sent
The hero out to be sold as a slave. The reason?
Iphitus was the only person he'd ever
Chosen to murder by stealth, and this was not
To be borne. If he'd taken revenge in an open way,
Zeus would have forgiven a just reprisal. The gods,
280   No less than men, dislike insulting behaviour.
Eurytus, then, and his sons have paid the price
For their arrogant rudeness, and all have gone to the grave.
What's more, their city's enslaved. These women you see here,
After a sorry change of fortune, now
285   Are assigned to you. Those were your husband's orders,
Which I, as his faithful servant, am carrying out.
As for himself, as soon as he's offered the sacrifice
Due to his father Zeus for Oechalia's fall,
You can reckon that he'll be here. Of all the auspicious
290   News I've brought, you'll be best pleased with that.
CHORUS LEADER:
My lady, now your joy is assured. These captives
Are here already, and Heracles soon will arrive.
DEÏANIRA:
Yes, in conscience, I must be glad to hear
295   That all is well with my husband. It has to follow.
And yet, when I think about it, there's still the fear
That our good luck may suddenly be reversed.
I, my friends, feel deeply sorry to see
Those ill-starred prisoners, here in a foreign land,
300   Exiles who've lost their fathers and lost their homes,
The daughters of free men, maybe, but now condemned
To a life as slaves. O Zeus, who turns the tide
Of battle, may I never see you strike

A child of mine like this, or if you must,
I pray you do it when I'm not here to see!                    305
Seeing these women fills me with such foreboding.
    [*She approaches one of the women.*]
Unhappy girl,²⁵ please tell me who you are.
Have you a husband? Children? You look as if
You're still too young – though nobly born, I'd say.
Lichas, who is this girl? Who were her father            310
And mother? Tell me; I feel more sorry for her
Than all the others. She shows great dignity.

LICHAS:
How would *I* know? Why should you ask? Perhaps
She comes from one of Oechalia's better families.        315

DEÏANIRA:
The royal house? Eurytus' child, maybe?

LICHAS:
Can't say. I didn't go out of my way to ask.

DEÏANIRA:
Did you hear her name from one of her friends on the road?

LICHAS:
No, I was quietly getting on with my job.

DEÏANIRA:
Well, poor child, you tell me your name yourself.        320
It's really sad that I don't know who you are.

LICHAS:
You won't get very much out of her, I fear.
You know, ever since she left her ruined country,
We haven't heard her utter a single word.
She has been in misery over her wretched lot,            325
Endlessly crying her eyes out. Certainly she's come
Down in the world, but we shouldn't press her too far.

DEÏANIRA:
Very well, we had better leave her alone and allow her
To pass indoors in peace. I wouldn't want                 330
To add to her pain myself. It is bad enough
As it is. Let's all go in. You'll want to be busy
For your return, while I arrange things here.
    [*The prisoners, soldiers and* LICHAS *start to move towards*

*the house and gradually pass offstage. The* MESSENGER
*advances and stops* DEÏANIRA.]

MESSENGER:

335  Wait here a moment first! A word in private.
You need to learn what people you're taking indoors,
And be made aware of things that you ought to know
But haven't been told. *I* know the whole of the truth.

DEÏANIRA:

What is it? Why are you trying to stop me?

MESSENGER:

340  Just wait and listen. My earlier news
Was worth your attention. This will be too.

DEÏANIRA:

Do you want me to call the others back,
Or simply to speak with me and these women?

MESSENGER:

With you and them I can be quite open.
Forget the others.

DEÏANIRA:

345                              They've gone now. Speak.

MESSENGER:

All the information that fellow gave
Just now was totally wrong. Either he lied,
Or else he wasn't telling the truth before.

DEÏANIRA:

What? You must explain what you mean.

350  I don't understand a word you've said.

MESSENGER:

I heard that man declaring, before a host
Of witnesses, this: It was all for that beautiful girl
That Heracles sacked Oechalia's lofty towers
And conquered Eurytus. Love was the only god

355  To charm him into this warlike expedition,
Nothing to do with penal servitude out
In Lydia, under Omphale, nothing to do
With Iphitus' death when he hurled him down from the walls.
Lichas has changed his story, omitting Love.

In fact, when Heracles failed to persuade her father
To let him have the girl as his secret bedmate,                    360
He trumped up some excuse or other, and then
Invaded her land and sacked her city. Now,
As you see, he has come back home with the lass in tow.            365
It has all been carefully planned, my lady. She
Won't be a slave – you mustn't imagine that.
It's hardly likely, given that furnace of lust.

That's why, dear madam, I felt you had to know
The facts, as I chanced to hear them from Lichas' lips.            370
What's more, there were plenty of others who heard him
    speaking,
Right at the heart of Trachis' meeting place.
They could challenge him, too. If my news isn't welcome,
I'm sorry for that – but still I've told you the truth!
DEÏANIRA:
Oh god, what's happening to me? I'm so distressed!                 375
What lurking pest am I harbouring under
My own roof? God, oh god! Can she be so lacking
In all distinction, as Lichas who brought her swore?
MESSENGER:
I'll say! Her birth is just as illustrious
As her beautiful face. She's Eurytus' daughter, once               380
Called Iole. Lichas never chose to inform
You so – he didn't go out of his way to ask!
CHORUS LEADER:
What underhand behaviour! A lie like that
Deserves more condemnation than other wrongs.
DEÏANIRA:
Oh women, what should I do?                                         385
This news – I'm cut to the quick!
CHORUS LEADER:
Go to Lichas; demand the truth. Perhaps
He'll give you an explanation, if you press him.
DEÏANIRA:
You're right. I'll go at once.

MESSENGER:

390 What about me? Should I go or stay?

DEÏANIRA:

Please stay. Here's Lichas in person,
Leaving the house of his own accord.

[*Re-enter* LICHAS *from the palace.*]

LICHAS:

Madam, what message may I take Heracles?
Tell me, I'm on my way, as you see.

DEÏANIRA:

395 You took so long to arrive, and now how quickly
You're rushing off, before we've spoken again!

LICHAS:

If you wish to ask any questions, I'm at your service.

DEÏANIRA:

Will you really give me the honest truth?

LICHAS:

Zeus be my witness, I shall, if I know.

DEÏANIRA:

400 Who, then, is the woman you came with here?

LICHAS:

She's from Euboea. I've no idea
Who her parents are.

MESSENGER [*coming forward*]:

                                        You! Look here!
Who do you think you're talking to, man?

LICHAS:

Why on earth should you ask me that?

MESSENGER:

Come on, reply, if you have the wit!

LICHAS:

405 I'm addressing the lady Deïanira,
Daughter of Oeneus, Heracles' wife,
My mistress – unless my sight is deceived.

MESSENGER:

Just what I wanted to hear you say.
Your mistress – yes?

LICHAS:

That's quite correct.

MESSENGER:

Well, then, what do you think the correct reward                    410
If your treatment of her is found to be incorrect?

LICHAS:

How incorrect? What are you quibbling about?

MESSENGER:

Quibbling! It's you who are doing that.

LICHAS:

I'm going. I've been a fool
To listen to you so long.

MESSENGER:

You won't until you have answered one brief question.           415

LICHAS:

Ask what you wish. You have a tongue in your head.

MESSENGER:

That female prisoner you've taken into the house –
I suppose you know who I mean?

LICHAS:

Of course, why ask?

MESSENGER:

Didn't you say this girl, whom you pretend                          420
To know nothing about, was Iole, Eurytus' daughter?

LICHAS:

Said it to whom, and where? Your witnesses, please.
Who'll testify to hearing me make that statement?

MESSENGER:

You said it in public. A huge great crowd in the middle
Of Trachis' meeting place heard that much from you.

LICHAS:

Very well.                                                          425
They *said* they heard it. Giving a rough impression
Is not the same as an accurate statement of fact.

MESSENGER:

A rough impression! Didn't you claim on oath
That you were bringing the girl to be Heracles' woman?

LICHAS:

430  On oath? His woman? For god's sake, my dear lady,
Tell me, who on earth is this interloper?

MESSENGER:

A witness, who heard you say it was lust for her
That caused Oechalia's ruin. It wasn't destroyed
By Lydia's queen, but Heracles' flagrant passion.

LICHAS:

Tell this fellow to go, my lady. No sane

435  Person bandies words with a man who's sick!

DEÏANIRA:

No, I beg you,[26] by Zeus whose lightnings flash
Atop Mt Oeta, don't cheat me or hide the truth.
You know I'm not a hard, ungenerous woman.
I understand the ways of the world, and human

440  Nature is never constant in its desires.
You can't engage in a boxing match with Love.[27]
Who'd be such a fool? Love governs even the gods
At his own sweet will. He certainly governs *me*.
Why not another woman just like myself?

445  Love is a sickness. If I get angry with my own
Husband for having caught it, I'm utterly mad.
There's no sense either in being angry with *her*.
She's doing nothing to be ashamed of or harmful
To me. I can't be jealous. No, if you're telling

450  Lies on my man's instructions, you've learned a bad lesson.
Perhaps you're teaching yourself to lie. In that case,
People will doubt your word when you want to be trusted.
Please tell me the whole truth. Look, you're not a slave!
For a freeborn person like you to be called a liar

455  Is real disgrace. And you won't get away with your lie.
There are many to whom you've talked who'll talk to me.
If you're afraid, your fear's misguided. Indeed,
*Not* learning the truth is what would give me distress.
But *knowing* – what's so dreadful in that?[28] Hasn't Heracles

460  Taken dozens of other women to bed?
None of them ever received hard words or reproaches
From *me*. Neither would Iole, even if

She were pining away with love herself. Didn't
I pity her more than the others as soon as I saw her?
Her beauty's ruined her life, and she was the poor            465
Unwitting cause of her home town's sack and enslavement.
Well, blow wind! But to you I'll say: If you must
Tell lies, then tell them to others, but never to me!

CHORUS LEADER:
Do as she says. She's right. You'll have no cause             470
To fault her kindness, and I shall be grateful, too.

LICHAS:
Well, dear lady, I see you think as a mortal
Should and show some feeling for human weakness.
I'll hide the truth no longer and tell you all.
Yes, it is just as this man says: the girl                    475
Inspired the terrible passion that shot through Heracles.
She was the cause that led to her father's desolate
Realm, Oechalia, facing capture and ruin.
I need to add, in my master's defence, that he never
Denied his love or ordered me to conceal it.                 480
No, I took it upon myself to lie, because
I felt afraid this story would give you pain.
If you account this wrong, then I was at fault.

Since, however, you *are* aware of the whole truth,
Please, for Heracles' sake and your own no less,             485
Accept this girl in your house and try to act
On the tolerant words you used just now towards her.
Your husband's prowess may be supreme in everything
    else,
But his love for her has proved his utter defeat.[29]

DEÏANIRA:
Yes, be sure, that is what I'm minded to do.                 490
No point in nursing a sickness that's self-imposed
By fighting a losing battle against the gods.
Let's go inside now. You must be given my message
And also carry a gift,[30] in fitting response
To the ones he sent. You must not leave empty-handed         495
After arriving here so richly attended.

*[Exeunt* DEÏANIRA *and* LICHAS *into the palace, the* MESS-
ENGER *by a side entrance.*[31]]

# CHORAL SONG 1

CHORUS:
> What a víctory the Cýprian góddess[32] will álways béar
>     awáy!                                              *[Strophe]*
> Bést be sílent
500 Of the góds, and of hów she beguíled the Olýmpian lórd of
>     áll,
> Hádes the kíng of the dárkness,
> Ór Poseídon[33] sháker of eárth with his trídent.
> Síng we of Deïaníra
> And the méttlesome rívals who stróve for her hánd,
505 Of stróng blóws, clóuds of dúst that fílled the lísts,
> Áfter the fíghters éntered.

> One a ríver god stróng in the fórm of a foúr-legg'd búll,
>     with hórns                                    *[Antistrophe]*
> Shárp and tówering,
510 Acheloüs from Óeniadáe. And he fáced the són of Zéus,
> Héracles, wíelding his cúrved bow,
> Brándishíng two spéars and the clúb he had bórne from
> Thébes. Then uníting in óne mass,
> They attácked and they lócked in the héat of desíre;
515 While Lóve's gréat quéen alóne, with stáff in hánd,
> Júdged the dispúte betwéen them.

> And thén there were póunding físts,[34] twángings
>     of bów,                                              *[Epode]*
> Cláshing hórns in a whírl of confúsion.
520 Then wréstlers' grápplings ládder-like,[35] blóws from the
>     bull's báttering fórehead,
> Groánings and grúntings on bóth sides.
> While that lóvely maiden
> Crówned a dístant híllside,

Sítting in fear. Whó should bé her máster?                          525
For mé, I téll the tále as thóugh I'd wátched thére.³⁶
But shé, the fáir príze they sóught to táke hóme,
· Could ónly wáit with thróbbing héart –
Góne her móther, her lífe uptúrned,
Lóst like a cálf abándoned.                                         530


# SCENE 3³⁷

[DEÏANIRA *re-enters from the palace accompanied by an
attendant holding a casket.*]

DEÏANIRA:
My friends, while Lichas is bidding farewell indoors
To the captive women, I've slipped outside to you,
Partly to say what I have contrived³⁸ to do,
But also to claim your sympathy in my plight.                       535


This girl, no longer an *innocent* girl, I think,
Is now installed. I've allowed her to come on board,
As a merchant accepts an extra item of freight,³⁹
To destroy my peace of mind. Now there are two of us,
Under a single blanket, awaiting the arms
Of a single lover. That's the wages Heracles –                      540
Faithful, noble man as I thought – has sent me
For looking after his home in his lengthy absence.
I can't be *angry*. This malady strikes him far
Too often for that. But living together in one house,
Sharing the self-same partner – what woman could stand
For that? Her beauty, I see, is fast approaching                    545
Its full perfection, while mine is fading away.
A man's eye's greedy to pluck the flower of youth,
But cast on an older woman, it turns away.
This makes me afraid that Heracles will be called                   550
'Deïanira's husband, Iole's man.'
Yet, as I've said, resentment isn't a course
For a sensible woman. Friends, I have found a way
To rid myself of this fear. I'll tell it you now.

555 Long years ago, in days gone by, I received
A gift which I hid away in a brazen urn.
I was still a girl, and it came from the centaur[40] Nessus,
A horse with the shaggy front of a man. As he
Was dying, I took my gift from his bleeding wound.
Nessus was running a ferry across a river,
560 The deep Evenus, and charging a fare. His passengers
Didn't cross in a rowing- or sailing-boat.
He carried them all in his arms. He carried me too,
When my father, Oeneus, sent me away from home
And I first accompanied Heracles as his bride.
I was riding on Nessus' shoulders, but when we'd reached
565 Midstream, he started to fondle my body. I screamed
For help, and at once Zeus' son turned round and shot
An arrow, which whistled its way to the centaur's chest
And lodged in his lungs. With his dying breath, the beast
Gasped out, 'Now listen, Deïanira! This
570 Is how you will gain from being ferried by me
As my final passenger, if you'll do what I say.
Take the clotted blood from around my wound,
Where Heracles' arrow, dipped in the Hydra of Lerna's[41]
Murky venom, struck. That blood will give you
575 A charm for Heracles' heart, and he'll never look
At another woman to love her more than yourself.

Since Nessus' death, dear friends, I've kept it locked
Away in my house, and I've remembered it now.
580 I've smeared the blood on this tunic, applying it all
Just as the centaur told me while he lived.
Everything's ready. I wouldn't wish to become
An expert or take lessons in evil magic –
I hate all women who try it. But if, by a gentle
Charm, I'm somehow able to overcome
585 This beautiful girl and win back Heracles' love,
The remedy's now prepared – unless you think
I am being foolish. If so, I'll leave it alone.
CHORUS LEADER:
Well, if you firmly trust your charm will work,

Your plan, in my opinion, is not unsound.
DEÏANIRA:
All I'm certain about is this: it *seems*                              590
A good idea, though I haven't tested it out.
CHORUS LEADER:
You'll only know by acting. Whatever you think,
You'll have no means of judging, unless you try.[42]
DEÏANIRA:
We'll know before very long. Here's Lichas, now
At the door already. He'll soon be off. Just keep      595
My plan a secret. Even a shameful act,
If carried out in the dark, won't lead to shame.

     [LICHAS *re-enters from the palace.*]

LICHAS:
Please give me your orders, lady Deïanira.
This long delay now means that I am late.
DEÏANIRA:
I've been attending to the matter, Lichas,            600
While you were speaking with the women indoors.
This casket holds a full-length robe for Heracles.
Take it to him and say it's a present from me,
With these instructions: Nobody else should wear it
Before he does, nor should it be exposed             605
To the shining sun or the heat of a fire in a sacred
Precinct or household shrine, till Heracles stands
In the public gaze and displays this robe to the gods
On a solemn day when bulls are slain on the altar.
I made a vow that, if ever I saw or heard             610
He was safely home, I'd dress him up in this robe
And show him off to the gods in new attire
For a grand new rite. In proof that it comes from me,
I've put my seal on the box. He'll know it at once.   615

Now be on your way, and first observe the messenger's
Rule: Don't strain to overdo your duty,
And then make sure you perform my errand as well
As you have done his, to earn our thanks twice over.

LICHAS:

620 By Hermes, god of heralds, as I discharge
My duties fairly, I promise I shan't fail *you*.
I'll bring this casket to Heracles as it is,
And tell him about your vow, to clinch the matter.[43]

DEÏANIRA:

Be on your way at once. You understand
625 Quite well, I think, the way things are at home.

LICHAS:

I do, and will say that all is safe and sound.

DEÏANIRA:

And then, about the girl. You know because
You saw, how very warmly I made her welcome.

LICHAS:

Yes, yes, I was amazed and truly delighted.

DEÏANIRA:

630 What else is there to tell? I fear it would be
Too soon to add how much I'm longing for him,
Before I'm certain that he is longing for me.[44]

[*Exeunt* LICHAS *by a side entrance, and* DEÏANIRA, *followed
by her attendant, into the palace.*]


# CHORAL SONG 2[45]

CHORUS:

O hárbours and rócks of Tráchis,                    [*Strophe 1*]
Óeta's héights, and áll who dwéll
635 Close bý to Thermópylae's hót springs,
Bý the círcling márgin of Mális' láke,
Where Ártemis' spírit háunts the báy,
And fár-famed cóuncils of Gréeks
Assémble neár the Gréat Gates.[46]


640 The glórious sóund of píping                    [*Antistrophe 1*]
Sóon shall ríse alóng these cóasts
Once móre in a sóng of good ómen,
Jóyous líke the stráins of the lýre divíne.

For Zéus' and Alcména's míghty són
Is hástening báck to his hóme
With spóils of pérfect prówess.                                    645

He was lóst on the ócean, góne from hóme,          [*Strophe* 2]
As we wáited in féar a wéary twélve-month,⁴⁷
While nó one knéw where he míght be stráying.
Áll the whíle, his lóving wífe                                      650
In hársh, crúel gríef and néver-énding wóe,
Bewáiled her fáte and píned awáy.
Now Wár crazed with lúst has
Fréed her from sádness and páinful dáys.

Bring him hóme, bring him hóme and rést            655
     not, oárs,                                   [*Antistrophe* 2]
Of the ship that cárry the héro wéstward,
Until you sét him ashóre in Tráchis,
Báck from Cápe Cenáeum's héarth,
Where mán's vóice cláims he óffers thánks to Zéus.
We práy he cómes in hót desíre,                                    660
Inflámed by that lóve-charm,
Mélted by Néssus' sweet dýing gíft.⁴⁸

# SCENE 4⁴⁹

[*Re-enter* DEÏANIRA *from the palace.*]

DEÏANIRA:
Women, I'm so afraid! Perhaps I have gone
Too far in all I have just being doing.

CHORUS LEADER:
Dear lady, Deïanira, tell us why.                                  665

DEÏANIRA:
I cannot say. My hopes were all for the best,
But I fear I shall soon be shown to have done great harm.

CHORUS LEADER:
Not harm in the gift you sent to Heracles?

DEÏANIRA:
Yes, my friends! I must warn you all.
670   Don't act in haste when the way is dark.
CHORUS LEADER:
Why are you frightened? Please explain, if you can.
DEÏANIRA:
A curious thing has happened. If I describe it,
Women, you'll be completely amazed. The stuff
I used just now to anoint the festal robe,
675   A pad of wool from a fleecy sheep – it has vanished!
It wasn't consumed by anything from indoors,
But simply devoured itself. It crumbled to dust
On top of a slab in the court. So you know exactly
How it occurred, I'll tell you at greater length.

680   I disregarded none of the careful instructions
The centaur gave me, when Heracles' poisoned barb
Was painfully trapped in his side. They could have been
Graven in letters of bronze on my memory's tablets.[50]
685   He told me to keep the ointment safe in a secret
Corner, away from fire and the sun's hot rays,
Until the time when I came to apply it fresh.
I did as he said; and now, when the need arrived,
I plucked a tuft of wool from one of our sheep,
690   Then went indoors on my own and spread the charm.
Next, I folded the present up and placed it,
Away from the sun, inside the box that I handed
Over to Lichas, as you observed. But while
I was going inside again, I saw an omen
Too strange for words, beyond all comprehension.
695   I must have thrown the tuft of wool right into
A patch of sunlight. And as it started to heat,
The whole of it shrivelled up and crumbled to powder
There on the ground, just like the sawdust you see
700   In a workman's shop. Then from the earth where it lay
Exposed, blisters of foam came bubbling up,
Like the purple juice of luscious grapes, new-cut
From the vine and drenching the ground at pressing-time.

Oh, how wretched I am! My mind's in a whirl!                 705
I only see I've done the most dreadful thing.
Now, I ask you, why would the dying centaur
Have shown any kindness to *me*, because of whom
He was dying? No, he wanted to kill the man
Who shot him, and so bewitched me into believing him.       710
I have learned the truth too late, when it's no more use.
If I'm not somehow wrong, I'll prove my husband's
Death and destruction – none but I, heaven help me!
I know the arrow which wounded Nessus could even
Harm old Chiron,[51] and he was a god. Whatever            715
Creatures on earth it touches die. Black poison
There in the blood! It passed through Nessus' wound
And must kill Heracles too – so *I* believe.

Howbeit, I am resolved, if Heracles falls,
Then Deïanira's death must follow, too.                      720
For a woman who prides herself on her noble birth,
Life with a ruined name is not worth living.
CHORUS LEADER:
Such fearful sights must needs give cause for alarm,
But don't foresee the worst before it happens.
DEÏANIRA:
In such mistakes what else can one foresee?                  725
There is no hope of good to reassure us.
CHORUS LEADER:
When we go wrong without intending it,
Allowance can be made – and so for you.
DEÏANIRA:
Only an innocent could argue that.
Find trouble for yourself, and then you'll know.             730
     [*Enter* HYLLUS *from a side entrance.*]
CHORUS LEADER:
Better to say no more for now – unless
You want to speak to your own son. Hyllus,
Who went in search of his father, has now returned.
HYLLUS:
Oh Mother! Grant me a wish – just one of three!

735  I wish you were dead, or alive but not my mother,
     Or else that you'd change to a woman with more of a heart!⁵²
     DEÏANIRA:
     Hyllus, what have *I* done to make you hate me?
     HYLLUS:
     He was your husband, my father!
740  You've murdered him – today!
     DEÏANIRA:
     My boy! What does this outburst mean?
     HYLLUS:
     No less than the truth. It's there.
     You cannot undo what's done.
     DEÏANIRA:
     Hyllus, how do you know? Who told you?
745  How can you say I've done such a hideous deed?
     HYLLUS:
     No one told me. I saw it myself
     With my own eyes – Father dying in agony!
     DEÏANIRA:
     Where did you find him? How were you with him?

     HYLLUS:
     Right! If you have to know, I must tell it all.
750  After the sack of Eurytus' glorious city,
     He left with the arms he'd captured and spoils for sacrifice.
     Euboea ends in a sea-washed headland, Cape
     Cenaeum. There, to my great delight, I first
     Caught sight of him, tracing the line of a grove
755  With an altar precinct to honour his father Zeus.
     He was making ready to cut the throats of numerous
     Beasts, when Lichas, his trusty herald, came
     From home, bearing your present, the fatal robe.
     My father put on the garment, precisely as you
     Instructed, and then began the slaughter of twelve
760  Unblemished bulls, the pick of the spoil reserved
     For starting the rite – though in all he'd gathered a
         hundred
     Victims of various kinds before the altar.

At first the doomed man uttered the prayers serenely,
Proudly displaying his richly embroidered robe.
But when the bleeding flesh of the bulls grew hot                765
In the flames, which were also fed by the resinous logs,
The sweat broke out on his skin, and the tunic clung
To his sides, as tightly as if a craftsman had glued it
To all his joints. A convulsive pain came over
His limbs and gnawed right into his bones. A deadly,            770
Malignant viper's poison was eating him up.
At once he shouted out for the wretched Lichas,
Who had no part in the crime which *you* committed.
'What is this trick?' he yelled at him. 'How did you come
To bring this robe?' Bewildered, the poor man stammered         775
It came as a gift from you, which he'd delivered
Intact. When his master heard him, a tearing pain
Seized hold of his lungs. He grasped his servant's foot
By the ankle and flung him out to a lonely rock
Which rose from the sea. The herald's skull was broken         780
In splinters, his blood was sprinkled over the crag,
And globules of milky brain seeped out through his hair.
The crowd broke silence[53] in a groan of horror,
Seeing them both, one sick and the other destroyed.
No one would dare come close to the stricken man,              785
As he fell to the ground or leapt to the sky in his wild
Convulsions, shouting and howling. The cliffs all round,
The mountains of Locris and capes of Euboea resounded.
At last he gave up. He'd fallen to earth so often
And raised such cries to the heavens, bemoaning his ill-starred 790
Choice of a fiend like you for his bride and the proud
Alliance with Oeneus' house that had wrecked his life.
Then, through the clouds of smoke that were swirling round
     him,
He raised his rolling eyes, and he saw me weeping,            795
There in the crowd of people. He looked towards me
And called, 'Come here, my son! Don't run away
From this horror, even if you must die beside me.
No, lift me up and take me away, I hope
Where no one else can see me. If pity prevents                 800

Your doing that, at least you can ship me out
Of Euboea as soon as you can. I can't die here.'
That charge was enough. We put him on board a boat
And managed somehow to bring him ashore, still racked
805 And roaring, in Trachis. You all shall see him soon –
Alive, maybe, if he isn't already dead.

That is the crime you planned and committed against
My father, Mother. You're now convicted. I pray
The avenging spirit of Justice will make you suffer
No less – if my prayer is right. And it *must* be right.
810 The right to curse you is granted to me by *you*.
You've murdered the very greatest man in the world,[54]
The like of whom you never shall see again.
     [*Exit* DEÏANIRA *into the palace.*]
CHORUS LEADER:
Going without a word? You surely know
Your silence argues your accuser's case.
HYLLUS:
815 Oh, let her go – and a fair wind blow her
Far from my sight! Why should a woman
Pride herself on a mother's name,
If she never acts as a mother should?
No, let her go, and luck go with her. I wish her
820 All the joy and pleasure she's giving my father!
     [*Exit* HYLLUS *into the palace.*]

# CHORAL SONG 3[55]

CHORUS:
       Behold, O maidens, suddenly brought to our door,   [*Strophe 1*]
       That word of the oracle, spoken
       Long ago in deep foreknowledge,
       The message of fortune that after the twelfth long year[56]
            had spanned
825    Its number of months, there would come to the true-born
            son of Zeus

Rest from his painful labours.
Trúe the wórd now,
Wafted home into harbour.
Hów could ányone lónger
Obey a týrannous máster
When once his eyes are darkened?                              830

For íf a clóud of múrder is swírling aróund,     [*Antistrophe 1*]
Through Nessus' insidious scheming,
Íf his sídes are stéeped in póison,
The poison which issued from death and the shimmering
    serpent reared,
This day that he looks on the sunlight must surely be his    835
    last,
Locked in the Hydra's monstrous
Grip of terror,
Wildly goaded and tortured.
Words of guile are erupting
In red sóres on his bódy,
As Black Hair wreaks his vengeance.                          840

All this pain poor Deïanira                        [*Strophe 2*]
Had never foreseen, but an onrush
Of mischief, when that rival
Came to bed in her own house.
She herself did the fatal deed,
But nów bewáils hávoc wróught by a stránger's wíles,         845
Rues that ominous meeting.
Nów the déw of her pále tears
Is moistening her fair cheeks,
While Fáte as she advánces reveals tréacherous,
Tempéstuous destrúction.                                     850

Break, break forth, you fountains of tears!       [*Antistrophe 2*]
The disease has infested the hero.
Alas! He never suffered
Súch great hárm from a déadly
Foe or roused such pity before.                              855

Oh cúrse the black-póinted spéar in the frónt of wár,
Spear which prodded the fair girl
Down Oechalia's mountains
And brought her to Trachis' walls!
860     While Cýpris, the gods' hándmaid who says néver a word
Póints to her new tríumph.


# SCENE 5[57]


[*A cry of lamentation is heard offstage.*][58]
CHORUS I:
Is it my foolish fancy, or did I hear
A cry of grief, echoing through the house?
CHORUS 2:
865   What is it?
It surely has a meaning – that sound of dismal
Lamentation. It speaks of trouble within.
CHORUS LEADER:
Now look! Our lady's nurse, with downcast eyes
870   And furrowed brow, is coming to give us news.
         [*Enter* NURSE *from the palace.*]
NURSE:
Children! What fearful sorrow it was doomed
To bring us – the present sent to Heracles!
CHORUS LEADER:
      Oh Nurse! What fresh mischance is this?
NURSE:
Deïanira's gone on her final journey –
875   Without stirring a foot!
CHORUS LEADER:
You cannot mean – her death?
NURSE:
                              It's true.
CHORUS LEADER:
She's *dead*, poor lady?
NURSE:
                         Yes, she's dead.

CHORUS LEADER:
The poor, lost soul! How, oh, how did she die?
NURSE:
It was cruel, so horribly cruel!
CHORUS LEADER:
But tell us,
What was the fate she met?                                      880
NURSE:
She killed herself – with a two-edged sword!
CHORUS:
    What passion, or what sickness, struck,
    Drove the point of a sharpened blade
    Into her heart? A second death,
    Now by a weapon of iron!                                 885
    Do you say that she did it alone, then?
    Tell us how she planned it.
    It cán't be trúe! You sáw thís víolent áct?[59]
NURSE:
Oh yes, I saw it. I was standing there.
CHORUS:
    Saw what? How? Please tell us.                          890
NURSE:
She dealt the blow herself, with her own hand.
CHORUS:
    You méan thát?
NURSE:
                Beyónd dóubt.
CHORUS:
    Oh, what a deadly child she bore,
    That cáptive gírl, the néw bríde!
    She bóre the hóuse a fóul fíend![60]                     895
NURSE:
Too true. If you'd been there close by to see
What Mistress did, you'd have pitied her all the more.
CHORUS LEADER:
And could a weak woman's hand have dared this thing?
NURSE:
With dreadful daring. I'll tell you all that happened,

900 Then you can witness it too. She'd gone alone
Inside the house, and when she saw that her son
Was making ready a loose-strung stretcher before
He left to meet his father, she hid herself
Where no one else could see her. Then falling down
Before the household altars, she loudly wailed
905 They'd all be left untended. She wept to touch
The old familiar objects she had used,
And while she wandered through the different rooms,
She'd spy a servant who'd been close to her,
And weep again, poor lady, as she looked
910 Into his eyes, lamenting her own fate,
And for the family hearth, now fatherless.[61]

But when she'd finished walking round, I saw her
Suddenly heading straight into Heracles' chamber.
I quietly watched in the shadows, where I couldn't
915 Be seen myself, and then observed her carefully
Spreading covers on to her husband's bed.
That task completed, she suddenly sprang on top
And sat there in the middle of the bed.
A flood of burning tears burst out once more
920 As I heard her say, 'My bed,[62] my bridal chamber,
Farewell for ever now. You'll never welcome
Me again, to sleep here in this room.'

With these sad words, she clutched the golden pin
That held her dress at the shoulder over her breasts
925 And wrenched it out, to expose her arm and the whole
Of her left side. I ran as fast as I could
To tell her son what his mother was trying to do.
There and back we hurried, but during that while,
We found she had stabbed her side with a two-edged sword,[63]
930 Right through to her heart. When Hyllus saw her, he uttered
A cry of terrible grief. He knew, poor boy,
That his own great anger had driven her to this act.
He'd learned the truth too late from one of the servants:
The centaur was all to blame; his mother had sent

The robe with no idea what harm she was doing.                          935

At that the wretched boy abandoned himself
To every kind of lament, as he mourned his mother.
He covered her lips with kisses, clung with his body
Close to her side[64] and lay there, sobbing his heart out.
'Oh, what I fool I was! My harsh reproach                               940
Was false!' he wailed. 'I've lost my father and mother,
Both at a single blow. They're gone forever!'

That's how things are in the house. I have to say,
If you try to plan your life two days ahead
Or further, you're a simple fool. You cannot                           945
Count on tomorrow until you've survived today.[65]
   [*Exit* NURSE *into the palace.*]


# CHORAL SONG 4[66]

CHORUS:
   Whose sórrow should Í be laménting fírst?        [*Strophe 1*]
   Whose súffering hóld for a dírge to cóme?
   Áll that I knów is bóundless gríef.

   One hórror is hére to be séen withín,        [*Antistrophe 1*]  950
   Anóther disáster will sóon appéar,
   Présent and fúture bóth one wóe.

   Ah, would that a wind might blow,             [*Strophe 2*]
   A wind with power to waft me from my homeland,
   Away to dwell in far-off climes, and spare my eyes.               955
   The sudden sight of Zeus' great son
   Alone would awaken terror,
   Make me faint and gazing die.
   For they sáy that in páin that can nót be assuáged
   He's coming before the house here –                               960
   Wonder past all speaking!

So soon they're arrived! I raised                    [*Antistrophe 2*]
My piercing song, my nightingale, so near them!
A band of strangers, all unknown, is marching here.
965     And what must this procession bode?
Such silent yet heavy footsteps
Speak a care for one they love.
*Aiái*! Their appróach is quíet as the gráve.
What cán I belíeve? Is Héracles
970     Dead, or peacefully sleeping?
[*During Antistrophe 2,* HERACLES *enters, carried on a litter
by bearers led by an* OLD MAN. *At the end,* HYLLUS *enters
from the palace.*]


# CLOSING SCENE[67]


HYLLUS:
    *Oímoí*![68] Dear Father, how wretched I am!
    Oh, what will become of me? *Óimoi*?
OLD MAN:[69]
    Silence, boy! You mustn't stir up
975     Your father's pain in his cruel, wild state.
    He is barely alive. Now curb your tongue
    And be quiet!
HYLLUS:
                    Do you mean, old sir, that he still lives?
OLD MAN:
    Do not wake him up when he's fast asleep
    Or rouse his sickness out of its lair!
    It is constantly coming
    And going, my son.
HYLLUS:
                    This blow is far
    Too heavy to bear. My mind's in a frenzy!
        [HERACLES *wakes.*]
HERACLES:
    O Zeus![70]
    Where have I come? Who are these people

I see, as I lie tormented by pain                                                        985
Unceasingly. Help me, god! The fiend
Is starting to gnaw me again. Ah!

OLD MAN:

Didn't I warn you? Far, far better
To hide your feelings and not to scatter
The mist of sleep                                                                        990
From his head and his eyes!

HYLLUS:

How else can I bear
To look on this vision of horror?

HERACLES:

Cenaeum, where my altars stood,
I wish I had never set eyes on you! Such,
Zeus knows, were the gracious                                                            995
Thanks you returned for my offerings!
What cruel wrong you have done me, wrong!
To face this eruption
Of madness which cannot be charmed away!
What worker of spells or of healing skills                                               1000
Will calm this torturing plague but Zeus?
I never could see such a marvel.
   É! É!⁷¹                                                     [Strophe]
  O god, lét me bé!
  Mercy, be merciful!
  Leave me to sleep in peace!                                                  1005
  How to endure such pain?
   [OLD MAN *tries to move him.*]
Don't touch me, man, don't try to turn me,
You'll kill me, you'll kill me!
You've now disturbed what was lulled to rest.
Ambushed, pounced on again! It's attacking me! Where do          1010
  you think you've
Sprung from, Greeks, you vilest of men in the world, for
  whose sáke I
Laboured, purging the sea of monsters, purging the
  woodlands,

Wearing my poor life out? And now, when I'm helplessly
     stricken,
No one will burn my body or draw his sword to relieve me.
     É! É!
     All unwilling to come?
1015     Cut off my head, I say!
     Stifle this cruel pain!
     Finish my life! God, god!

OLD MAN:

Hyllus, you are his son. What he asks is a task too hard for a
Weak old man like me. You must help him yourself. You are
     younger
And stronger than I.

HYLLUS:

1020                         My hands are here, but I haven't the
     power,
Power within or outside myself, to inflict the blow that will
Make him forget his agony. That is for Zeus to accord him.


HERACLES:

     Oh, where, whére's my són?                    [*Antistrophe*]
     Come to me, come to me!
1025     Lift me and hold me close.
     Mercy, O god, I pray!
     It's rearing up once more, this pain.
     It will tear me apart,
1030     This angry, dangerous, deadly beast!
Help me, Pallas Athena![72] Again it's destroying me! Dear son,
Pity your father and draw your sword on me – no one will
     blame you.
1035 Strike me below my neck and heal this torment with which
     your
Godless mother has driven me mad. I wish I could see her,
1040     Próstrate, rúined as shé ruined mé, like thís! God of mércy,
          Hades, brother of Zeus,
          Put me to sleep, to sleep!
          Finish my wretched life,
          Grant me a speedy end.

CHORUS LEADER:
I shudder to hear[73] our master in such distress.
So great a hero, racked by such great pain!                    1045
HERACLES:
How many burning labours,[74] cruel indeed,
My hands, this back, have painfully undergone!
Yet neither Zeus' wife, Hera, nor the vile
Eurystheus ever imposed such a fierce ordeal
On me – this woven robe, the devilish net
Which Deïanira, with her treacherous eyes,               1050
Has fastened to my shoulders, and now I'm dying.
Plastered against my sides, it has gnawed its way
Right into my flesh, it is sucking out the breath
Inside my lungs, and now it has drained my fresh
Life-blood to the final drop. The whole of my body's      1055
Wasted, crushed in these unspeakable chains.
Those warriors on the plain, that host of earth-born
Giants,[75] those savage beasts, and all the lands
I came to, Greek or barbarian, purging monsters –        1060
None of them ever did this much; but a feeble
Woman, without a drop of masculine blood,
Alone and swordless, managed to bring me down.

Hyllus, my son, now prove you are indeed               1065
My true-born son. Don't honour your mother's name
Above your father's. Fetch that woman from home
And pass her into my clutches with your own hands.
I need to know if it hurts you more to see
My mangled frame or hers, when I've fairly punished her.
Come on, my boy, don't shrink! Show me some pity,      1070
As others pity me. Here I am, sobbing
And crying away like a girl. No one could say
He ever saw great Heracles weeping before.
I faced my hardships without so much as a whimper.
But now, instead, I'm found a feeble woman.              1075

My son, come here, stand close beside your father,
And see how I've been brought to this dreadful pass.

I'll take these coverings off and show you. Look!
Look all of you! Gaze on my tortured body,
1080    Observe the wretched Heracles' pitiful state!
            *Aiaí*, áh the páin! *Aiaí*!
That burning spasm once again! It has pierced me
Through my sides. It won't allow me to rest,
It seems – this wretched, racking, gnawing plague!
1085        O king of the underworld, take me!
            Lightning of Zeus, now strike!
Brandish your bolt, lord! Father, launch it powerfully
Down on my head. It's eating me up once more;
It has bloomed, it has broken out. Oh hands, my hands,
1090    My sturdy back and chest, my loyal old arms!
You were the famous arms whose strength subdued
The lion that haunted Nemea and scourged the flocks,
A creature none would dare to approach or face.
You slew the Hydra of Lerna; you overcame
1095    Those wild half-men who walked on horses' legs,
The violent, lawless, super-mighty centaurs.
You killed the Erymanthian boar, and fetched
The monster dog[76] up from the underworld,
The dread Echidna's invincible whelp, with three
Fierce heads. You slew the dragon who closely watched
1100    The golden apples away in the farthest west.
I braved all these and countless other labours,
And no man claimed a victory over you.
But now my limbs are useless; I'm torn to rags,
Unseen disaster's ransacked my whole being,
1105    Though I was called the child of a peerless mother,
The son of Zeus who reigns among the stars.
But be assured of this: though I am nothing
And have no power to move, even as I am
I'll get my hands on that woman. Just bring her here.
1110    She must learn her lesson and cry this truth to the world:
In death, as in life, I punished evil-doers.
CHORUS LEADER:
Unhappy Greece, what sorrow I see ahead
For you – to lose so great a man as this!

HYLLUS:
Father, you're silent now, and I can reply.
Ill though you are, please listen to what I say.                          1115
I ask of you no more than you ought to give.
Just hear me out and allow your anger to cool,
Else you will never learn how wrong you are
In both your wishes and the rage you feel.

HERACLES:
Say what you like and then have done. I'm ill,                            1120
And can't make out a word of all your riddles.

HYLLUS:
I want to tell you about my mother – how
She is, and how she unwittingly went astray.

HERACLES:
You treacherous cur! Those words to my face? How can you
Dare to mention the mother who killed your father?                        1125

HYLLUS:
You have to know how she is. I can't say nothing.

HERACLES:
You can't, when I think of all the harm she's done.

HYLLUS:
You'll understand when you know what she's done today.

HERACLES:
Go on. But take good care not to prove disloyal.

HYLLUS:
Very well. My mother's dead. She has just been killed.                    1130

HERACLES:
Who did it? Ill-omened words! The gods are at work.

HYLLUS:
She wasn't murdered. She killed herself.

HERACLES:
Too early! *I* should have killed that woman!

HYLLUS:
Even you would relent if you knew the whole truth.

HERACLES:
Knew what? You puzzle me. Say what you mean.                              1135

HYLLUS:
Her mistake was fatal, but her intentions were good.

HERACLES:
You call that *good* – to kill your father?
HYLLUS:
She saw the girl you'd taken and thought a love-charm
Would win you back. But her plan completely failed.
HERACLES:
1140   Love-charms in Trachis? Who dispenses *them*?
HYLLUS:
The centaur Nessus convinced her long ago
That a charm like that would drive you mad with love.
HERACLES:
I see! I see![77] Heracles' end has come.
No more to live, no more to feel the sun!
1145   At last I have some inkling where I stand.
Now go, my son. You've lost your father now.
Summon your brothers and sisters to me here,
And call Alcmena, my poor mother, who slept
With Zeus for nothing. I want you all to hear
1150   My final words and share the oracles I know.
HYLLUS:
I fear your mother is not in Trachis. She's living
Close to the sea at Tiryns. Some of your children
She's taken with her; the rest are still in Thebes.
But all of us who are here will do whatever
1155   Is needed, Father, and help you as best we may.
HERACLES:
Well, then, my son, here's what you have to do.
You're mine, and now's the time for you to show
The stuff you're made of.
                              Many years ago
It was foretold me from my father Zeus,
1160   No living person should ever cause my death,
But one already dead who lived below
In Hades. So, the centaur-beast has made
That prophecy true: the dead has killed the living.[78]
1165   And this accords with later oracles,
Which I'll reveal – the new chimes with the old.
Up at Dodona,[79] I once visited

Zeus' mountain shrine and met the Selli,
Priests who sleep upon bare earth. I heard
My father's talking oak and wrote the words
Down on a tablet. They said that at this time,
This present time, I'd be at last released                          1170
From all the labours laid on me. I thought
That meant fair days. But all it signified
Was death – my death. The dead are labour-free.
These prophecies are coming true, my son.
Your task is now to stand at Heracles' side.                        1175
Don't raise my curses by a long delay.
Give me your willing help and show you've learned
That best of rules, obedience to your father.

HYLLUS:
I'm frightened, Father. Such blind promises
Are hard to give, but still I'll do as you ask.                     1180

HERACLES:
First place your hand in mine to give your pledge.

HYLLUS:
What promise are you forcing me to make?

HERACLES:
Obey me, boy! Give me your hand now, quickly!

HYLLUS:
It's here, then; take it. I shan't oppose your wish.

HERACLES:
Swear by the head of Zeus, whose seed I am . . .                    1185

HYLLUS:
What must I swear? You have to tell me that.

HERACLES:
Swear that you will perform the task I give you.

HYLLUS:
I, Hyllus, swear this oath. Zeus be my witness!

HERACLES:
And pray for punishment[80] if you break your oath.

HYLLUS:
I'll need no punishment, as I'll keep my oath.
But still I make that prayer.                                       1190

HERACLES:

                            So then.
You've been to Oeta and Zeus' holy place,
High on the mountain top?

HYLLUS:

                            I have.
I've often sacrificed at the altar there.

HERACLES:

That is the place[81] where you must bear me now.
Do it yourself, with any friends you choose.
1195  Erect a pyre of branches cut from the strong,
Deep-rooted oak and wild male olive trees
Felled to the ground, and on that lay my body.
Then take a torch of burning pine and set
The pyre alight. I want to see no tears
Of mourning. If you're Heracles' son, you'll do
1200  My bidding without one tear or cry of lament.
Or else I'll still be there, beneath the earth,
Waiting to haunt you with my curse forever.

HYLLUS:

No, Father, no! How can you be so cruel?

HERACLES:

It's what has to be done. If not, you'd better
1205  Find a new father. You're my son no more.

HYLLUS:

I say again, you're cruel. You're asking me
To be your murderer and defile myself.

HERACLES:

No, no, not I. You'll be my healer, son,
Since you alone can cure me of all this pain.

HYLLUS:

1210  How can I cure you by setting fire to your body?

HERACLES:

Well, if you shrink from that, do all the rest.[82]

HYLLUS:

Yes, Father. I shan't refuse to carry you there.

HERACLES:

And will you prepare my pyre, as I've instructed?

HYLLUS:
So long as my own hands play no part in the work,
I'll see to it all. You can rely on me.                                    1215
HERACLES:
That will be good enough – a generous gift.
Now promise me one more favour, small this time.
HYLLUS:
However great it is, I promise to do it.
HERACLES:
Well, then, you know the girl, King Eurytus' daughter?
HYLLUS:
It's Iole whom you mean, if I take you right.                               1220
HERACLES:
Yes, Iole. This is my firm instruction, Hyllus:
When I have died, if you wish to do your duty
And to fulfil the oath you've sworn your father,
Take this girl as your wife. You can't refuse me.
No other man must be allowed to wed                                         1225
The woman who lay in Heracles' arms but you.[83]
You, son, must be the one to marry her.
Now say you will. You'll meet my chief demands;
Don't spoil that gift by refusing one small thing.
HYLLUS:
Oh god!
I know that anger's wrong with a man who's sick.                            1230
But how could anyone sane agree to that?
HERACLES:
You sound as though you'll not do a thing I say.
HYLLUS:
Look! Iole, no one else, must be held to blame
For my mother's death and for bringing you in turn
To this terrible pass. Only a man who suffered                              1235
From some demonic sickness could choose to do
As you ask. Oh Father, I'd rather die myself
Beside you than make a home with my deadliest foe.
HERACLES:
It seems this fellow won't even show respect
For his father's dying wish. Be careful, though!

1240    The curse of heaven awaits your disobedience.
        HYLLUS:
        Oh god! Your crazing sickness
        Must soon be plain to the world.
        HERACLES:
        Yes, it had gone to sleep,
        And you're waking it up once more.
        HYLLUS:
        I wish I knew what to do!
        HERACLES:
        Obey your father. That's all.
        HYLLUS:
1245    But what you are teaching me now is wickedness.
        HERACLES:
        Wickedness? Not if you'll make me happy.
        HYLLUS:
        Is this your final, solemn command?
        HERACLES:
        Yes, I command it, and call the gods
        To witness my word.
        HYLLUS:
        I cannot refuse you, then. The gods will know
1250    My action's yours. I'll do my duty, Father,
        To you and prove my noble nature.
        HERACLES:
        The way to end. And please, my son, perform
        Your service quickly. Lay me upon the pyre
        Before the tearing, stinging pain returns.
1255    Make haste, men, lift me up. This is release
        From toil. It signals Heracles' final end.
        HYLLUS:
        Yes, nothing prevents your wishes being fulfilled.
        Your orders, Father, leave me without a choice.
        HERACLES:
        Come then,[84] my unyielding soul, do not wait
1260    To awaken the fearful demon again.
        Put a curb of steel, stone-set, on my lips.
        No cries of ill omen! The struggle ahead

Will be hard, but the end will be joyful.[85]
[*During the following lines, the litter carrying* HERACLES *is
raised and borne off by the bearers down a side entrance in
a cortège, led by the* OLD MAN.]

HYLLUS:

Followers, lift him! I ask you to show
Your hearts' understanding for me in this task.                    1265
For you know that the hearts of the callous gods
Feel nothing in all these sorry events.
They beget their sons and are called our fathers,
Yet look down calmly on our great pain.
No man has a vision of what is to come.[86]                        1270
But the present is fraught with sorrow for us here,
Shame for those hard gods,
Torment exceeding all for the hero
Who braves this fire of destruction.
     [HYLLUS *follows the cortège.*]

CHORUS LEADER:

Women, you need not stay by the house.                             1275
We have witnessed a strange apparition of death,
Now matched by a picture of pain unknown.
And all this story is great Zeus.[87]
     [*The* CHORUS *follows.*]

# AJAX

# Preface to *Ajax*

## THE TRADITION

Sophocles' audience knew Ajax well from Homer's *Iliad* as the greatest warrior on the Greek side during the Trojan War after Achilles. He was particularly associated in the epic with Odysseus and also with Hector, the greatest of the Trojan warriors. His story continued in the *Odyssey* (briefly) and the Epic Cycle, both of which referred to the episode that lies behind Sophocles' play: after Achilles' death, the hero's arms were awarded in a contest not to Ajax but to Odysseus, and the humiliation of this defeat drove Ajax to madness and suicide, followed by a dishonourable burial.[1]

Ajax was also a figure of hero-cult at Athens. He came from Salamis, an island close to the city, which had been part of Attica since the sixth century, and he was regarded as a major Athenian hero in Sophocles' time.

## SYNOPSIS

Before the action begins, Ajax, in mortification over the judgement of Achilles' arms, has made a solitary night-attack on the Greek army, with the intention of killing the generals whom he regards as responsible for his humiliation: Agamemnon and Menelaus (the two sons of Atreus) and Odysseus. He has been frustrated in this attempt by the goddess Athena, who has afflicted him with a delusional madness and so driven him to slaughter the Greeks' captured spoil of sheep and cattle, in the belief that they are his intended victims. The play shows Ajax first at the height of his dementia, then after he has returned to his senses and realized what he has done. He now sees suicide as the only means of preserving his honour. Despite the pleas of his friends and dependants, and after an apparent change of heart, he finally leaps on his sword.

The remainder of the tragedy is devoted to the discovery of Ajax's corpse and the issue of his honourable burial by his half-brother Teucer. This is strongly opposed by Agamemnon and Menelaus, but Teucer gets his way after the intervention of Odysseus. The drama ends in a solemn funeral procession.

# INTERPRETATION

Like *Women of Trachis*, *Ajax* is a strange and powerful play, impossible to date with any certainty and one that has attracted a variety of interpretations. What follows aims only to offer the first-time reader a few clues to the understanding of a complex work.[2]

Once again, the action appears to fall into two sharply divided parts: one concerned with the tragedy of Ajax himself and his death, the other with his burial. Here also, though, there are important themes and links which make for a unity and a progression within the whole.

An obvious line of interpretation sees the second part, culminating in Ajax's funeral, as a rehabilitation of the humiliated suicide to a point consistent with his historical status in Athens as a cult hero. Although there is no direct reference in the text to the establishment of a cult, this idea must surely be implicit and important. Certainly the restoration of Ajax to honour after his death contradicts the epic tradition about the treatment of his body.

Another approach looks back to the Homeric Ajax and the heroic code reflected in the *Iliad*. The cardinal values of this code are *aretê*, excellence in warlike exploits demanding great courage, and *timê*, the honour and social esteem in which a man with *aretê* is held. When Ajax fails to receive Achilles' arms, his status

as second in *areté* only to Achilles is seriously undermined, and
he believes he is bound in honour to reassert it. However, in his
planned assault on the Atridae, he takes the heroic code to an
unacceptable extreme; to murder the two generals and torture
Odysseus cannot be an honourable way of behaving. After he
has been frustrated by Athena, the realization that he has only
vented his rage on harmless animals is so humiliating that, if he
cannot live in honour, he must die in honour by committing
suicide.

At the same time, we can detect a contrast between the old
Homeric world with its aristocratic values and the contemporary
world of fifth-century democracy. The latter is represented posi-
tively in Sophocles' portrayal of Odysseus (in this play) and
more negatively by Menelaus and Agamemnon. Some critics have
viewed Ajax as the last of the great heroes, with Odysseus' victory
in the judgement of arms signifying a move to altered, and not
necessarily more admirable, criteria of excellence within the context of the city-state. This reading would account for the remarkable change of tone and style in the later scenes, and for the
element of satire in the treatment of the Atridae, whose political
pronouncements and offensive posturing lack the rationality and
self-knowledge shown by Odysseus.

Odysseus' moderation is obviously crucial as a foil to the
arrogance and excess of the play's hero. Ajax suffers from the
sin of pride (the state of mind often referred to by modern critics
as *hubris*[3]) that comes before a fall. He lacks the redeeming quality of *sophrosynê*, which basically means 'sound-
mindedness' and embodies the virtues of self-restraint and awareness of one's human limitations. This is the quality demonstrated
by Odysseus but missing in Ajax, as can be seen in the latter's
words and behaviour towards the other characters and, very
specifically, in what we learn about him from the Messenger
(757–78): his arrogant boasting had incurred the wrath of
Athena, who sums up the whole position herself in the final
words of Scene 1: 'The gods love those / Who know their place
[the people with *sophrosynê*] and hate ignoble men [those who
have betrayed their *areté* and breeding by dishonourable
behaviour].'

There are yet other strands in the play's conceptual texture. One is the ethic, common to the heroic and fifth-century worlds in ancient Greece, that is both assumed and challenged in all of Sophocles' plays: you do good to your friends and harm to your enemies. Intractable problems arise when those who have been your friends become your enemies. Ajax's friends and comrades became enemies in his eyes when the judgement of arms went against him, and those enemies, in the persons of Menelaus and Agamemnon, inevitably treat him as an enemy and inhumanely want to refuse his body burial.

Changes in relationships lead on to a further vital theme: the patterns of change and alternation that are to be observed in nature and the whole of human life.[4] This truth is, paradoxically, put into the mouth of the obdurate Ajax himself in his famous Deception Speech (see note 37). It underlies the reversal at the end of the play, when Ajax's humiliation is converted to honour – as the result of Odysseus' own conversion from Ajax's enemy to Ajax's friend.

The reason for Odysseus' conversion adds yet one more dimension. It is foreshadowed in Scene 1, where Odysseus admits to *pity* for Ajax in his ruinous madness (122–3) and acknowledges the insubstantial nature of all mortal existence (125–6). It is the theme that runs through the appeal of Ajax's concubine Tecmessa (485–524) for pity and consideration of herself and their child. Near the end, Odysseus argues for the recognition of Ajax's *aretê* and for obedience to the divine imperatives which demand that his body should be shown respect (1337–45). What is more, Odysseus will need those rites of burial himself (1365). If his compassion is not entirely altruistic, it still suggests a yardstick against which the other values explored in the drama can be measured.[5]

# CASTING

Unless Sophocles quite exceptionally made use of four actors, the protagonist combined Ajax with Teucer, so providing an element of continuity like the doubling of Deïanira and Heracles in *Women of Trachis*. For the other roles various combinations are possible, but the second actor is generally thought to have played Odysseus and Tecmessa. This would leave left Athena, the Messenger, Menelaus and Agamemnon to the third actor.

If this allocation is correct, Ajax's dead body would have been represented on stage by a dummy, and a mute would have had to stand in for Tecmessa after 1170. Other mutes would have played the child Eurysaces, various attendants and others taking part in the final procession.

# STAGING

The *skênê* represents Ajax's hut, the wooden building in which he and his dependants would have been quartered at one end of the Greek encampment by the sea (3–4). In the latter part of the play, this ceases to be functional and merely forms a background and sounding-board for the argument over Ajax's body. One *eisodos* could have stood for the approach from the rest of the Greek camp, the other the path to the wilder land along the shore. Athena's appearance at the beginning of the play is discussed in note 3 to the text.

At 347–8 the doors of the *skênê* are opened to disclose a tableau of Ajax sitting among the slaughtered sheep. Most scholars agree that this spectacular moment involved the *ekkyklêma*, the wheeled platform that could be propelled and withdrawn through the central entrance and was understood by convention to be presenting the effects of an event indoors.

A major, much debated problem arises over the staging of Ajax's death: we have to conjecture how the hero's suicide was contrived, whether on stage or just off; also how and where his body was supposed to be found by Tecmessa and then prominently displayed (in the form of a dummy[6]) in a position where it could be visibly present until the end of the play. The neatest and most practical solution, perhaps, is to assume that 'the trees close to the hut' mentioned in 892 were somehow represented in front of the *skênê* to the 'shore' side of the acting area. This need not have amounted to anything more than a masking 'wing' consisting of a flat painted with one or more stylized trees, behind which Ajax could have made his final exit at 865 and then be imagined to fall on his sword, to be subsequently discovered offstage by Tecmessa before being carried on as a corpse. For further details of this solution, see notes 53, 61, 63, 64. In note 69 I suggest a practical function for a balancing flat to the other side of the *skênê*.[7]

Most commentaries posit a change of scene to a lonely place away from the camp after the Chorus makes its unusual exit at 814, but it is hardly necessary to suppose this, if the above suggestion for a 'grove' is valid.[8] More important is the likelihood that the focus of action in the later scenes advances down from the *skênê* into the *orchêstra*, so reflecting the drama's change to a more contemporary, audience-orientated atmosphere.

## DRAMATIC TECHNIQUE

*Ajax* is commonly regarded as the earliest and most Aeschylean of Sophocles' tragedies, mainly because of the poetic richness of its earlier scenes. But words are not used in quite the same powerfully ominous way as in Aeschylus (see pages 9–10). The ambivalences in Ajax's Deception Speech are more dictated by the immediate context[9] than inherent in the way the drama works. Account has also to be taken of the marked change in pace and tone of the language in the later scenes concerned with the wrangle over his dead body. Teucer's confrontations with Menelaus and Agamemnon are far more like the *agônes*, or formal debates, that are a marked characteristic of Euripides' plays. In this case, the use of language in the theatre seems to be moving away from the idea that words in themselves have a kind of magical power to control events and towards the more sophisticated concept of rhetoric, the art which confers the power of controlling people's minds and emotions through argument. However that may be, the shift in style between the earlier and later scenes in *Ajax* (like the shift in the use of theatrical space) reflects the contrast between the nobler and more idealized atmosphere of the heroic world that Ajax represents and the pragmatic spirit of debate which belongs more to the contemporary world of Sophocles' audience. We can observe a more complex dramaturgy here than in *Women of Trachis* with its heavy reliance on straight narrative.

The notes on the play offer a commentary on Sophocles' control of the plot, especially in contriving a situation that allows Ajax to commit suicide, almost on stage, in the absence of the Chorus, and then for his corpse to provide a visual focus while the actor who has played him goes on to assume the role of Teucer.[10] The poet's dramatic imagination and skill are well exemplified in the memorable moments and surprises that he contrives and in his adroit sequencing of the different 'movements' in their distinct metres and emotional registers for soloists, Chorus or both. It is also interesting to see how Sophocles used his human resources – the three actors and the Chorus – to tell his story and engage his audience's responses. The power of the play depends to a large extent on the characters and personalities underlying the actors' different masks and expressed in their words and actions.

The protagonist had a magnificent opportunity in the title role. It demands a commanding stage presence and a large physique, together with the vocal power and stamina to perform four long iambic speeches, an extended lyric interchange in sung delivery with the Chorus and Tecmessa, and two comparatively short but striking runs of stichomythia. Adjectives and adverbs used to describe him in the text refer to his greatness, boldness, impetuosity, obstinacy, nobility, raw cruelty, thoughtless boastfulness – and to his isolation. His first entrance with his whip in manic exhilaration is hugely compelling, as we observe him with horror, gloating over his imagined victims and imperiously treating the warrior goddess Athena as a kind of underling. His next appearance is in a spectacular tableau surrounded by the sheep he has brutally slaughtered, now longing for his own death in the depths of his frustration and despair after realizing what he has actually done. After that, four long speeches serve in their different ways to emphasize his terrifying loneliness. Although only one of them is a soliloquy in the strict sense, the others are very largely solipsistic reflections. Even the address to Eurysaces suggests that

Ajax sees his little son as essentially an extension of himself. In what he says to the Chorus, he is solely concerned with his own requirements, while his stichomythic exchanges with the devoted Tecmessa lack tenderness and end in a violent outburst. Does Ajax show any compassion or self-knowledge? In the Deception Speech, perhaps (but see note 37). What we can say for sure about that speech is that it allows the actor a chance to establish a calmer, more rational and philosophical mood before the return to splendid self-assertion and grim vindictiveness in the Suicide Speech.

After his suicide, Ajax's body and presence had to be represented on stage by a prominently displayed dummy. Something of his spirit, though, lived on in the voice of Teucer, performed by the same actor, in confrontation with the Atridae. Teucer lacks his half-brother's greatness, the special demonic quality of a hero, but his speeches show much of Ajax's aggression, and the two are particularly linked by their common desire not to lose face in the eyes of Telamon, their father. Vocal continuity between the two roles could have contributed both to the drama's unity and to the sustaining of the audience's interest in the later scenes.

If the second actor combined the roles of Tecmessa and Odysseus, the two friends of Ajax (apart from the Chorus), we have another interesting double, though each part makes a strong impact in its own right. Odysseus on Ajax's trail in the opening lines, and then in fear of seeing his quarry in a state of wild madness, makes a striking figure from the outset. His unexpected pity for Ajax at the end of Scene 1 not only anticipates his surprising support for Ajax's burial in the closing scene but also leads on to the tender concern that runs through Tecmessa's narratives and her moving appeal. Tecmessa is the character who discovers Ajax's body and shares with the Chorus in the long operatic lament that follows. She is still present for the final rituals, though only in the physical form of a mute actor: But she is also there in the voice of Odysseus, whose gentle persuasions secure the outcome to which the play must tend and reassert the value of compassion.

The third actor played Ajax's adversaries in the drama. First, the formidably vindictive and merciless goddess Athena, who has struck the hero with his humiliating madness. Next, the Messenger, not characterized as hostile, but one whose chief function is essentially sinister: to relay the warning words of the prophet Calchas about Athena's continuing wrath against Ajax, with the reason for it. Lastly, Menelaus and Agamemnon, each in turn confronting Teucer with their different arguments, but similar offensiveness, so that the drama of Ajax in conflict with his foes continues in the actors's voices almost to the very end.

Sophocles' control of his medium is also evident in his use of the Chorus of Salaminian sailors. As always in Greek tragedy, the Chorus serves as an important link between the actors and the audience, as it guides the latter's responses to the action and personalities. The content of the Chorus's songs and its contribution to the dramatic continuum are explored in the notes.[11] Like the audience, the sailors display limited understanding, but they look to Ajax as their protector and indicate that we are being invited to admire their master for all his arrogance and brutality and to sympathize with him in his humiliation. Their singing and movement are integral to the emotional impact of the opera-like exchanges between them and Ajax or Tecmessa. Sophocles makes them Athenians by origin (202), and this helps to reinforce the more positive image of Ajax as one of the city's cult heroes. In their last main song (1185-1222), which expresses their weariness with war, they seem to be identifying more with the audience's preoccupations than with Ajax himself, but this can be seen as a subtle element in the dramatic process whereby Sophocles is finally drawing his disgraced hero into the rituals of the Athenian community.

# NOTES

1.   Heroes in epic are normally accorded an honorific cremation.
2.   I am particularly indebted here to the chapters on *Ajax* in Winnington-Ingram (1980), discussions by Pat Easterling in several sources, Peter Wilson's Introduction to the republished Jebb

edition (2005) and Jon Hesk's admirable book on the whole play (2003).

3.  The word was more commonly applied in classical Greek to specific *acts* of unwarranted aggression.

4.  Compare the images in *Women of Trachis* 112–19, 129–31.

5.  Compassion is also a fundamental theme in *Philoctetes*, though there it is conspicuously lacking in Odysseus and his plans are foiled by it.

6.  A dummy is necessary, as the actor playing Ajax has to reappear as Teucer.

7.  For my approach to this problem, I am particularly indebted to Scott Scullion's discussion in 'Three Studies in Athenian Dramaturgy' (Stuttgart 1994). There are parallels for an onstage 'grove' in Euripides' *Ion* and Sophocles' own *Oedipus at Colonus*. Scullion believes in property trees and bushes rather than a painted flat. There is, in fact, little evidence for either in fifth-century tragedy, but Sophocles was credited by Aristotle with the introduction of *skênê*-painting, an art about which a contemporary painter, Agatharchus of Samos, wrote a book. This is thought to mean the painting of architectural backgrounds in perspective on the stage building. It might, however, have included the painting of flats to the sides of the acting area immediately in front of the *skênê*. Such flats could have been used to facilitate side entrances and exits other than those along the main *eisodoi*. An entrance of this sort seems needed for Odysseus' sudden appearances at *Philoctetes* 964 and 1293; see *Ajax* notes 2, 69.

8.  If precise locality matters, it is more natural to imagine the two groups of sailors returning to the same spot at 866ff. to reunite after their futile search.

9.  See *Ajax* note 37.

10. See *Ajax* notes 37, 43, 50, 52, 53, 61, 65.

11. See *Ajax* notes 13, 19, 35, 44, 62, 84, 95.

# Characters

ATHENA
ODYSSEUS, *a Greek commander*
AJAX, *a great Greek warrior*
CHORUS *of sailors*
TECMESSA, *Ajax's captive wife*
MESSENGER, *Ajax's half-brother*
MENELAÜS, *a Greek commander*
AGAMEMNON, *Greek commander-in-chief*
EURYSACES, *the young son of Ajax and Tecmessa*
ATTENDANTS

[*Scene: Before Ajax's hut in the Greek encampment at Troy.*]

## SCENE 1[1]

[*Enter* ODYSSEUS *by a side entrance. He circles round the area in front of the hut, looking for tracks.* ATHENA *also appears.*]

ATHENA:[2]

I'm always spying you on the prowl, Odysseus,
Seizing the chance to strike a blow at your foes.
I see you now, by Ajax's hut, where his ships
Are posted to guard the end of the Grecian lines.
5   I've been watching you all this time, on your huntsman's
      trail,
Scanning the tracks he has newly scored, to see
If he's there indoors or not. You're sniffing about
Like a Spartan bitch and closing in on your quarry.
Ajax has just come home. His head is dripping
10  With sweat, his hands with the blood that his sword has spilt.
No need for you any more to be peering round
Inside this entrance. Tell me what lies behind
This busy search. I know the answer to give you.

ODYSSEUS:

Athena's voice! The god whom I love best!
15  Though you are out of my sight, your words are so
Distinct to hear. Their thrilling sound is like
The brazen blast of a Tuscan trumpet call.[3]

You're right again. I'm circling round on the trail
Of a foe – of Ajax, lord of the shield.[4] It's he,
None other, whom I've been tracking for all this time.                   20
During last night, he has performed the most
Astounding act against us – *if* it was he who did it.
Nothing is clear; we're wandering in the dark.
I've saddled myself with the task of making sure.

An hour or two ago we found that all                                     25
Our plundered sheep and cattle had been destroyed,
Slaughtered by some marauder, their herdsman with them.
Everyone puts the blame for this on Ajax.
What's more, a scout observed him bounding alone
Across the plain, with a dripping sword in hand,                         30
And then reported the facts to me. At once
I hurried along his tracks and identified some,
Though others left me confused and led me nowhere.
You've come at the perfect time. It's you who have always
Guided me in the past and will guide me now.                             35
ATHENA:
I know, Odysseus, and came a while ago
To guard the route and assist your hunt for clues.
ODYSSEUS:
Dear goddess, am I toiling in vain?
ATHENA:
No, it is Ajax's work, for sure.
ODYSSEUS:
What drove him into such frantic violence?                               40
ATHENA:
Anger at losing Achilles' arms.
ODYSSEUS:
Why vent his rage by attacking sheep?
ATHENA:
He thought *your* blood was fouling his hands.
ODYSSEUS:
What? Was he trying to harm the *Greeks*?
ATHENA:
He would have succeeded, if I'd been negligent.                          45

ODYSSEUS:
What was his reckless, daredevil scheme?
ATHENA:
A one-man raid under cover of night.
ODYSSEUS:
How close did he get? Did he reach his goal?
ATHENA:
He came as far as the generals' gates.
ODYSSEUS:
50  Then what forestalled his lust for blood?
ATHENA:
*I* did. I threw a cloud of delusion over
His eyes and so precluded his fevered joy,
Side-tracking him on to the flocks and the undivided
Spoil of jumbled cattle the men were guarding.
He set upon the horned creatures, hacking away
55  At their spines and strewing a circle of carcasses round him.
At times he imagined he'd caught the two Atridae[5]
Within his grasp and was striking them down, or else
He was killing another chief, and then one more.
As he raced around in his frenzied sickness, I
60  Kept goading and thrusting him into the nets of ruin.
At last, when he'd grown weary of wreaking carnage,
He tied together the cattle that still survived
With all the sheep, then brought them back to his hut,
Supposing them to be men, not a haul of beasts with
    horns.
65  And now they are roped indoors, he's lashing their bodies.

You too can take a look at his wild dementia,
I want you to cry it aloud to all the Greeks.
Wait there for a moment – you needn't be frightened, he
    won't
Be dangerous. I'll ensure that his eyes are turned
70  In another direction and can't detect you watching.
Hey, you! Stop trying to rope your prisoners' arms
Behind their backs. I'm summoning you out here.
Ajax, I say! Come out in front of this hut!

ODYSSEUS:[6]
Athena, what are you doing?
Don't call him out of doors!
ATHENA:
Be quiet! Don't earn yourself
The name of an arrant coward.                    75
ODYSSEUS:
Please, please, I implore you, don't!
Allow him to stay inside.
ATHENA:
What are you frightened of?
He was only a man before.
ODYSSEUS:
Yes, he was this man's bitter
Foe, and he still is now!
ATHENA:
Isn't a laugh at your foes
The sweetest laugh to enjoy?
ODYSSEUS:
I'll be happy enough
If he stays well indoors.                        80
ATHENA:
Are you scared to enjoy the view
Of a man in a state of madness?
ODYSSEUS:
I wouldn't have shrunk in fear
From looking, if he were sane!
ATHENA:
I promise he'll not set eyes on you
Even now, at close quarters.
ODYSSEUS:
How can that be, if he sees
With the eyes he has always had?
ATHENA:
*I* shall darken his vision,
However sharp it may be.                         85
ODYSSEUS:
Anything can be done,

I suppose, by divine contrivance.

ATHENA:
Be quiet, then, stand still.
And wait here, just as you are.

ODYSSEUS:
Very well, I'll wait. But I wish
I were safely out of the way.

ATHENA:
You there, now, Ajax! This is my second summons!
90  Why do you show such scant regard for your ally?
        [AJAX *enters from the hut, holding a whip.*][7]

AJAX:
Welcome, Athena! Welcome, daughter of Zeus!
How well you've stood at my side![8] I'll deck your temple
With golden spoils for this glorious catch of quarry.

ATHENA:
Well spoken, man! Now tell me about your raid
95  On the camp. Is your sword now reeking with Grecian blood?

AJAX:
So I can boast. I cannot deny it.

ATHENA:
You turned your hand on the sons of Atreus?

AJAX:
They'll never treat Ajax lightly again!

ATHENA:
They're dead, if I understand you right.

AJAX:
100  I've killed them. *Now* they can steal my arms!

ATHENA:
Well, then, what of Laertes' son?
Have you got him now? Perhaps he's escaped?

AJAX:
You're asking about that villainous fox?

ATHENA:
Yes, I am. I mean your rival, Odysseus.

AJAX:
105  I'm delighted to say, dear lady, he's sitting inside –
In chains! I don't want him to die just yet.

ATHENA:
What do you hope to gain from him first?
AJAX:
I'll tie him up to one of my roof posts . . .
ATHENA:
How do you mean to hurt the wretch?
AJAX:
Then lash his back till he bleeds to death! 110
ATHENA:
Poor wretch! Don't torture the man like that!
AJAX:
Have your way, Athena, in everything else,
But this is the price Odysseus has got to pay.
ATHENA:
Very well, if that's your pleasure, I leave him to you.
Go for him, do your worst, whatever you will! 115
AJAX:
I'm back to work – and leaving you one instruction:
Always fight at my side, as you've done today!
    [*Exit* AJAX *into the hut.*]
ATHENA:
You see, Odysseus, the gods can be so strong!
Where could you find a man more circumspect
Than Ajax, better in meeting time's demands? 120
ODYSSEUS:
No one I know. But, enemy though he be,
I'm bound to pity him[9] none the less, poor man!
He's crushed beneath the yoke of ruinous madness.
I'm less concerned for him than for myself.
All of us living on this earth I see 125
Are nothing more than ghosts or flimsy shadows.
ATHENA:
Such be your thoughts, then. Never utter
An arrogant word[10] yourself against the gods,
Nor be puffed up if you surpass another
In strength of arm or piles of hoarded wealth. 130
One day can humble and exalt again
The whole of human life.[11] The gods love those

Who know their place and hate ignoble men.[12]
> [*Exeunt* ATHENA *and* ODYSSEUS *by different side entrances.*]

## CHORAL ENTRANCE SONG[13]

[*Enter* CHORUS *of sailors.*]

CHORUS:
Son of Telamon, Ajax, whose home is the surf-ringed
135     Island of Salamis, throned on the sea,
When you prosper, I celebrate with you.
But if great Zeus smites or if poisonous slander
About you is scattered abroad by the Greeks,
Then I tremble in fear, wild-eyed, like a dove
140     That is trapped in the snare of the fowler.

So too, in the night that has now passed on,
Our ears were assailed by a babble of sound,
Crying shame to your men: you'd invaded the meadow
Where horses go wild and ravaged the cattle,
145     The spoil of the Greeks
Which their spears had won but was yet to be shared,
In the flashing might of your great sword.

Such whispering words of falsehood are poured
In the people's ears by crafty Odysseus,
150     And firmly believed. Any story of you
Will be quickly accepted. Each hearer delights
In the tale even more than the teller and gloats
In triumph at your misadventures.

If you aim your shafts at the great, you will not
155     Fall short of your target; but if you allege
Such things about *me*, you will never convince.
Jealousy steals on the powerful or rich.
Yet leave small men unruled by the great,
And you'll find them a perilous tower of defence.

For safety the weak must depend on the strong,                    160
As the strong must be loyally served by the weak –
Though fools can never be taught in their youth
To acknowledge the truth of this wisdom.[14]


It is fools who are noisily spreading these slanders,
And we without you, lord Ajax, are powerless                      165
To drive their vile accusations away.
For once they've escaped your imperious gaze,
They flutter and chatter like birds on the plain;
But if *you* were to swoop like a mighty vulture,
They'd scatter in fear of your sudden appearance                  170
And cower in motionless silence.


Rumour, O fount of my shame and dishonour!          [*Strophe*]
Was Artemis, daughter of Zeus,
Tauric goddess, bull-enthroned,[15]
The power who launched that strike on the bulls of the            175
     people?
Did shé resént some víctory whénce she wón no thánks,
Cheated of glorious spoils, perhaps, or lacking
Gifts for the prize of a deer?
Or maybe Ares, lord of the brazen cuirass,
Incensed by proud contempt for his aid in the fray,[16]           180
Sought revenge by guile in the night-time.


Ajax, how could you have knowingly
     ventured,                                      [*Antistrophe*]
Falling upon those flocks,
Gone so far astray unled?
The gods can send such sickness. But Zeus and Apollo,             185
Avert these evil slanders born of Grecian lips!
Íf by mystérious hínts they're brúiting fálsehood,
Whether the kings of the host
Or else that spawn of Sisyphus' profligate line,[17]
We beg you, lord, don't hide in your hut by the sea.              190
Guard, oh, guard your good reputation!

Come, you must rise from the seat                    [*Epode*]
Where now you're rooted fast,
Steering clear of the fight so long and kindling flames,
195    Flames of ruin as high as heaven.
So fearless your foes' spite rages,
As wind carries fire though the woodland vales.
They're jéering, all snéering,
200    And I am in constant grief.

## SCENE 2[18]

[*Enter* TECMESSA *from the hut.*]
TECMESSA:[19]
Sailors of Ajax, sprung from the earth-born
Sons of Erechtheus, monarch of Athens,[20]
All of us here, far away in Troy,
Who care for King Telamon's house, must grieve;
205    Since Ajax so fearful in greatness, so raw
In his strength, lies bowed
By the turbulent storm of his sickness.
CHORUS:
What crushing blow in the night has succeeded
The blow of the day?
210    Tell us, daughter of Trojan Teleutas.
You are the woman whom warlike Ajax
Won with his spear, whom he loves with devotion.[21]
You know, and can hint at an answer.
TECMESSA:
How can I relate what cannot be spoken?
215    You'll learn of disaster as fearful as death.
It was madness that seized our glorious Ajax
And struck him with ruinous shame in the night.
You can see them, the sacrificed victims, butchered
Inside his hut, all dripping with blood.
220    What omens to take for his future!
CHORUS:                                              [*Strophe*]
What néws is this, lády,

News of that fiery warrior, past
All bearing, past escaping,
Whispered abroad by the Danaan kings[22] and now                    225
Críed by the great vóice of the péople?
Ah mé, I féar, féar what is wáiting.
In a públic scándal
He'll díe, díe if in frénzy
He has ráised his bláck sword                                       230
To smíte áll of those cáttle dówn,
With all their mounted herdsmen.

TECMESSA:
Alas! So he'd come from the allied camp
When he drove those bound flocks home. Indoors,                     235
He cut their throats where they stood on the floor,
Or hacked their sides and broke them apart.
Next, grabbing a pair of white-hooved rams,
He severed the first's head, sliced off its tongue-tip
And tossed it away;                                                 240
But the other he tied upright to a roof-post,
Seized a great horse-strap, folded it double,
Then flogged the tup with a whistling whip;
While he cursed them and shouted abuse, such words
As a god, no man, must have taught him.                             245

CHORUS:                                                   [Antistrophe]
What's léft to us, sáilors?
All we can do is to cover our heads
And steal away to safety.
Else we must take to our oars at the benches and then
Láunch our ship óut to the hígh seas.                               250
I sée those kíngs, spéeding agáinst us –
Yes, the twó Atrídae,
With grím thréats. I am fríghtened!
They will stóne my máster,
And ús tóo! We must sháre his páin,                                 255
The monstrous fate that grips him.

TECMESSA:
He is mad no more; for the lighting flashes
Have ceased, and the violent wind has subsided.

The return to his senses has brought new pain,
260   As the vision of ruin that's self-inflicted,
When no one's with you to share the blame,
Strains tight on the cable of torment.

CHORUS LEADER:[23]
Well, if the fit has passed, it surely must
Be better for him. The talk should soon die down.
TECMESSA:
265   If you were given the choice, would you prefer
To grieve your friends, while feeling happy yourself,
Or share the sorrow you have brought to them?
CHORUS LEADER:
The double sadness, madam, must be worse.
TECMESSA:
Then his recovery means we all are lost.
CHORUS LEADER:
270   What do you mean? I hardly understand.
TECMESSA:
When Ajax was still suffering from his sickness,
His frenzy filled him with intense delight
While causing grief to us, his sane companions.
But now the malady's gone and he's restored,
275   He's utterly overwhelmed by his remorse,
And we're as troubled as we were before.
Surely this makes the misery twice as great.
CHORUS LEADER:
I must agree. I fear a blow from heaven
Has struck him down. How else, if Ajax well
280   Is still no happier than Ajax sick?
TECMESSA:
You have to understand, that's how it is.
CHORUS LEADER:
How did the madness first swoop down on him?
We share your grief. Please let us know the truth.
TECMESSA:
Ajax is part of you; so I'll tell you all.
285   It was dead of night, the hour when the evening braziers

Were flickering down, when he seized his two-edged sword
To leave the hut on a raid. There seemed no point,
So I remonstrated and said, 'What are you doing,
Ajax? Why are you sallying forth, unsummoned?
No messenger's come. There's been no trumpet call.                          290
Just now the whole encampment's fast asleep.'
He answered me curtly, with the trite refrain:
'It's silence, woman, suits a woman best!'
I stood rebuked and held my peace, while he
Rushed out alone. What happened there in the camp                           295
I cannot say. But he came back in with a line
Of hobbled bulls, herd-dogs and captured sheep.
Then he either severed his victims' heads, or cut
Their upturned throats or chopped right through their
    spines.
Others he bound in cords and tortured them,
As though he were laying into men, not sheep.                               300

At last he shot through the doors and yelled aloud
To a ghost outside, in spasms of loud abuse
Against the Atridae, then at Odysseus, crazily
Laughing over the shameful vengeance he'd gone
And taken. Next he leapt indoors again,                                     305
And slowly, painfully, got his reason back.
When he gazed around at the shambles inside the hut,
He pummelled his head and howled, then sank to the ground,
A wreck amid the wreckage of slaughtered sheep,
Tightly clutching his hair in his nails' clenched grip.                     310

He sat there for an age, completely dumb,
Until he went for *me*, with appalling threats
If I didn't explain the blow which had struck him down.
My friends, I took fright, and I told him all                               315
The havoc he'd wrought, as far as I understood it.
At once he broke into howls of anguished grief.
I'd never heard him wail like that before.
He always used to say that cries of lament
Were only for cowards and pusillanimous men.                                320

He'd never indulge in shrill outbursts of sorrow,
But moan, bull-like, in deep and muffled tones.
And now he's lying there in this wretched plight.
He won't take food or drink. He's sitting where
325  He collapsed, inert, surrounded by all the beasts
He's killed, and plainly set on some dreadful act.

Now, friends – this is why I've come out here – go in
And help him if you're able. Men in his state
330  Can be prevailed on by the advice of friends.
CHORUS LEADER:
Tecmessa, child of Teleutas, what strange blows
You say have driven our master into this trance!
AJAX [*offstage*]:
    Io, moi, moi.
TECMESSA:
I think he'll soon be even more possessed.
335  You must have heard that anguished cry of his.
AJAX:
Io, moi moi!
CHORUS LEADER:
He must be sick, or else he's shocked with grief
To see the work his former malady's done.
AJAX:
Son, son! Come here!
TECMESSA:
340  Oh god! Eurysaces, he's shouting for *you*.
What can he want? Where are you? Oh dear god!
AJAX:
Where's Teucer? I need him now! Must his pursuit
Of loot go on forever, while I die?
CHORUS LEADER:
The man seems sane enough. Now open up!
345  When he sees me, he may be more subdued.
TECMESSA:
I'll open up. There! You may look inside
To see his handiwork and the state he's in.

[*The hut door is opened and* AJAX *is revealed sitting among the slaughtered cattle.*[24]]

AJAX:[25:]                                                              [*Strophe 1*]

   Ió!
   It's you, sáilor fríends,
   You are the ónly ónes,
   The sole fríends who still
   Remain lóyal and trúe.                                           350
   Now look and see the hideous wave
   That's surging round to shut me in,
   Round in a squall of bloodshed!

CHORUS LEADER:
Tecmessa, your account seems all too true.
He's not in his right mind. This makes it clear.                       355

AJAX:                                                                  [*Antistrophe 1*]

   Ió!
   My crew, yóu who knów
   How ships sáil the séas,
   Who came abóard and rówed
   With such stréngth and skíll.
   It's you, it's you alone I see
   Can help me face this shame and pain.                            360
   Kill me beside these creatures!

CHORUS LEADER:
Ill-omened words! Evil cannot be cured
By evil. Do not add to ruin's pain.

AJAX:                                                                  [*Strophe 2*]

   Here's Ajáx the bráve, the bold-héarted mán,
   Who never blénched in fíght against fúrious fóes,               365
   And now he fláunts his pówer on poor hármless béasts!
   Oh, how they'll laugh! How I've been brought to shame!

TECMESSA:
I beg you, Ajax, lord, don't say such things.

AJAX:
Get out! You shift your ground and graze elsewhere!
*Aiai! Aiai!*                                                          370

TECMESSA:
For god's sake, listen! Show a little sense!

AJAX:
>    How wretched I am! Those damned
>    Hell-hounds have slipped right through my hands.
>    I struck the cattle with crumpled horns,
375  The góats in their glórious flócks,
>    And spílt the ánimals' bláck blóod.

TECMESSA:
Why go on grieving, then? What's done is done.
There's no escape, it can't be otherwise.

AJAX:                                          [Antistrophe 2]
>    You vile wrétch who sées, who hears áll that góes,
380  You catspáw of évil, Laértes' són,
>    The army's pile of dung, its ground córn of cráft,
>    You must be laughing at me now for joy!

CHORUS LEADER:
Laughter and tears come round as god decides.

AJAX:
I'd like to see him, ruined though I am –
385  *Io moi moi*!

CHORUS LEADER:
Speak carefully, sir! You know what straits you're in.

AJAX:
>    O Zeus, who begat my line,
>    I wish I could destroy that man,
>    That hateful, crafty, scheming fox,
390  Destróy those two pówerful kíngs,
>    And thén could méet my ówn déath!

TECMESSA:
Embrace me in your prayer. Let me die, too!
Why should I have to live, if you are dead?

AJAX:                                          [Strophe 3]
>    Ió!
>    O dark, nów my líght!
395  O grim glóom of héll, you are my shíning sún!
>    So táke me, táke me home dówn belów
>    To líve with yóu. I can't lóok for hélp –
>    So undeserving I've sunk to be –
400  To gods above or mortal men on earth.
>    No, that mighty power,

Pallas, child of Zeus,
Tortures me here to death.
Where should I escape?
Where apply for rest?
If these slaughtered beasts                                   405
Bode the death of all
My honour, friends,
And if my hunt was crazy work,
The whole Greek host may raise their swords
And drive them inside me!

TECMESSA:
Ah wretched me! That a man of worth should speak              410
As he would never have stooped to speak before.

AJAX:                                              [Antistrophe 3]
Ió!
You rough stráits of séa,
You ocean cáves and wóods where sheep gráze nearbý,
For lóng, how lóng, for too lóng an áge
You hóld me hére to wage wár at Tróy.                         415
But now no more while I breathe the breath
Of life, no more. You can be sure of that.
Old Scamander, broad
Stream that flows nearby,
Kinder to other Greeks,                                       420
Never shall you see
Ajax here again,
Soldier whose true like –
I shall boast aloud –
Troy never saw
Arise from all the land of Greece.                            425
And now what fate has brought me low!
My honour is all lost!

CHORUS LEADER:
I can't gainsay, not yet allow your words.
Your wretched situation leaves me baffled.

AJAX:[26]
Aiai![27] Who would have thought the name by which            430

I'm known would match my wretched fate so well?
Now I can say *aiai* for Aias yet again.
And then once more. Such is my piteous plight.
My father, here on Trojan soil, achieved
435 The highest prize for valour in all the host
And went home crowned with glory.[28] I, his son,
Came after him to Troy; I was as strong
A soldier, and my deeds were no less fine.
But now I'm facing death, disgraced and stripped
440 Of honour by the Greeks. And yet I reckon
I know this much: if Achilles were still alive
And here to award the prize of his own arms
For martial prowess, no one could have seized hold
Of them in place of me. Instead, the Atridae
445 Spurned my triumphs and fixed the award to go
To an outright scoundrel. If a mind unhinged and distorted
Vision had not diverted me from my purpose,
They'd never have rigged the vote like that again.
My sword was ready to strike them down, but the grim-eyed
450 Daughter of Zeus, the invincible goddess,[29] struck
Me down with a fit of madness and foiled my plan.
My hands are red with the blood of these poor creatures,
While *they* are crowing over their lucky escape –
455 Not by design of mine. When a god's against you,
Even a low-born weakling eludes your clutches.

So now, what shall I do? I'm clearly hated
By all the gods; the army of Greece detests me;
And so does the whole of Troy and its blood-stained plains.
460 Should I make for home across the Aegean Sea,
Desert my ships and leave the Atridae to it?
How could I show my face before my father,
Telamon? How could he endure the sight
Of me, appearing naked, without the prize
465 For which he won his own great crown of glory?
Not to be borne! Suppose, then, I approach
The Trojan walls, to fight them one to one,
And do some feat before I die in the end –

The way, I think, to make the Atridae smile!
Impossible. I need to find a venture,                    470
To *prove* to my old father that his son
Has not inherited a coward's heart.
It shames a man to wish his life prolonged
When life is dogged by unrelenting pain.
Day follows day; it's one move forward, one              475
Move back from death. What joy is there in that?
I wouldn't count a person of any worth
Who likes to warm himself on empty hope.
A noble man must either live in honour
Or else have died in honour. That is all.                480
CHORUS LEADER:
Ajax, no one could call you insincere
At any time. You always speak from the heart.
Hold back, though. Listen to your loyal crew's
Advice and put these gloomy thoughts aside.
TECMESSA:[30]
Ajax, my master, nothing afflicts mankind                485
More harshly than the force of destiny.
My father was free-born, as powerfully rich
As any man in Troy. I'm now a slave.
The gods must have determined this, but more
Your conquering hand. You took me to your bed           490
And made me yours, so now my loyalty's all
To you. I beg you, in the name of Zeus
Who rules our hearth, I beg you by the love
That binds the two of us together, don't
Expose me to your enemies' cruel abuse                  495
By making me over to another man.
The day you die and leave me all alone
Must be the day the Greeks seize hold of my arms
And force me off, with your own child, to lead
A slave's existence. One of my masters then             500
Will fling this cruel taunt: 'Look there, it's Ajax's
Woman! He was the strongest man in the army!
What an enviable life she led, but she's now reduced
To menial chores!' That will be my bad luck,

505 But you and your son will face these shameful gibes.
Show some respect, sir: for your father, whom
You are abandoning in his sad old age;
Respect your mother in her life's long stint,
Who prays so often for your safe return.
510 Show pity too, my lord, for your own son.
Deprived of the care he needs, cut off from you,
He'll live with guardian parents to whom he's nothing.
Just think what misery you'll bequeath to him
And me after your death. I've nowhere now
515 To turn, except to you, who devastated
My native country, since another fate
Sent both my parents down to live in Hades.
What country could I ever have but you?
What wealth? My whole life's in your hands.
520 Please give some thought to *me*! Surely a man
Should not forget the pleasure he has enjoyed.
One kindness always breeds another kindness.
If you meet with good and let the memory fade,
You cannot be counted noble any more.

CHORUS LEADER:
525 Ajax, I wish you shared the pity I feel
Myself. You'd then commend Tecmessa's words.

AJAX:
She'll be commended by me for sure, so long as
She brings herself to do as I instruct.

TECMESSA:
Dear Ajax, I shall do whatever you say.

AJAX:
530 Then fetch my son here now. I want to see him.

TECMESSA:
Yes – but I sent him out. I was afraid.

AJAX:
When I was stricken down? Is that what you mean?

TECMESSA:
I feared, if the poor child met you, he might be killed.

AJAX:
Yes, my evil genius could well have done it!

TECMESSA:
At least I took good care to stave off *that*.                    535
AJAX:
I thank you for the foresight that you showed.
TECMESSA:
Then tell me, please, how can I help you now?
AJAX:
Please let me see him here and talk to him.
TECMESSA:
Of course. The servants are minding him close by.
AJAX:
Well, then, what stops his coming along at once?                 540
TECMESSA [*to offstage*]:
    My child, your father's calling. Whichever servant
    Is holding him by the hand, please bring him here.
AJAX:
Is he coming, or just ignoring what you say?
TECMESSA:
Look! The man is bringing the boy here now.
    [*Enter an attendant with* EURYSACES *from a side entrance.*]
AJAX:[31]
Lift him! Lift him up to me here! He won't              545
Be frightened to see this welter of fresh-spilt blood
If he's truly his father's son. He needs to be quickly
Broken into his father's wild, rough ways
And made to become like me. My son, I pray
That you'll be luckier than your father was,             550
But still take after him in everything else.
If so, you'll be a fine man. There's one thing, even
Now, I envy you for: you have no inkling
Of all this chaos. Life's at its sweetest when you
Feel nothing, when you don't know about joy or pain.       555
But once you do, you'll need to find a way
Of showing your father's foes the stuff you're made of.
Meantime, let the wind blow gently. Grow, young plant!
Cherish your life and bring your mother joy.
None of the Greeks, I know, will ever subject you          560
To brutal harm, even when I'm not here.

I'll leave my brother Teucer to guard the gate,
And he will take good care of you – even though
He's now off hunting the enemy far away.

565 Now, my warrior friends, my crew of sailors,
Here is the charge of love I'm laying on you
And Teucer together: carry him my instruction
To take this child to my home and hand him over
To Telamon and my mother, Queen Eriboea.
570 Then he can look after them when they grow old,
Until they die. And Teucer must see my weapons
Are not set up as a prize for competition
By the officials or that bane of mine,
Odysseus. You, my son, must have the shield
From which you take your name, Eurysaces.
575 Keep it and wield it by this strong-stitched loop;
No spear can break its cover of seven hides.
The rest of my arms lie with me, in my grave.

Make haste, Tecmessa. Take the child and close
The doors. You mustn't lament outside the hut.
580 Quick, bolt up! You women are so emotional!
Good doctors don't chant dirges and incantations
Over a wound that needs a surgeon's knife.
CHORUS LEADER:
This busy haste of yours makes me afraid.
Your words are now so sharp. I feel uneasy.
TECMESSA:[32]
585 Ajax, my master? What do you mean to do?
AJAX:
No inquisitions! You must control yourself.
TECMESSA:
I'm desperate! I beg you, by your son,
By all the gods, don't leave us in the lurch.
AJAX:
You're being tedious. Cannot you understand?
590 There's nothing I owe now to any god!

TECMESSA:
You must not say that!
AJAX:
                              Talk to men with ears!
TECMESSA:
Have *you* no ears?
AJAX:
                              You've said too much already.
TECMESSA:
I'm frightened, sir!
AJAX:
                              Attendants, shut those doors![33]
TECMESSA:
Be gentle, Ajax!
AJAX:
                    Woman, you must be crazy
If you imagine you'll school my temper now!                    595
     [*Exit* AJAX *into the hut.*][34]


# CHORAL SONG 1[35]

CHORUS:
    Famous Salamis, you, my island,              [*Strophe 1*]
    Stand proud in the waves that beat your shores,
    Bright star of the world for all time.
    While I, alas, longing year after year for home,          600
    Must wait and wait, sleeping cold on the grassy
       mountain,
    Incessantly through the countless months.
    The time wéars me awáy,
    My hope túrns to despáir.                                   605
    Soon I shall páss the gáte
    And sink to the hideous shades of Hades.

    More pain now to beset us! Ajax,               [*Antistrophe 1*]
    The master we serve, is sick past cure,                    610
    Struck down by his god-sent madness.

You sent him out, island home, long ago to thrive
In furious war. Now he broods like a lonely shepherd,
615    And all of his friends are filled with grief.
While those féats of his árm,
Those great glórious déeds,
Have perished áll unlóved
620    And counted for nought with the vile Atridae.

His móther, tóo, wórn and wéak in her léngth of
    dáys,                                                      [Strophe 2]
625    Hair whíte with áge, soón must héar of the fátal síckness
Eating away his reason.
Wildly she'll shriek aloud!
Wrétched lády, she won't gríeve like a géntly
630    Pláintive níghtingale, but wáil her lamént in shríll-toned
Anguish. Then, with a dull thud,
Blows will rain from her clenched fists,
Bosom-bruising; and last she'll tear that white hair.

635    Poor mádman, fár bétter hídden in Hádes'
    glóom!                                                     [Antistrophe 2]
Of áll the Gréek sóuls who tóiled in the wár at Tróy
He came of the noblest lineage.
Gone are the calmer moods,
640    Ónce his náture. His mind's frántic and wánders.
Hápless Télamon, what néws of your són awáits you,
Struck by ruinous madness,
Cursed as Aeacus' sons were
645    Never doomed until now – save only Ajax!


# SCENE 3

[*Re-enter* AJAX *from the hut, carrying his sword.*][36]
AJAX:[37]
Time in its long, uncounted course, brings forth
The hidden truth, then hides it all from the light.
Nothing's beyond man's hoping; awesome oaths

And stubborn wills can still be overcome.
Take me, for instance, me. I once was so                          650
Grimly determined, hard like tempered steel,
But now I've lost the manhood in my tongue.[38]
This woman's changed me. Yes, I pity her.
How can I leave her widowed and my son
An orphan, at the mercy of my foes?

No, I'll go down to the meadows by the shore
To wash myself and purge away my stains,                          655
And so escape Athena's dangerous wrath.
I'll find a place untrodden by human foot
And dig a hole to bury this sword of mine,[39]
This hatefullest of weapons, where none can see it.
Hades can guard it in the night below.                            660
For ever since my hand received this sword,
This gift of Hector, my worst enemy,
The Greeks have never done me any good.
The ancient proverb's true: an enemy's gift
Is an empty gift and brings a man no joy.                         665

In future, then, we'll know to yield to the gods
And learn how to revere the sons of Atreus.[40]
They rule, and I submit. Oh yes, I must.
All that is awesome and most powerful
Gives way to recognized prerogatives:[41]                         670
The winter's snow-strewn paths make room in time
For summer's fruits; and night's eternal round
Resigns for day's white steeds to light her flame;
The breath of awesome winds can lay to rest
The roaring sea; and sleep that conquers all                      675
Unlocks its chains and cannot keep its hold.
Must we not also learn to know our place?
*I* must. I've newly come to understand,
The enemy we're bound to hate today
Will one day be our friend; and while I hope                      680
To serve and help my friend, I know he'll not
Remain my friend forever. People find

That comradeship's a haven they cannot trust.
No, all of this must turn out well. Tecmessa,
685   Go indoors, and pray that what my heart
Longs for may be fulfilled – through to the end.[42]
        [*Exit* TECMESSA *with* EURYSACES.]
You, my good comrades, show me the same regard
As she. When Teucer comes, ask him to prove
His care for me and loyalty to you, too.
690   I'm going on the journey I must take.
You do my bidding, and soon, perhaps, you'll learn,
For all I suffer now, I'm safe and well.
        [*Exit* AJAX.][43]


# CHORAL SONG 2[44]

CHORUS:
        I thrill with longing,[45] on wings of joy I soar on
            high,                                        [*Strophe*]
        Ió, ió, god Pán!
695   O Pán, spírit who róams the séas,
        Cóme to us from the rocky ridge
        Where snow beats on Cyllene's[46] heights. Appear, lord,
        Master who sets the gods a-dancing!
        Join with me, beat your feet,
700   Wave your arms, as you dance in Crete or Nysa![47]
        Now is the time for me to revel.
        Cross the Icarian Sea from Delos,[48]
        Be wíth me, Lórd Apóllo,
        To publish your healing power!
705   Be wíth me nów, trúe to your lóving kíndness!


        The god of warfare has now dispelled my cloud
            of grief.                                    [*Antistrophe*]
        Ió, ió! Once móre,
        O Kíng Zéus, we can seé the líght.
        Dawn's fáir whiteness illumes the shíps
710   That speed over the sea so fast. For Ajax,

Setting his grief aside, has newly
Paid to the gods their due:
Sacrifice and respect for the laws of heaven.
Time has the power to quench or kindle.⁴⁹
Nothing I'd call beyond our saying,                          715
When Ajax, past all hoping,
Has suffered a change of heart
And céased his fierce féud with the sóns of Átreus.


# SCENE 4

*[Enter* MESSENGER *from a side entrance.]*⁵⁰
MESSENGER:
Friends, I have news to give you. First of all,
Teucer has just returned from Mysia's heights.                   720
As soon as he'd entered camp and reached headquarters,
The whole Greek army yelled at him, all at once.
They'd spotted him while he was still far off and crowded
Round him, every man of them, raining curses                      725
From all directions: 'You're the brother of Ajax!'
They cried. 'He's just gone mad and attacked the army!
We'll stone your body to shreds and have your blood.
You won't be able to stop us!' They'd reached the point
Where swords were drawn from their scabbards and ready to     730
    strike.
The brawl, indeed, had run as far as it could,
When the older men intervened and calmed the others.
Where's Ajax now? I need to report this to him.
The master's always owed the truth in full.
CHORUS LEADER:
He left not long ago. His mood has changed,                      735
And his thoughts are firmly set on some new course.
MESSENGER:
In vain! In vain!
The man I come from must have sent me out
Too late – or else I've been too slow in coming.

CHORUS LEADER:

740  Why all this urgency? How have you failed?

MESSENGER:

Teucer's instructions were to keep his brother
Inside his hut until he arrived himself.

CHORUS LEADER:

He has gone, I fear. His mind has changed for the better,
And now he wants to make his peace with the gods.

MESSENGER:

745  The foolish, foolish man! That is, if Calchas'
Prophecies must contain a germ of wisdom.

CHORUS LEADER:

What did he say? And what do you know to tell us?

MESSENGER:

This much I know, as I was there in person.
Calchas detached himself from the sons of Atreus

750  Where all the chiefs were sitting round in council,
And greeted Teucer kindly by the hand.
The priest then charged him strongly, by hook or crook,
To hold Ajax inside his hut today,
While daylight lasts, and not to let him out,

755  If he wished to see his brother alive again.
Divine Athena's anger, he explained,
Would only dog his steps this one more day.
The prophet went on to say that lives which grow
Too great or yield to folly come to grief

760  Through cruel calamities sent by the gods.
If you're born human, you must not entertain
Thoughts higher than a human being should.
Ajax displayed his folly the very moment
That he set out from home. His father's parting
Words were: 'Son, let your ambition be

765  To fight to win, but always with god's help.'[51]
He boastfully and thoughtlessly replied,
'Father, with god's help even a nobody
Can win a victory. I don't need god's help.
I trust I'll land the fish of fame without it!'

770  Those were his boastful words. Another time,

When the goddess Athena was urging him on and said,
'Ajax, now use that hand of yours and *kill*!'
He made her this unspeakably rude retort:
'You can assist the other Greeks, my lady!
The battle-line won't break where *I'm* on hand.'                         775
That speech incurred Athena's pitiless wrath.
His mind had flown beyond his human limits.

If, however, he's still alive today,
We might, with god's help, manage to save him yet.
That's what the prophet said. Teucer at once                              780
Rose to his feet and sent me straight to you
With these instructions. If I'm too late and Calchas
Knows his art, Ajax is now no more.
CHORUS LEADER:
Tecmessa, unhappy ill-starred creature!
Come out and hear what this man says.                                     785
Bad news! We're on the razor's edge.
        [*Re-enter* TECMESSA *with* EURYSACES.]
TECMESSA:
Oh, why must you call me from my rest again?
I'd thought our troubles were over. They're unrelenting!
CHORUS LEADER:
Listen to this man here. He's just arrived
With news of Ajax. It's made me deeply worried.                           790
TECMESSA:
Oh god! What is your news, man? Are we lost?
MESSENGER:
I don't know about you, but I'd be concerned
For Ajax's safety if he's not indoors now.
TECMESSA:
He's out! I'm on the rack! What do you mean?
MESSENGER:
Teucer's instructions are to keep him well                                795
Inside his hut. Don't let him out on his own.
TECMESSA:
Where's Teucer? Why is he saying that?

MESSENGER:
He's just arrived. If Ajax *has* gone out,
He thinks this time he's going to his death.
TECMESSA:
800  Oh, help me, god! Who told him that?
MESSENGER:
The prophet Calchas. He says today's
The day. It brings his death or life.
TECMESSA:
Stand by me, friends, at this momentous time!
Find Teucer, some of you. Get him to come here quickly.
805  The rest must scour the country along the bay
To east and west. Please go and try to find
Where Ajax has unhappily ventured out.
I realize now that I misjudged my man:
He loved me once, but now he's cast me off.
What shall I do, my child? I can't sit here.
810  I must go too, as far as my strength will take me.
      [*She motions* EURYSACES *back inside the hut.*]
Let's be away, make haste! No time for rest,
If we hope to save a man who's set on death.
CHORUS LEADER:
We're ready to go. That's not an idle promise.
We'll run as fast as our legs will take us.
      [*Exeunt* TECMESSA *and the divided* CHORUS *by the two
      side entrances.*][52]


# SCENE 5

[*Re-enter* AJAX.][53]
AJAX:
815  There stands the slaughterer,[54] where its cutting edge
Can serve me best – if a man has time to reflect.[55]
It was the gift of Hector, the foe turned friend,
The man I hated most and loathed to see.
It's planted in the enemy soil of Troy,
820  Fresh-sharpened on the iron-consuming stone.

And I have carefully placed it, so the point
Can do its work most kindly and kill me quickly.

I'm well prepared, then. Next you, Zeus, must be
The first to help me, as you rightly should.[56]
The boon I'm claiming is not much to ask.                                    825
Despatch a man to take the unhappy news
To Teucer. He must be first to lift my body
When I have fallen upon my sword and while
The blade's still wet with blood. Let none of my enemies
Find me before my brother and throw me out
On open ground as prey for the dogs and birds.                               830
This, Zeus, I beg of you. And I also call
On Hermes, guide of the dead beneath the earth,
To put me fast to sleep when with a swift,
Unwrithing leap I've run my body through.

I summon now the eternal virgin powers                                       835
Who never fail to mark what mortals suffer,
The dread long-striding Furies.[57] They must learn
How Atreus' sons are killing wretched Ajax.
Pounce down on those vile men as they deserve.
Destroy them utterly, as you see me                                          840
Falling self-slaughtered. So may they die themselves.[58]
Come, demons of vengeance, swiftly. Taste their blood.
Spare not a single life in the whole Greek army!

And you, O Sun, who drive your chariot through                               845
The heavenly heights, when you sight my native land,
Draw in your golden reins and bear the news
Of Ajax's fatal madness and his death
To my old father and my unhappy mother.
Poor woman, when she hears this sad report,                                  850
Her cries of grief will echo throughout the city.

But why indulge in these futile laments?
The task must be begun and quickly ended.
O Death, Death, come and visit me now![59]                                   854

I greet the light; I greet the sacred soil
860 Of Salamis, my own home; my father's hearth;
And glorious Athens[60] with its race akin
To mine; I greet the springs and rivers here;
The plains of Troy, who have sustained my life.
Farewell! That's Ajax's final word to *you*.
865 The rest can all be told to the dead below.
[*Exit* AJAX.][61]

## SECOND ENTRANCE SONG

[*Half the* CHORUS *re-enters by a side entrance.*][62]
CHORUS A:
It's toil and pain and pain and toil!
Whére, whére?
Where have I not trudged my way?
No place can tell me where our captain can be found.
870 Now listen, there!
There! That thudding sound again!
[*The other half of the* CHORUS *returns by the opposite side entrance.*]
CHORUS B:
It's us, your fellow-sailors on the voyage to Troy.
CHORUS A:
What néws, fríends?
CHORUS B:
We've searched for tracks along the fleet's whole western flank.
CHORUS A:
875 What lúck thére?
CHORUS B:
Only a load of toil and nothing we could *see*.
CHORUS A:
And *we* have covered all the region to the east,
But could not find a sign of Ajax anywhere.

# LAMENT

CHORUS: [*Strophe*]
    Oh say whére he ís! Perhaps sómebody knóws,
    Who in his húnt for físh must face tóil at níght.    880
    Whát of the nýmphs of the hílls,
    Or fair spríte who háunts
    Óne of the Bósporus' stréams?
    They might have spied that angry man
    Coming towards them there.
    No reply! Toil without end!
    It is too hárd that Í should roam hére and thére,
    Strúggling on, néver to fínd the tráil,
    Never to catch one glimpse of that enfeebled man.   890

TECMESSA [*offstage*]:
*Io moi moi*!

CHORUS LEADER:
Who cried so loudly from the trees close to the hut?[63]

TECMESSA:
*Io*! Ah me!

CHORUS LEADER:
I see Tecmessa there, our master's captive bride,
Poor lady, fraught with anguish, as her cry proclaims!   895
    [TECMESSA *enters from the trees*.][64]

TECMESSA:
My friends, I'm lost, confounded! My whole life's destroyed!

CHORUS:
    Oh, whý, whý?

TECMESSA:
Ajax is lying here. His blood is flowing fresh.
He's fallen on his sword and plunged it in his heart!

CHORUS:
    Sháll I see hóme agáin?   900
    I sáiled with you, cáptain, to Tróy.
    Nów you've kílled me, wrétched mán.
    Lády, you're wrétched tóo!

TECMESSA:
That's how it is with him, and we must cry *aiai*.
CHORUS LEADER:
905   Who could have helped the unhappy man to die like this?
TECMESSA:
He did it by himself. It's all too plain. The sword
Is planted in the ground and proves he fell on it.
CHORUS:
        Óh, I was blínd and mád!
        Só, then, you shéd your blóod
910     Alone, áll alóne,
        Withóut your fríends. And Í was so wítless and déaf
        And nóticed nóthing. Whére, whére's
        Ájax the óbdurate nów,
        That mán of the sád name?
        [*During the next few lines,* AJAX's *body is carried on stage
        and laid down in a central position.*]
TECMESSA:
915   You must not look at him.[65] No, I'll cover him up
Completely in this enfolding cloak, since no
True friend of his could bear to see the blood
That's spurting up to his nostrils, streaming black
From his deadly wound, the wound he dealt himself.
920   Oh god, what shall I do? Which of your friends
Will lift you up for burial? Where is Teucer?
If he came now, he'd be in time to compose
His fallen brother's limbs. Ill-fated Ajax,
Brought down from such a mighty height, you ought
To be lamented even among your foes!
CHORUS:                                              [*Antistrophe*]
925     The blow hád to fáll, to swoop dówn at lást.
        That stubborn héart of yóurs was long dóomed to réap
        Tóil upon límitless tóil.
        I heard áll your críes,
        Críes through the níght and the dáy,
930     Those cries and groans of savage wrath,
        Hatred for Atreus' sons,
        Uttered in deadly grief.
        That was a fátal tíme, the first sóurce of wóe.

Cúrse the black dáy when they héld the gréat                935
Judgement of arms to choose the bravest Greek at Troy!

TECMESSA:
*Io moi moi!*

CHORUS LEADER:
Your grief, I'm sure, is nobly sprung and deeply felt.

TECMESSA:
*Io moi moi!*

CHORUS LEADER:
I cannot wonder, lady, at that second cry.                  940
The loved one you're bereft of was so great a man!

TECMESSA:
You may think so, but I must *feel* it all too well.

CHORUS:
    Too trúe, trúe.

TECMESSA:
Alas, my child, to what a yoke of slavery
We're bound! What masters now will rule the two of us!       945

CHORUS:
    Hów could they bé so hárd?
    Those Átreïd génerals cán't
    Tréat you wíth such mónstrous spíte.
    Mércy, now, gód forfénd!

TECMESSA:
The gods have played their part in what we're suffering *now*.   950

CHORUS LEADER:
I know. They've made you bear an all too heavy load.

TECMESSA:
Yes, Zeus' dread daughter Pallas sows the seeds of pain
As sharp as this to make Odysseus' heart rejoice.

CHORUS:
    Cúrsed be his sóul's dark éye![66]
    Hé will be glóating nów,                          955
    That tough, hárdy mán.
    He láughs and mócks agáin and agáin at the héro's
    Gríef that mádness bróught fórth.
    Héaring the tále, the Atrídae
    Jóin in the láughter.                             960

TECMESSA:
Well, *let* them laugh and take delight in Ajax's
Miseries. Even if they failed to miss him
During his life, they may perhaps lament
His death when they need him on the battlefield.
It's shallow minds that never recognize
965  The good things they enjoy until they're lost.
His death has hurt me when it has given them joy –
Though he himself is glad. He has secured
All that he longed to win, the death he wanted.
Why, therefore, should they laugh at his demise?
970  His death is the gods' concern, not theirs, not theirs.[67]


# SCENE 6[68]


TEUCER [*offstage*]:
*Io, moi, moi!*
CHORUS LEADER:
975  Silence! I think that must be Teucer's voice.
His loud cry hits the mark of this disaster.
        [*Enter* TEUCER *by a side entrance.*]
TEUCER:
Oh Ajax, dearest brother, my life's light!
Are all your dealings ended as rumour says?
CHORUS LEADER:
He's gone for ever, Teucer. That's for sure.
TEUCER:
980  He's gone! Then fortune's treated me so cruelly!
CHORUS LEADER:
That's how it is –
TEUCER:
                          Ah wretched, wretched me!
CHORUS LEADER:
And you must grieve.
TEUCER:
                          His rash and violent hand!

CHORUS LEADER:
Too violent, Teucer.
TEUCER:
                              Help me, god! His child!
Where can I find him, tell me, where in Troy?
CHORUS LEADER:
Alone beside the huts.
TEUCER [*to* TECMESSA]:
                                Then bring him here                    985
As quickly as you can. The enemy mustn't
Snatch him up like a robbed lioness' cub.
Hurry and do your part. You know the world
Delights to mock the dead when they are down.
     [*Exit* TECMESSA.]⁶⁹
CHORUS LEADER:
Teucer, before he died, your brother asked          990
That you should mind his child, as you are doing.
TEUCER:
Of all the sights that I have ever seen
This is the one most painful; and of all
The journeys that I ever made, this last
Has hurt me most, oh Ajax, dearest brother!        995
I only heard the news about your death
When I was busily trying to track you down.
The rumour shot through all the Greeks, as though
It came from a god,⁷⁰ that you were dead and gone.
On hearing it still far away, I gave
A silent groan. But now I'm here to see           1000
The truth with my own eyes, I'm desolate!
Oh god!
Remove the cover. Let me face the full
Horror of what he did. That bitterness,
That bold aggression still upon your face!
What pain your death has sown for me to harvest!   1005
Where can I turn? Whom can I dare approach?
You were in trouble and I brought no help.
Won't Telamon, your father as well as mine,

Receive me home with shining, happy eyes,
1010 When he sees me come without you? Yes, oh yes!
He never likes to smile, even when he's
In luck. He'll not mince his words, not he.
He'll pile up all the insults he can find
On the bastard son he got from his campaigns.[71]
I'll be the unmanly coward who let you down,
1015 You, dearest Ajax, or played a dirty trick
To win your power and house when you were dead.
That's what he'll say, the crotchety old man
Who'll pick an angry quarrel out of nothing.
Then lastly he'll disown me and throw me out,[72]
1020 No longer free, but branded as a slave.

So much for home; while here in Troy I have
A crowd of bitter foes, and scant support;
And all that's gone, I've found, now you are dead.
Oh god, what can I do? How can I draw
1025 You off this sharp, light-catching sword-point? Look!
This sword was Hector's![73] He was the killer, then,
Who took your life away. Although he'd died,
He was meant, you see, to destroy you in the end.[74]

Sailors, compare[75] the fates of these two men.
It was by the belt Ajax presented to him
1030 That Hector was strapped to Achilles' chariot-rail
And steadily mangled till he breathed his last;
While Ajax used this sword which was Hector's gift
1033 In the fatal fall that has now destroyed him too.
1036 I, then, should say the gods contrived his death,
As they contrive all else for humankind.
If anyone dissents from this opinion,
He can cling to his own view, I to mine.

CHORUS LEADER:
1040 No more for now. You'd better be thinking how
You'll bury Ajax – and what you'll argue next.
I spy an enemy coming, who may well laugh
At our misfortunes like the bully he is.

TEUCER:
Who is the officer you can see out there?
CHORUS LEADER:
It's Menelaus, for whom we sailed to Troy.                    1045
TEUCER:
You're right. Close to, he's easily recognized.
    [*Enter* MENELAUS, *attended, from a side entrance.*]
MENELAUS:
You there! Don't lift that body up, I tell you.
It's not your business. Leave it where it is!
TEUCER:
What do you mean by that absurd demand?
MENELAUS:
It's my decision and the commander-in-chief's.              1050
TEUCER:
Be good enough to give me a proper reason.
MENELAUS:
When we brought Ajax here from home, we thought
He'd prove our friend and ally. In the event
We've found him a worse foe than all the Trojans.
He set his mind to murder the whole Greek army             1055
And made a night foray to strike us down.
Had this wild sally not been foiled by one
Of the gods, we should have fared as he has done
And now be ignominiously flat on the ground,
While he would still be living. Fortunately,                1060
The god diverted Ajax's violent energy
On to the sheep and cattle. So that's why
No one can have the power to lay his body
To rest in a grave. No, he must be thrown out
On the yellow sand to feed the hungry seabirds.[76]         1065
And so I'll have no stormy threats from you.
Maybe we couldn't control him while he lived,
But now he's dead, we surely will, whether
You like it or not. *Our* hands will put him straight.
He never used to listen to what I said.                     1070

It's most degrading for a common subject
Not to cooperate with the powers that be.
Law and order will never prevail in a city
Where fear's not well established. Nor can discipline
1075   Be maintained in an army without the backing
Of fear[77] and proper respect. However large
A man's physique, he has to understand
The slightest accident can bring him down.
If you feel fear and have a sense of shame,
1080   Then you'll be safe. But arrogant and self-willed
Behaviour, when it's allowed, can only drag
The ship of state, after an easy voyage,
Down to the ocean's bottom in the end.

I want foundations of appropriate fear.
1085   We mustn't suppose that we can do as we please
And never pay the price of our pleasure in pain.
Life goes by turns.[78] Ajax has had his round
Of blazing arrogance. It's my turn now to be proud!
And I solemnly warn you not to bury his body,
1090   Unless you want to bury yourself beside him.
CHORUS LEADER:
Menelaus, beware of laying down the law,
However wisely, and then displaying pride
Yourself in violent treatment of the dead.
TEUCER:
Sailors, I'd never be surprised again
If someone humbly born then goes astray,
1095   When men supposed to be of noble birth
Are so wrong-headed in their arguments.
Let's start again, now. Do you really say
That you brought Ajax here to help the Greeks?
Didn't he sail to Troy of his own free will?
1100   Are you this man's superior? What right have you
To lord it over the force he brought from Salamis?
You're king of Sparta, not in charge of us.
There's no chain of command that entitles you
1104   To discipline him or him to discipline you.[79]

No, govern your own people and chastise *them*                    1107
With your pompous lectures. Whether it's you or your brother
General who says me nay, I'll bury Ajax
As I well should. I'll not be cowed by your threats.              1110
It was not to retrieve your wife that he joined the war,
Like all your suffering minions. He was bound
By oath[80] and not by any pledge to you.
He never had any respect for insignificant
Nobodies. So you can come back here with a larger                 1115
Body of heralds. Come with the general himself.
While this is your tune, no noise of yours will shift me.

CHORUS LEADER:
This kind of talk won't make the trouble better.
Harsh words can sting, however well deserved.

MENELAUS:
That archer[81] seems to think he's quite a man!                  1120

TEUCER:
I'm not the master of a menial skill.

MENELAUS:
You'd boast much louder if you had a shield.

TEUCER:
Put on full armour! I'd still stand up to *you.*

MENELAUS:
What courage your little tongue is giving you!

TEUCER:
Self-confidence is fine, if you're in the right.                  1125

MENELAUS:
Was it right for him to kill me and be honoured?

TEUCER:
Kill? That's strange. Have you come back to life?

MENELAUS:
The god has saved me. In Ajax's eyes, I'm dead.

TEUCER:
The gods have saved you. Treat them with some respect.

MENELAUS:
Would I be one to slight the laws of heaven?                      1130

TEUCER:
Yes, if you're here to stop the dead being buried.

MENELAUS:
I bury a public enemy? Out of the question!
TEUCER:
Did Ajax ever confront *you* as an enemy?
MENELAUS:
We loathed each other, and you knew that well.
TEUCER:
1135   Yes, you were found to have rigged the vote against him.
MENELAUS:
His loss was down to the jury, not to me.
TEUCER:
You're good at covering up your dirty tricks!
MENELAUS:
Someone's going to suffer for that remark.
TEUCER:
No more, I fancy, than the pain I'll give.
MENELAUS:
1140   I'll say just this: Ajax must not be buried.
TEUCER:
And *I* will say just this: he *shall* be buried.
MENELAUS:
A story.[82] I once observed a loud-mouthed man
Who urged his crew to sail in wintry weather.
But when the gale blew up, he'd lost his voice.
1145   He wrapped himself inside his cloak, and any
Sailor who liked could walk all over him.
The same will happen to you and your loud mouth:
A huge great storm will suddenly blow from a tiny
Cloud and extinguish all that noisy rant.
TEUCER:
1150   And I observed an exceedingly stupid man,
Who'd gloat offensively over his neighbour's troubles.
Then someone rather like me, of similar temper,
Gave him a look and spoke to him like this:
'You'd better not mistreat the dead, my man,
1155   As, if you do, you're sure to come to grief.'
The poor ass got his warning face to face.
I see him now and, so it appears to me,
He's you – none else. That wasn't much of a riddle!

MENELAUS:
I'm off. I can't have people knowing I merely
Gave you a reprimand, when I might have whipped you!                1160
TEUCER:
Very well, be off. It's just as shaming for me
To listen to fools who tell ridiculous stories.
    [*Exit* MENELAUS *with attendants.*]
CHORUS LEADER:
  I am sure that an angry contest's ahead.
  Quickly, Teucer, as fast as you can,
  You must see to a trench in the soil for a grave,              1165
  Where Ajax can rest in the cold, dank earth,
  For his everlasting remembrance.
TEUCER:
Look, at the very time they're needed, here
They are approaching, Ajax's wife and child,
To pay the funeral rites to his wretched body.                     1170
    [*Enter* TECMESSA *and* EURYSACES.]
Come here, Eurysaces. Come here and stand
Close by your father. You're going to be a suppliant.[83]
You'll kneel and rest one hand on him, and then
I want you to take a lock of hair from me,
One from your mother, and also one of your own.
These locks will make your supplication strong.                    1175
If anyone from the army tries to force
You away from this dead body, he has my curse:
For evil doom on evil deed, I pray
He'll have *his* body thrown, unburied, over
His country's border; then that all his race
Will be cut down to the roots, exactly as
I now cut off this lock of my own hair.
Hold it, my boy, and take good care of it.                         1180
Now kneel, and hold your father's body tight.
Let no one move you away. You, sailors, don't
Stand by like women. You must be men and help
The child till I return, when I've prepared
A grave for Ajax, even if all forbid it.
    [*Exit* TEUCER.]

# CHORAL SONG 3[84]

CHORUS:

1185    Whén will I, whén will I, whén will I céase    [Strophe 1]
    Cóunting the years, cónstantly róaming réstless?
    Must the weary hours of this wretched soldier's life
    Never, never come to an end,
1190    Here on the boundless plains of Troy,
    In sadness and shame for all us Greeks?

    Whó was he, whó was he, whó was the mán?    [Antistrophe 1]
    Whý could he not mélt into áir, or plúmmet
1195    Down to Hades? Why did he need to teach the Greeks
    How to band in murderous arms?
    Toil that ever engenders toil!
    That mischief-maker destroyed mankind.

    Alas! That master of war    [Strophe 2]
1200    Róbbed me of all pléasure in life,
    Gárlands and wine quáffed from deep góblets.
    He stífled the sweet dróne of the pipe,
    Cóst me my rest, néver to sleep soúnd in the níght-time.
1205    And lóve's jóys, oh, lóve's jóys he has stólen fróm me.
    So here I must lie neglected,
    Hair sodden with drenching dew.
    Hów can I ónce forgét
1210    That Tróy's glóom is aróund me?

    Till lately Ajax the bold    [Antistrophe 2]
    Shíelded me from féar in the night,
    Sáw that the foe's wéapons could not hárm me.
    But nów he has been dóomed to a harsh
1215    Déstiny. What jóy is there still léft for my cómfort?
    I lóng, lóng to sáil hóme and to páss the héadland,
    Where cypresses face the ocean
1220    That washes the shore beneath
    Sunium's lofty heights,[85]
    And gréet hóliest Áthens.

# CLOSING SCENE[86]

[*Re-enter* TEUCER.]

TEUCER:
I've hurried back as I've seen the commander-in-chief,
Agamemnon, speeding over there towards us.
He's clearly out to unleash his foolish tongue.                               1225

[*Enter* AGAMEMNON, *attended.*]

AGAMEMNON:
You there! I'm told you've dared to open your mouth
In those appalling insults quite unscathed –
Yes, you, I mean the captive woman's boy.
My goodness, if you'd had a noble mother,
You *would* be prancing round and talking big!                              1230
You're bad enough when you're a nobody,
Taking another useless nobody's side
And swearing we have no authority over
Achaean soldiers and sailors here, or you.
Ajax, in your book, sailed under his own
Command. That's surely a gross impertinence                                  1235
To come from a slave's mouth. What kind of man
Inspires you to bark out these arrogant claims?
Where has he gone or stood where I have not?
Is he the only man the Greeks can call on?
It looks as if we made a bad mistake
In throwing out the award of Achilles' arms
To open competition among the Greeks,                                        1240
If Teucer's always going to vilify us
And you lot won't agree, even when beaten,
To accept a verdict reached by majority vote.
You losers will either rain abuse on us,
Or else, no doubt, you'll stab us in the back.                               1245
Rules, on this basis, can never have any force,
You know, if we reject legitimate winners
And then advance the also-rans to the front.
We can't have that. It's not the thugs with broadest                        1250
Backs who prove the most reliable troops.

It's brain, not brawn, that always rules the day.
An ox with huge flanks only needs a tiny
Lash to keep it ploughing the furrow straight.
1255 That medicine's shortly on its way to you,
I see, if you can't acquire a little sense.
Ajax no more exists, he's now a shade.
But you are recklessly acting above your station
And talking out of turn. Be sensible.
You'd better realize who you are and bring
1260 Along some friend to help you[87] – a freeborn person
Who'll put your case to us on your behalf.
I honestly couldn't follow what *you* say,
As I don't understand your barbarous tongue.
CHORUS LEADER:
I wish you'd *both* be sensible,
1265 And have no better advice to offer.
TEUCER [*sighs*]:
How quickly gratitude towards the dead
Trickles away and proves its treachery!
Ajax, you won't receive another thought,
However slight, from the king for whom you risked
1270 Your life so often on the battlefield.
All that you've done is lost, thrown overboard.
What a stupid speech that was of yours, Agamemnon!
Do you remember *nothing*? What of the time[88]
When all of you were trapped inside your lines?
1275 The rout had taken place and you by then
Were helpless. Only Ajax came to your rescue.
The fire was already raging round the sterns
And over the quarterdecks, and Hector was leaping
Wildly across the trenches on to the hulls.
1280 Who held those dangers off? The man whom you
Said never went where you'd not gone yourself.
Don't you think he was doing his duty then?
And what about later on, when he confronted
Hector in single combat? Did he do it
Because he was ordered? No, he was picked by lot.
1285 He hadn't cast a runaway coward's lot,

Like a lump of soggy earth, in the plumed helmet,
But one that was going to jump out lightly first.
Ajax performed these exploits, and I assisted him,
Teucer the slave, the barbarian woman's boy.
How can you have the face to call me that,                         1290
You wretch? Don't you know that your father's father,
Pelops, originally came from Phrygia, another
Barbarian country, while your own father, Atreus,
Served his brother the most unholy meal
Of his children's flesh?[89] Your mother was born in Crete,        1295
And she was consigned by the father whose loins produced her
To feed the fish when he caught her in bed with a lover.
You're one to taunt me with my origins!
My father is the famous Telamon, who
Achieved the highest distinction in the army                       1300
And won my mother to share his bed. She
Was King Laomedon's daughter, and Heracles
Presented her to *him* as his special prize.[90]
Can I, the high-born son of high-born parents
On both sides, bring disgrace on my blood relation,               1305
The man who's lying here so sadly dead,
Whom you are all for throwing out unburied
And not ashamed to say so? Understand
That if you cast out Ajax, you'll be casting
Out the three of *us* to lie beside him.
I'd sooner die fighting before the army                            1310
On his behalf than for your woman's sake –
Or should I say your brother's woman? So!
Look to your own position, not to mine.
If you do me harm, you'll wish you'd played the coward
Rather than stood so rashly up to *me*.                            1315
        [*Enter* ODYSSEUS.]
CHORUS LEADER:
Odysseus, sir, your coming's timely, if you're
Not here to join this quarrel but break it up.
ODYSSEUS:
What's it about? I heard the two kings shouting
Over this brave man's body from far away.

AGAMEMNON:

1320  Yes, lord Odysseus. Teucer has just been throwing
      The most disgraceful insults at us both.

ODYSSEUS:

What insults? I can forgive a man for engaging
In violent words when he's been insulted first.

AGAMEMNON:

I did insult him, as he's insulted me.

ODYSSEUS:

1325  What has he done to you to cause offence?

AGAMEMNON:

He refuses to let this body go unburied
And means to inter it in defiance of me.

ODYSSEUS:

Can you permit a friend to speak the truth
And still support you, as he always has?

AGAMEMNON:

1330  Speak on. I'd be a fool not to permit it.
      You are my loyallest friend among the Greeks.

ODYSSEUS:

Then listen. In god's name, don't allow yourself
To treat the body of Ajax so unfeelingly
And cast him out unburied. Violent hatred

1335  Should not prevail so far that you violate justice.
      Ever since I won the arms of Achilles,
      Ajax was my worst enemy in the camp.
      But even so, for all his animosity
      Towards myself, I cannot show him dishonour.
      I have to admit I thought him the most outstanding

1340  Soldier among us Greeks who came to Troy,
      Except Achilles. You'd be unjust to show
      His body disrespect. You'd be destroying
      The laws of heaven, not Ajax himself at all.
      When a good and brave man dies, it can't be right

1345  To injure him, however much you hate him.

AGAMEMNON:

Odysseus, are you fighting *me* for him?

ODYSSEUS:
I am. I hated him when it was right to hate.
AGAMEMNON:
And shouldn't you kick his body now he's dead?
ODYSSEUS:
One shouldn't triumph, friend, in an ill-won victory.
AGAMEMNON:
Piety doesn't come easily to a king.                                        1350
ODYSSEUS:
To follow a friend's advice is not so hard.
AGAMEMNON:
The good man listens to his superiors.
ODYSSEUS:
Now wait. By yielding to your friends – you win.
AGAMEMNON:
Think of the kind of man you're backing now.
ODYSSEUS:
He was my foe, for sure. But he once was noble.                            1355
AGAMEMNON:
What next? Have you such respect for an enemy's
    corpse?
ODYSSEUS:
His valour moves me more than his enmity.
AGAMEMNON:
That is a most capricious way to think!
ODYSSEUS:
Our minds can change towards our fellow-men.
AGAMEMNON:
Would you approve my making friends like Ajax?                             1360
ODYSSEUS:
I don't like to approve a stubborn will.
AGAMEMNON:
You'll turn us into cowards right away.
ODYSSEUS:
No, no. The whole of Greece will call you just.
AGAMEMNON:
Are you telling me to allow this corpse's burial?

ODYSSEUS:
1365    I am. I'll need those rites one day myself.
AGAMEMNON:
That's how it always goes – each man for himself!
ODYSSEUS:
But why should I work more for anyone else?
AGAMEMNON:
Very well. It can be your doing, none of mine.
ODYSSEUS:
Whichever way, the act will do you credit.
AGAMEMNON:
1370    Well, you can rest assured, for *you* I'd offer
Even greater favours.[91] But Ajax still
Remains my hated foe, below in Hades
As here on earth – though you may do as you wish.
        [*Exit* AGAMEMNON *with attendants.*]
CHORUS LEADER:
If anyone after this, Odysseus, says
1375    You're not a wise man – well, he's just a fool.
ODYSSEUS:
I also promise, Teucer, that from today
I'll prove as strong a friend as I was once
An enemy. I should like to help with all
The burial rites for Ajax here and join
1380    In all the tributes due to the greatest men.
TEUCER:
Oh great Odysseus! I can only thank you
For your kind words. You've foiled my expectations.
You were the Greek my brother hated most,
But you alone have offered him active help.
1385    You haven't brought yourself to fling abuse
At Ajax in his presence, a living person
Against a dead, as did that lunatic general,
He and his brother, who came and tried to throw
His body out, profaned, without a burial.
I pray the Father who rules this sky above,
1390    The vengeful Fury and fulfilling Justice,
Destroy these evil men and let their bodies

Suffer the evil and the ill-deserved,
Profane exposure they proposed for Ajax.
But as for you, sir, son of old Laertes,
Though I can hardly let you touch his bier,
In case I thereby give offence to the dead,                          1395
Please join in all the rest,[92] and if you wish
To bring some soldiers, I shall not object.
I'll see to everything else. But be assured,
To us you've proved yourself a man of honour.

ODYSSEUS:
I'd hoped to take full part, but if that's not                       1400
Your wish, I shall respect that wish and go.
   [*Exit* ODYSSEUS.]

TEUCER:
  Now enough.[93] We have lingered for far too long.
  You there, make haste to be digging the grave,
  While some put a bowl to be licked by the flames
  On a high-raised tripod and heat the water                   1405
  For ritual washing.
  One company bear from the hut the fine armour
  He wore to protect him behind his shield.[94]
  Boy, you are young, but this is your father,
  So help me as far as your strength will allow.
  You may lovingly put your hands on his side,                 1410
  And we'll lift him together. His lungs are still warm
  And pumping the power of his black blood forth.
  Come, everyone present who claims to be Ajax's
  Friend, make haste and be gone on your way
  In final service to this great man.                          1415
  You never followed a greater.

CHORUS:
  When mortals have seen, much truth can be learned.
  But until he has seen, no man can divine
  What will come or the fate which awaits him.[95]              1420
    [*Exeunt all in solemn procession.*]

# ELECTRA

# Preface to Electra

## THE TRADITION

The essentials of the myth inherited by Sophocles were derived from Homer and his epic successors, then developed by the Greek lyric poets and the dramatist's predecessors in tragedy.

Agamemnon, king of Mycenae, led the expedition to Troy to recover Helen, the wife of his brother Menelaus, who had eloped with the Trojan prince Paris. So that his fleet could sail, Agamemnon was compelled to sacrifice his daughter Iphigenia to the goddess Artemis. On his return home from the sack of Troy ten years later, he was murdered by his wife, Clytemnestra, and her lover Aegisthus, who then became the rulers of Mycenae.

Agamemnon's young son, Orestes, had escaped into exile at the time of his father's death. Grown to manhood, he returned to Mycenae on the orders of the Delphic oracle, to take revenge on his father's murderers, first making contact with his unmarried sister Electra. After killing his mother and Aegisthus, Orestes was pursued by the Furies to Delphi, where he was purified by the god Apollo, and then to Athens, where he was tried and acquitted by a court of citizens.

## SYNOPSIS

Electra, one of Agamemnon's surviving daughters, continues to mourn publicly for her dead father and to pray that her exiled brother, Orestes, will return home to avenge Agamemnon's murder. Treated as a slave by the usurpers Clytemnestra and

Aegisthus, Electra is contrasted with her sister Chrysothemis, who offers no resistance and so enjoys a comfortable life.

The plot springs from Orestes' secret return to Argos and the execution of a cunning stratagem, based on a false report of his own death, to kill his mother and her lover. Electra, however, is not initially made aware of this plan, and the main action of the play is concerned with her individual plight and the impact of Orestes' trick on her emotions and personality.

## INTERPRETATION

The traditional myth of Orestes, who killed his mother to avenge his father, made a perfect subject for a drama that would excite an audience and give it something to think about. To the Athenian of the fifth century BC, justice demanded that crime should be punished, and the normal basis of morality was to do good to one's friends and harm to one's enemies. At the same time, to shed the blood of one's own kin, especially the mother whose body had given one life, entailed appalling personal pollution. The Orestes story, therefore, not only had great emotional potential in the theatre but also raised disturbing questions about the ethics of retribution in general. We are lucky, uniquely in this case, to have inherited contrasting treatments by each of the three great tragic poets from Athens in the fifth century BC.

The first of these treatments, undoubtedly influential on Sophocles, was by Aeschylus, who used the huge canvas of the trilogy form in his *Oresteia* to present the issues in the broadest possible perspective. This astonishing work, first performed in 458 BC,[1] explores the self-defeating and self-perpetuating character of retributive justice based on violent revenge. When Orestes kills Clytemnestra as a sacred duty, commanded by Apollo, in the second play of the trilogy *(Libation Bearers)*, it comes as the climax of a long chain of crime and retribution in the house of Atreus, going back through two generations. The inexorable law is that 'the doer must suffer,' and the divine agents of the retaliatory process are the terrifying Furies, known as Erinyes, who themselves hound down Orestes, after he has murdered his mother, in the third play *(Eumenides)*. The chain of crime is broken and a solution to the problem of the blood feud is worked out in the context of the city-state, when Orestes is formally tried and acquitted by a court of Athenian citizens. In Aeschylus' grand conception, human beings learn by their suffering and are able to progress to a new kind of justice based on the laws of the *polis*, which still allow a place to the Furies (now known as Eumenides, or Kindly Ones) in the life of the community.

We do not know for sure whether Sophocles' treatment of the Orestes myth preceded or followed Euripides' *Electra*, though recent scholarship[2] tends to favour an earlier date for the Euripides play (about 420 as against 413 for the Sophocles). Both poets, however, composed their tragedies as single plays with a number of formal features in common. Both chose to concentrate the dramatic action on Orestes' retributive murder of Clytemnestra and Aegisthus, by contrast with Aeschylus' much wider scope. And both assigned the protagonist's role to Orestes' sister, Electra, whose function and significance are much more limited in Aeschylus' *Libation Bearers*.

Euripides was less concerned to explore revenge than matricide as such. He was evidently repelled by the idea that the god of Delphi, Apollo, could have commanded such a deed from his holy oracle. He looks at the mother-murder in human terms and represents Orestes as a reluctant hero driven to this appalling deed by a dominating sister whose circumstances have warped her personality and natural instincts. The murders of Aegisthus and Clytemnestra are both performed in a discreditable, non-heroic way, emphasized by the victims each being invested with some redeeming features. The aftermath for both Orestes and Electra is essentially revulsion and remorse. The Furies get a formal mention in the closing scene, but are given little emotive value. The poignant picture at the end is of a brother and sister, previously separated emotionally by their egocentric preoccupations and now united by their common guilt, being forced by their individual destinies to say farewell and part.

Sophocles' treatment of the myth is more elusive and difficult to pin down. Indeed, there have been widely differing views of his *Electra*'s moral slant. On the face of it, the issue is quite uncomplicated: Orestes plans and executes the killing of his mother with ruthless efficiency, and there is no aftermath of his being hounded by the Furies or stricken by frightful remorse. In Aeschylus and Euripides, the murder of Clytemnestra comes after that of Aegisthus and is presented as the climactic horror, but Sophocles, with his different emphasis and for his own dramatic reasons, reverses the order. Looked at superficially, he seems to have reverted to the Homeric account of Orestes' revenge in the *Odyssey*, where it is treated as laudable and final. Hence the famous description of the play by A. W. Schlegel as 'a combination of matricide and good spirits', which might be paraphrased as 'matricide without tears'.

Some modern accounts, however, have looked deeper and found this melodramatic interpretation too simplistic. This *Electra*, unlike Euripides', is not about matricide as such and has more to do with revenge in general. Electra is indubitably the leading character, and Orestes' drama is secondary to hers. Tears are shed in plenty during the course of the action, and there is no escaping the tragic *pathos* of the whole, the predominant mood of suffering. Indeed, of the three dramatic treatments of the Orestes myth, this one is arguably not the cheerfullest but the most unrelentingly grim. Orestes may not see the Furies after the murder, but the Furies are there at several points in the play, both specifically in the poetic language and implicitly in the theme of tragic retaliation, which is all-pervasive. As in Aeschylus, they feature no less than the Olympian god Apollo, whose authority also broods over the sinister action.

The retaliation motif calls for further elaboration. The picture we are offered by Electra right from the start is of a noble nature *compelled* by loyalty to her father to adopt an aggressive stance towards her mother which is impious and excessive. Her lamentation for the dead Agamemnon is bound to be extended indefinitely while his murderers remain unpunished and secure in their usurped power. Moreover, the vituperation and harsh treatment that Clytemnestra and Aegisthus mete out to her enforce a retaliatory response of non-cooperation and active defiance. The interesting thing is that Electra herself is aware of her excess, but sure at the same time that she has no choice but to behave towards her mother as she does. In this she is contrasted with her sister Chrysothemis, who is prepared to accept a subordinate position and compromise with the usurpers. By one set of norms, Chrysothemis is behaving 'wisely' or 'sensibly' in coming to terms with a situation that she has no power to alter, and by the same criteria Electra is behaving 'foolishly'. In terms of piety to her father, though, Electra is showing the truer 'wisdom'.

The constant iteration of the retaliation motif suggests that Sophocles was less concerned with retribution as a one-moment *event* and more as a continuous *process*. The recurrent Erinyes imagery also carries the implication that revenge is as ruinous to its human agents as it is to its victims. So while the play's action appears to show Orestes and Electra finally triumphing over their foes, the tragedy is that, by a hideous irony, they themselves are destroyed morally as the drama progresses.

This is not so obvious in the case of Orestes as he features less prominently than Electra. But we may note the hard military tone in which he outlines his murder plan in the prologue and, if the translation's assignment of the dialogue is right, his deliberate ignoring of the moan from indoors which might have reminded him that Electra and her feelings should come into his calculations. He cynically rejects the notion that a false report of his death could be a bad omen for himself, but, by the end of the play, we may feel that there is an ironical sense in which he has been dead from the outset in terms of common humanity. When he eventually meets Electra, he briefly responds to his sister's grief as she weeps over the urn containing his supposed ashes, but, once the recognition has taken place, he greets her rapturous outpourings with cautious reserve. After he has killed his mother and her lover, his final exit line is blood-chillingly vindictive.

The process of Electra's tragedy is worked out much more elaborately and is the primary focus of dramatic interest. Much hinges on the point that Orestes does not involve his sister in the plot and leaves her to an extremity of despair under the devastating impact of the false news that he has been killed in a chariot race. Her practical reaction to this blow is to conceive the crazily unrealistic idea of winning glory by killing Aegisthus single-handed, if Chrysothemis refuses (as she does) to help her. After that, Electra's great speech of mourning over the urn emphasizes how close to nothingness she feels. When she eventually realizes that Orestes *is* alive, her contrasting joy knows no bounds, and all rationality remaining in her seems lost. The drama's horrific climax is her shout to Orestes, at the moment of Clytemnestra's murder offstage, to strike her mother a second time.

In the portrayal of Electra, there are passages where Sophocles seems deliberately to be reminding his audience of his Antigone,[3] another uncompromising heroine who holds unswervingly to the categorical imperative of familial piety. Similarly, Chrysothemis' utilitarian ethics vividly recall those of Ismene in the earlier play. The final intertextual echo of *Antigone*, though, is the really telling one. In her last lines of an extremely long part, Electra tells Orestes (by implication) to expose Aegisthus' body to be devoured by the dogs and vultures. This surely connotes the total loss of her humanity. Degraded from Antigone to Creon, she is as morally annihilated as the Theban king. Not only has she consistently contravened the famous Greek precept of 'nothing in excess', she has also ceased any longer to 'know herself'.[4]

The view, then, that regards Sophocles as shelving the moral aspect of revenge in the Orestes story misses the depth and subtle irony of this disturbingly powerful tragedy. He follows Aeschylus in exploring the universal problem of revenge, but he is also, like Euripides, interested in the personalities of the individuals who perpetrate revenge and in what it does to them in the process.

# CASTING

The role of Electra will have been a 'star role' for Sophocles' first actor. After a solo entrance, the character remains on stage, with one very short break (1384–97), until the end of the play. The second actor must (very interestingly to us) have combined the parts of Orestes and Clytemnestra. The third played the Old Slave, Chrysothemis and Aegisthus, another intriguing variety of roles. An additional (mute) actor performed Pylades. Other extras were attendants accompanying Clytemnestra and Orestes.

# STAGING

The *skênê* will have represented the palace at Mycenae, with the central doorway serving for entrances from and exits into the house. Clytemnestra's covered corpse in the closing scene was probably shown on a mechanical device known as the *ekkyklêma*, which rolled out of the central entrance on to the acting area in front of the *skênê*.

# DRAMATIC TECHNIQUE

Sophocles was as original in his dramatization as he was in his treatment of the inherited myth. As a theatrical experience, *Electra* can be among the most moving of all surviving Greek tragedies. Paradoxically, for a very large part of the piece, the plot is at a standstill or else nudged forward by false starts which do not come to anything. One critic, G. H. Gellie,[5] has observed that it is only when the male characters are around that anything seems to happen; the bulk of the play consists of women in argument or lamentation. Yet in performance, the play has an organic progression and a quality of suspense that make it increasingly absorbing. The opening is strong and upbeat, while the rapid pace of the final scene is almost unbearably exciting after the gradual but highly emotional build-up. The central figure of Electra, in her extremities of love and hatred, grief and joy, makes the drama powerfully compelling, and it is not surprising that the role has attracted several distinguished actresses in modern times.

Overall shape apart, no less remarkable is the poet's masterly use of tragedy's form and conventions to contribute to the total impact. The rhetoric of the great long speeches is full of strikingly vivid detail and suggests the adversarial atmosphere of the law courts or a public debate. The false messenger's speech is a tour de force: we are swept up in the Old Slave's exciting description of Orestes' fatal chariot race while knowing at the same time that it is all a pack of lies. Stichomythia, too, is brilliantly employed to articulate the conflict between Electra's and Chrysothemis' ethical standpoints and make this vibrantly theatrical. The choral songs are not intrusive interludes, but a crucial part of the drama's seamless movement. Their imagery and taut rhythms capture the mood of the moment, whether sinister or pathetic, and help to bring out the deeper significance of the action. At certain points, Sophocles takes Electra herself into lyric mode to express the intensity of her sorrow or joy.

# NOTES

1. It seems highly likely that the *Oresteia* was revived at some point in the 420s, as Sophocles, Euripides and the comic playwright Aristophanes evidently assumed their audience's familiarity with it.
2. A very helpful discussion can be found in Jenny March's commentary on *Electra* (Warminster 2001), pp. 21–2.
3. See *Electra* notes 27, 53, 71.
4. The two precepts were carved on the temple of Apollo at Delphi. Apollo is the god who dominates the divine background to this play. See *Electra* note 3.
5. In *Sophocles: A Reading* (Melbourne 1972).

# Characters

OLD SLAVE, *Orestes' tutor*
ORESTES, *son of Agamemnon*
ELECTRA, *daughter of Agamemnon*
CHORUS *of women of Mycenae*
CHRYSOTHEMIS, *Electra's sister*
CLYTEMNESTRA, *mother of Orestes and Electra*
AEGISTHUS, *Clytemnestra's second husband*
PYLADES, *Orestes' friend*
ATTENDANTS

## SCENE 1[1]

[*Enter* OLD SLAVE, ORESTES *and* PYLADES]
OLD SLAVE:
Son of Agamemnon, commander-in-chief at Troy,
Now you are here in person, to see what you always
Longed to see. Look! The land of your dreams,
The ancient plain of Argos, the sacred grove
5   Where Io[2] was plagued by the stinging gadfly. There,
Orestes, the forum of Apollo,[3] the wolf-killing god.
To the left the famous temple of Hera.[4] The place
We have reached you may call Mycenae,[5] rich in gold,
10  And here the palace of Atreus,[6] rich in blood.
From here, some years ago, when your father was murdered,
Your sister Electra handed you into my care.
I carried you off, I saved your life, and then
I brought you up as my own, until you reached
Your prime of manhood, to avenge your father's murder.

15  So now, Orestes – and you, his faithful friend,
Pylades[7] – settle your plan of campaign quickly.
Black night is over, the stars have fled, the sun's
Bright rays are waking the birds to their dawn chorus.
20  Get all your talking done before any man
Ventures abroad. This is the final crossroads.

The time for flinching is past. To action now!
ORESTES:
Good man! The truest of my followers! How well you prove
Your loyalty to us. Like an old thoroughbred warhorse          25
Who never loses his spirit in the stress of battle,
But keeps his ears pricked up, you urge us on
And lend your own support in the very front line.
Well now, I'll tell you what I've decided. You
Pay careful attention to what I say and put me                 30
Straight if I miss the mark. When I went
To the Delphic oracle[8] to ask precisely how
I ought to take revenge on my father's murderers,
Apollo made a response which is quickly told:                  35
    *Not with the might of shielded host*
    *Shall Justice see her purpose done.*
    *By lone deceit and stealthy craft*
    *Must blood be shed and victory won.*
That was the oracle we heard. Let us act accordingly.
Your role must be to enter the palace here
When the right moment takes you in, to reconnoitre             40
The situation and come back to us with a clear report.
Your age and long absence will make you hard to recognize.
They won't suspect those grey hairs. Spin them a yarn
That you're a stranger from Phocis, sent by Phanoteus,         45
Who happens to be the strongest of their military allies.
Give them the news, with an oath to back it up,
That Orestes is dead, killed in a fatal accident,
Flung from his running chariot at the Pythian Games.[9]
That's the story you'll tell. And now for us.                  50
First, we'll pour libations[10] on my father's grave,
As the god instructed, and crown it with curling locks[11]
Cut from my head, before we retrace our steps,
Bearing with us the urn of bronze which I think
You also know is lying concealed in the brushwood.             55
Our crafty tale will bring them the glad tidings
That my body has been cremated and now consists
Of nothing but charred remains. What harm does it do me
To say I'm dead? None, if the outcome proves

60  My real salvation and wins me a glorious prize.[12]
In my opinion, no word can be a bad omen
If it leads to gain. A false report of death
Is a trick I've often seen used by clever philosophers.
They come back home again, and their prestige
65  Is higher than ever. So it will be with me.
I swear this news of my death will allow me to live
And shine like a star on my foes in time to come.

Now, earth of my fathers, gods of this land,
Welcome me home. Grant success to my mission,
You also, house of my fathers. Sent by the gods,
70  I come in the name of justice to purify *you*.
Let me not leave this land dishonoured. May I
Be lord of my wealth and establish my house anew.

Enough of words. It's over to you, old friend.
Be off, and see to your appointed task.
75  We'll to our business, too. It's time. And with men,[13]
In any operation, time is the great controller.
ELECTRA [*from within*]:
*Io moi moi!* So wretched!
OLD SLAVE:
Listen! I thought I heard one of the servants
Moaning softly behind the doors, my son.
80  'So wretched!' – could it be Electra? Ought we to stay
Where we are and listen while she laments?[14]
ORESTES:
No, no! Apollo's orders first. The proper
Start must be libations at my father's grave.
85  That is the way to victory and to success.

[*Exeunt* ORESTES *and* PYLADES *by one side entrance, the*
OLD SLAVE *by the other.*]

## ELECTRA'S MONODY[15]

[*Enter* ELECTRA *from the palace.*]
ELECTRA:
Holiest sunlight,
O sky who enfolds the earth, you've heard
My songs of grief so often,
So often marked the beating
Of blows rained full on my bleeding breast,                90
When the mists of the dark lift in the morning.
Through the nights I have kept my vigil of tears.
My hateful bed in a house of pain
Is witness to all my laments for my poor
Wretched father, alas! Far from his homeland               95
Murderous Ares[16] refused him a grave.
My own dear mother, she and her mate
Aegisthus, as woodcutters fell an oak,
They split his skull with a murderous axe.
And I alone, Father, in sadness                            100
Am left to pour pity upon you,
So sadly, shamefully murdered.
But I shall never
End my dirges and bitter laments
While I still see the twinkling,                           105
All-radiant stars and the daylight,
Nor cease to keen like the nightingale[17]
Who killed her young, crying my sorrow
To the world here by the royal gateway.
O hear me, all you gods of the dead,
Hades, Persephone, Hermes below.[18]                       110
O hear me, power of my father's curse,
And you, the dread Furies[19] of vengeance,
Who spy the shedding of kindred blood
And robbing of beds in secret lust,
Come to me, succour me, punish my father's                115
Murder most foul,
And home to my arms send me my brother.

Alone I am weak, powerless to shoulder
120    The heavy load of my suffering.


## ENTRY OF THE CHORUS[20]

[*Enter the* CHORUS *of Mycenean women.*]
CHORUS:                                                [*Strophe 1*]
        O child, child of a wretchedly hard
        Mother, Electra, why are you still
        Chanting these insatiable songs of grief,
125      Crying for King Agamemnon, godlessly
        Caught in the trap by your mother's own treachery,
        Betrayed to death by a wicked hand? So perish the man
        Who déalt thát blów, if Í may práy só.

ELECTRA:
        Daughters of noble fathers,
130      You've come to console me in all my misfortunes,
        I know it, I feel it, I see it so clearly.
        But how could I willingly fail in my duty
        And cease to bewail my ill-fated father?
        No, my friends, whose kindness will always give friendship
            for friendship,
135      Leave me to my distraction,
        Leave me, I beg you.


CHORUS:                                            [*Antistrophe 1*]
        But how, how will dirges and prayers
        Help to summon your father back,
        Up from the Lake of Death which none escapes?
140      No, in your limitless grief you are fatally
        Parting from reason for pain without remedy.
        This sighing offers no release from suffering's chains.
        So whý, whý cóurt such sénseless ánguísh?

ELECTRA:
145      None but a fool forgets their
        Parents grievously gone to the underworld.
        Closer to my sad heart is the nightingale,

Bird who heralds the springtime, crazily,
Constantly moaning for Itys, for Itys.[21]
O Niobe,[22] queen of sorrows, I count you immortal in          150
  blessedness,
Tombed in the frozen rock face,
Weeping and weeping.

CHORUS:                                                   [Strophe 2]
You're not the only one,
Daughter, to know bereavement's pain.
Others are in your house. Your grief exceeds theirs,           155
The ones who share your father's blood, who still live,
Yes, your sisters, Chrysothemis and Iphianassa.[23]
He lives who is sheltered from sorrow,
Happily coming to manhood.                                     160
The famous land of Mycenae
Soon will welcome him back to his heritage.
The hand of Zeus will guide him home – Orestes!

ELECTRA:
Orestes, ah! I never tire of waiting,
So wretched and so lost – no child, no husband –               165
Drenched in my tears and doomed to perpetual
Misery. Can he remember the wrongs he has
Suffered and what he has heard of me? Which of his
Messages reach me without disappointing me?                    170
He álwáys lóngs to cóme,
But néver thínks fit to énd his lónging.

CHORUS:                                                  [Antistrophe 2]
Courage, you must take heart,
Daughter. Zeus is still great in heaven.
Nothing escapes his watchful eye and strong rule.              175
Assign to *him* the fury of your harsh rage.
Curb your anger with those you hate, you need not forget
  them.
Time is a god of healing.
The seaboard pastures of Crisa[24]                             180
Harbour your noble brother,

Son of the great Agamemnon, who cares for you.
So does the god who reigns by the river Acheron.[25]

ELECTRA:

185   No, most of my life has trickled past and left me
Without any hope. All my strength is ebbing.
Wasting to nothing without any children,
Needing the sheltering love of a husband.
I work as a slave in the house of my father,

190   As though I were just a contemptible foreigner.
I weár méan shábby clóthes
And éat stánding bý mysélf at méaltímes.

CHORUS:                                                              [Strophe 3]

That cry on the king's homecoming,
That pitiful cry at the fatal feast,

195   When the bronze axe struck and felled him down
And the blood ran down the flagstones.
It was guile that instructed; the killer was lust.
In monstrous union they brought to birth
That monstrous shape, whether mortal or god

200   Brought their scheme to ripeness.

ELECTRA:

Of all the days that I ever lived
That was the one most hateful,
That night of horror, night which saw

205   The monstrous feast.
What did my father feel
When he saw those two hands looming near –
Those hands that have now betrayed me too,
Captured and destroyed my life?
May Zeus the great Olympian god

210   Exact the punishment they deserve!
Those who committed such wickedness never
Should live to enjoy their splendour.

CHORUS:                                                          [Antistrophe 3]

Take care, you've said enough now!
You must see how your ruinous plight,

The shame of your present wretched state,                        215
Is all of your own making.
Your trials are worse than they need to be.
Your sullen soul keeps breeding wars
Which cannot be won. Don't fight with the strong.
Hów can yóu come néar them?                                       220

ELECTRA:
They *must* be fought! I'm left no choice.
Their crimes dictate my actions.
I know my passion all too well,
But I shan't cease
Plaguing them while I live.                                       225
My dearest sisters, what person of sense
Would say you were right? How can I now
Listen to kind, consoling words?
Leave me, my comforters, leave me alone.
These knots are never to be untied.                              230
I'll never find any relief from my sorrows,
My dirges cannot be reckoned.


CHORUS:                                              [*Epode*]
Dear child, I wish you kindly.
Please trust me like a mother.
Your folly's breeding ruin.                                       235

ELECTRA:
How can this evil allow moderation?
How *can* it be right to betray the departed?
How is it human to be so faithless?
I want no praise from impious men,
No home with them of quiet ease,                                  240
If noble blood still runs in my veins.
Shall I fail my father, stifling my cries,
Clipping the wings of grief?
Múst his córpse in the gróund
Wretchedly waste away,                                            245
Feebly count for nothing?
Múst his kíllers glóat,
Never to pay with blood for blood?

Then death to conscience,
250     And mán's féar of gód[26] is áll forgótten!

## SCENE 2[27]

CHORUS LEADER:
Electra, I'm as much concerned for your good
As I am for myself. If what I say is wrong,
You have your way. We're always there to help.
ELECTRA:
Women, all these laments of mine must make
255  Me seem so very embittered. I feel ashamed.
I'm forced to do it, though. You must forgive me.
A woman of noble birth could not act otherwise,
When she sees the troubles that haunt her father's house
260  Not fading away but growing day and night.

First, there's my mother. For all our natural ties,
We're bitter enemies. Next, I have to live
In my own house beside my father's murderers.
*They* give me my orders, and it rests with them
265  Whether I eat or starve. Moreover, what
Do you imagine my days are like when I
Can see Aegisthus sitting on my father's throne,
Wearing the same royal robes and pouring
270  Libations at the hearth-stone where he killed him?
Lastly, I have to witness this crowning outrage:
My father's murderer sharing my father's bed
With that brazen mother of mine – if it's still proper
To call the woman who sleeps with him my mother,
275  Who has the gall to live with that polluting
Criminal and lacks all fear of avenging Furies.[28]

Indeed, she appears to exult in her behaviour.
She has established the day when she trapped and
        murdered
280  My father, and set it apart for dancing and sacrifice

Every month to the gods who preserve the city.
And I must watch and wretchedly weep in my room,
Pining, lamenting aloud for the feast obscenely
Held in my father's name – all by myself, 285
As I may not even cry to my heart's content.
This 'noble' woman is there to bawl me out
With taunts like these: 'You god-forsaken bitch!
Are you the only daughter whose father's died?
Are you the only mourner alive on earth? 290
I hope you rot, and pray that the gods below
Will keep you weeping forever!' So much for her insults –
Except when she hears a rumour saying Orestes
Will soon return. That sends her berserk,
And she yells in my face, 'I blame *you* for this. 295
It's all your work. You stole Orestes out of my hands
And smuggled him out of Argos. I'll make you pay!' –
Yapping away, and her royal consort is there
Beside her to egg her on in similar vein – 300
That poisonous, gutless coward, who fights his battles
With women's help. Oh, I am sick and weary,
Weary of waiting for Orestes to come back home
And end all this. His never-ending delays 305
Have shattered every hope that I might have had.
In face of this, my friends, what room is there
For moderation or respect? With evil all
Around you, nothing but evil is left to do.
CHORUS LEADER:
Electra, is Aegisthus close enough to hear
You talking to us? Or is he away from home? 310
ELECTRA:
He certainly is. I shouldn't be straying out
Of doors if he were at home. He's now in the country.
CHORUS LEADER:
In that case I can speak to you more freely. 315
ELECTRA:
He's out. What do you want to know?
CHORUS LEADER:
Well, then, your brother – what about him?

Is he on his way or still delaying?

CHORUS LEADER:
320   A man may hesitate before a heavy task.

ELECTRA:
*I* never hesitated when I saved his life.

CHORUS LEADER:
He's too noble to let you down.

ELECTRA:
I trust so, else I shouldn't have lived so long.

CHORUS LEADER:
Say no more now. Here is your sister Chrysothemis –
325   She's Agamemnon's daughter as much as your mother's –
Coming out of the palace. Her hands are holding
Grave-offerings ritually paid to the dead.

     [*Enter* CHRYSOTHEMIS *from the palace.*]

CHRYSOTHEMIS:
Here you are again, holding forth
At the palace gateway! Electra, what are you doing?
330   Haven't you learned by now? Your anger's pointless,
Don't indulge it for nothing. I must admit
This situation distresses me too. If only
I had the strength, I'd show them how I feel.
335   But things are bad. It's wiser to trim my sails,
Not pose as a threat without any power to harm.
I wish you'd do the same. I know full well
That right is on your side, but if I want
340   To be free, our lords and masters must be obeyed.

ELECTRA:
Chrysothemis! How can you forget the father
Whose child you are and only think of your mother?
All the lectures you've been reading to me
345   Were written by her. They're not words of your own.
You have to choose: either to be a 'fool' like me,
Or else to be 'wise' and forget your proper family.
You said just now that if you could find the strength,

You'd show your hatred towards these people. But when 350
I champion our father, so far from lending a hand,
You try to thwart me – cowardice into the bargain!
Now tell me (or I'll tell you), what good would it do
To abandon all this mourning? I still have my life,
Not much of a life, I know, but enough for me.
By annoying *them*, I show respect to the dead, 355
If the dead can enjoy respect. You'd have me think
You hate them, but your hatred's a hollow sham.
You're really aiding and abetting your father's murderers.
I'd never submit to them, even if they gave me
All the lovely presents you now enjoy. 360
Keep your delicious food and life of luxury!
The only sustenance I need is a clear conscience.
I wouldn't want your privileges. Nor would you
If you had any sense. Very well. Instead of being known 365
As great Agamemnon's child, you can be called
Clytemnestra's daughter. Then people will know the truth:
You've betrayed your murdered father and your own family.

CHORUS LEADER:
Stop wrangling, please! You both have more 370
To gain from listening to each other.

CHRYSOTHEMIS:
Electra's tirades are nothing new to me.
I'd never have opened my lips if I hadn't heard
That serious trouble is on its way. They're going
To put an end to her lengthy lamentations. 375

ELECTRA:
All right, tell me the worst. If it's more frightful
Than the trouble I'm in now, I'll hold my tongue.

CHRYSOTHEMIS:
Well, I'll tell you all that I know myself.
Their plan is this: if you won't stop lamenting,
They'll send you where you'll never see the sun, 380
Buried alive in a cave across the frontier,
To chant your miseries there. You'd better think
About it carefully. Don't blame me when you suffer

Later on. You need to be sensible now.

CHRYSOTHEMIS:

385 Is *that* what they've planned to do with me?

CHRYSOTHEMIS:

It certainly is. As soon as Aegisthus returns.

ELECTRA:

All right, let him come, the sooner the better.

CHRYSOTHEMIS:

Electra! How can you pray for that?

ELECTRA:

Let him come, if that's what he means to do.

CHRYSOTHEMIS:

390 What do you want to happen? You're mad!

ELECTRA:

I want to escape, away from you all.

CHRYSOTHEMIS:

Have you no care for the life you have?

ELECTRA:

Oh, what a splendid life that is!

CHRYSOTHEMIS:

It would be so if you knew any sense.

ELECTRA:

395 Don't teach me how to betray my friends!

CHRYSOTHEMIS:

I'm only saying give in when you're beaten.

ELECTRA:

*You* can grovel. That's not *my* way.

CHRYSOTHEMIS:

At least it's better than falling through folly.

ELECTRA:

I'll fall if I must, for my father's sake.

CHRYSOTHEMIS:

400 Father will forgive us, I know.

ELECTRA:

Only a coward would talk like that.

CHRYSOTHEMIS:

But won't you listen to *my* advice?

ELECTRA:
No! I hope I'm never so foolish!
CHRYSOTHEMIS:
Very well, I'll go, on the way I was sent.
ELECTRA:
Where are you off to? Who are those offerings for?                        405
CHRYSOTHEMIS:
They're Mother's libations for our father's grave.
ELECTRA:
Libations? She's sending libations to her deadliest enemy?
CHRYSOTHEMIS:
The man she killed – that's what you really meant.
ELECTRA:
Who put the idea in her mind? Who told her to do it?
CHRYSOTHEMIS:
I *think* she was distressed by a frightening dream.                      410
ELECTRA:
Gods of our fathers, be with us now – at last!
CHRYSOTHEMIS:
Are you encouraged because you know she's frightened?
ELECTRA:
Describe the dream, and then I'll tell you.
CHRYSOTHEMIS:
I only know a very little . . .
ELECTRA:
Just tell me that. One little word                                         415
Can floor or set a person up for good.
CHRYSOTHEMIS:
They say she saw our father beside her again,
Restored to life. He then took hold of the staff
He used to carry and now Aegisthus wields,                                 420
And planted it on the hearth. This sprouted up
And grew to a leafy branch which overshadowed
The whole of Mycenae. So much I learned
From someone present when she revealed her dream
To the god of the Sun. That's all I know, except                          425
That our mother's frightened enough to send me out.[29]                   427

ELECTRA:

431   Chrysothemis, don't put any one of these things
On our father's grave. No man or god would approve.
Funeral offerings and libations for him
Coming from *her*, his hateful enemy? No,
Cast them out to the winds, or dig a trench
435   And hide them deep in the earth where none can reach
Our father's resting place. Let them be buried
Treasure, stored in Hades for her own funeral.
She must be the most hard-bitten woman alive!
440   How else could she be trying to crown the grave
Of the man she *killed* with these malignant offerings?
Do you imagine his buried corpse will take
Such tributes kindly? She killed him without respect
445   Like an enemy, butchered his limbs[30] and washed the blood
From her sword by smearing it on to her victim's head.
You can't suppose these gifts can atone for her guilt.
They won't. Leave them alone. Instead, Chrysothemis,
Offer a few strands cut from the ends of your hair,
450   And from poor me – not much of a gift, but still
It's all I have – this prayer of a lock and plain
Unjewelled girdle. Then kneel on the ground and pray
That he himself will come from the world below
And graciously champion us against our foes;
455   And pray that his son Orestes gains the upper
Hand and lives to trample upon his enemies;
So that hereafter we may crown his grave
With richer gifts than those we now accord him.
I think, indeed I think that *he* was minded
460   To send her this ugly dream. Be it so or not,
Chrysothemis, do this service to help yourself,
Do it to help me, do it to help the dear, dear
Father of us both, who lies in the house of Hades.

CHORUS LEADER:

Your sister's right. You know where your duty lies.
465   I'm sure you'll have the sense to follow her lead.

CHRYSOTHEMIS:

I will. Duty is not to be argued over,

But quickly done. I'll go about it now.
But please, my friends, you mustn't give me away.
If Mother finds out, I'll live to regret my boldness.                    470
    [*Exit* CHRYSOTHEMIS *by a side entrance.*]


## CHORAL SONG 1[31]

CHORUS:
    Óh my áuguring soul! Whát can it méan?    [*Strophe*]
    Unless my judgement is all awry,
    Jústice sént this díre dréam,                                     475
    And she'll be here, triumphantly bearing spoils of right.
    She'll hóund them dówn. Sóon, my chíld, they'll páy the
        príce.
    I féel it nów. Cóurage
    Swells in my heart to hear this                                   480
    Sweetly breathing spell of dreams.
    Can hé forgét? He néver sh* áll, that gréat lórd, kíng of
        Gréece.
    The áncient wéapon thréatens stíll, that brónze-fórged,       485
        twó-edged áxe
    Which cruelly dealt that ruthless, shameful, murderous blow.

    Néar now! Trámping of feet, póising of hánds!    [*Antistrophe*]
    That fearsome Fury[32] who lurks in wait,                         490
    Véngeance ármed with brónze cláws!
    Those frenzied sinners rushed to a union stained with
        blood
    And stéeped in guílt, cúrsed in lóve and cúrsed in béd.
    And só, be súre, cóurage!                                        495
    Never, oh, never shall we
    See this portent fail to strike
    That kíller and hér accómplice. Íf this níght-sént, ghóstly
        síght
    Comes nót to dúe fulfílment, thén my sóul's déep éye is       500
        blínd;
    All ominous dreams are vain, all oracles empty words.

When Pélops[33] in past áges                          [*Epode*]
505     Won the ráce with his cháriot,
        What néver-ending sórrow
        Strúck this lánd!
        When Mýrtilus, his hélper,
        Was drówned beneath the ócean
510     Tossèd héadlong from his cháriot,
        He cúrsed the race of Pélops
        And díed in great ánguish.
        Sínce that dáy
        This pálace has been háunted
515     By súffering and ánguish.


# SCENE 3[34]


[*Enter* CLYTEMNESTRA *with an attendant from the palace.*]
CLYTEMNESTRA:
Out and about again, it seems, and off the leash!
Aegisthus isn't at home to keep you under control
And stop you shaming your family out of doors.
As he's away, you won't take any notice
520     Of *me* – although you've often said in public
That I'm a harsh and oppressive tyrant who treats
Both you and yours with insolent disregard.
Insolent I am not. If I curse you,
It's due to the taunts you're always hurling at me.

525     Your constant pretext is simply this: I killed
Your father. Yes, I did. I'm well aware of that
And won't pretend to deny it. Justice determined
His death; I wasn't alone. And you should have taken
The side of Justice, if you'd had any sense.
530     Listen! This father of yours whom you're always lamenting
Committed the most barbaric crime: he sacrificed
Your sister[35] to the gods. Iphigenia's birth
Never cost him the pains of labour that I went through.
Very well. Now answer this question. Why did he sacrifice her?

To help the Greeks? But they enjoyed no right                    535
To kill a daughter of *mine*. Or did he kill
My child to help his brother Menelaus?
In that case, didn't he owe me some satisfaction?
Menelaus had two children of his own. Their lives
Should have been forfeit first, because they belonged            540
To him and to Helen, for whom the war was fought.
Or was it that Hades had some strange desire
To glut his belly on my children rather than hers?
Perhaps Agamemnon had now transferred his love
To his brother's children and lost all interest in mine?         545
What a perverse and callous father that would make him!

That's how I see it, even if you disagree.
Iphigenia would say the same if she
Could speak for herself. No, for my own part,
I view the past with no misgivings at all.
You may believe I'm wrong, but do make sure                      550
You're right yourself before you criticize others.
ELECTRA:
This time you shan't maintain you made this offensive
Speech of yours because I attacked you first.
With your permission, might I straighten the record
In my dead father's defence and my sister's too?                 555
CLYTEMNESTRA:
You certainly may. I wish you always began
In a tone like that. You'd be a pleasure to listen to.
ELECTRA:
Very well, then, listen. You say you killed my father.
What admission could be more shameful than that,
Whether or not justice was on your side?                         560
I put it to you, it wasn't justice that drove
You to kill him. No, you were seduced by the evil man
Who is now your partner. Ask Artemis, the hunter
Goddess, why she becalmed the fleet at Aulis,
As none of the winds would blow. What was she punishing?
I'll give you the answer. We can't cross-question *her*.         565

My father, as I've been told, was out on a hunt
In Artemis' sacred grove, when his footfall startled
A dappled stag from its covert. After he'd shot it,
He accidentally let fall some boastful words.
570 This made the goddess angry, and so she held
The Greek fleet up, to make my father atone
For the stag by sacrificing his daughter.
That's how it occurred. It was the only solution.
The ships couldn't sail back home or across to Troy.
575 He sacrificed Iphigenia[36] under compulsion;
With great reluctance. It wasn't for Menelaus.

Even if it were true, as you maintain,
That he did it to help his brother, did that entitle
You to murder him? What was your justification?
580 Blood for blood,[37] I suppose. But by laying down
That law, aren't you making a rod for your own back?
In all fairness, you'd be the next to die.

Look now, isn't your pretext entirely specious?
585 Be kind enough to explain the motive behind
The crowning scandal of your present conduct –
Sleeping with the assassin whose help you engaged
To murder my father, and having children by him,
Ousting the lawful offspring of your previous
590 Legitimate union. How could I accept that?
Or will you agree that this was another way
Of avenging Iphigenia? If that's what you're honestly
Saying, it couldn't be more disgraceful. You don't
Avenge a daughter by marrying one of your enemies.

595 But I'm not even allowed to speak my mind.
You're constantly sounding off that I'm bad-mouthing
My mother. In fact, I reckon you treat me more
As a mistress would than a mother. I lead such a wretched
600 Life, continually bullied by you and your paramour.
As for your exiled son Orestes, who barely

Escaped your clutches, what an abysmal life
*He* leads! You've often accused me of bringing him up
To be your avenger. Yes, if I'd had the strength,
I'd have done it, you can be sure. Denounce me for *that*                    605
To the world. Call me whatever names you choose:
Disloyal, loud-mouthed, totally lacking in shame
Or respect! If such behaviour reflects my nature,
The world can say, 'She takes after her mother'!

CHORUS LEADER [*to* ELECTRA]:
I see she's fuming with anger. She looks to me                               610
No longer concerned whether she's in the right.

CLYTEMNESTRA:
Why should *I* feel any concern for *her*
When she has hurled these insults against her mother?
She's old enough to know better. Utterly shameless!
Don't you believe she'd stoop to anything?                                   615

ELECTRA:
Let me assure you, however it looks to you,
I *am* ashamed of my actions and very aware
Of being untrue to myself. But your hostility
And cruel treatment force this behaviour on me.                             620
Shameful ways are learned by shameful example.[38]

CLYTEMNESTRA:
You impudent creature! *I'm* to blame, I suppose.
*My* words and actions inspire your long tirades.

ELECTRA:
The speeches are yours, not mine. It's you
Who perform the actions, and they discover the words.                       625

CLYTEMNESTRA:
I swear by Artemis,[39] you'll pay for this insolence
As soon as Aegisthus comes home.

ELECTRA:
You see?
You gave me permission to speak my mind
And are now too furious even to listen.

CLYTEMNESTRA:
Won't you allow me just to offer sacrifice                                   630

Undisturbed? I let *you* get to the end.
ELECTRA:
By all means, carry on! Sacrifice away!
I shan't interrupt. My lips are locked.
CLYTEMNESTRA [*to the attendant*]:
Lift up my sacrifice of fruit, that I may offer
635   Prayers to Apollo at his altar here
For deliverance from my present fears.
Phoebus Apollo, thou my defender,
Hear my secret prayer.
No friends are here beside me,
Nor is it right and proper
To unfold all to the light
640   While *she* is standing near,
Lest with her spiteful, chattering tongue
She sow the seeds of reckless rumour
Through all the city. So hear me thus,
For only thus can I speak.
These visions that came to me last night,
645   These doubtful dreams, Lycean Lord,
If they boded good, grant them fulfilment;
If evil, let them rebound on my foes.
If any by craft would steal the wealth
That I now enjoy, let it not be.
Vouchsafe me always to live as I am,
650   With life unharmed, to govern the house
Of Atreus' sons and all this realm,
To dwell in prosperous joy with the friends
I love, who presently share my home,
And with those of my children who bear
No malice against me nor cause me pain.
655   These prayers, Lycean Apollo, graciously hear
And grant us our humble requests.
For the rest, thou art a god and surely
Knowest it all, though I be silent.
All things must needs be seen by the sons of Zeus.
        [*Enter the* OLD SLAVE *from a side entrance.*]

OLD SLAVE:
Women of Argos, would I be right in thinking                    660
That this is King Aegisthus' palace?
CHORUS LEADER:
It is, sir. Your guess is correct.
OLD SLAVE:
Am I also right in supposing this lady
To be his wife? She bears herself like a queen.
CHORUS LEADER:
Perfectly right. You can speak to her here.                     665
OLD SLAVE:
Good morning, my lady. I am the bearer of news,
Good news, from a friend, to you and Aegisthus.
CLYTEMNESTRA:
That is an excellent omen. But first
Tell me who sent you here.
OLD SLAVE:
Phanoteus of Phocis – with an important message.               670
CLYTEMNESTRA:
What is it, sir? Tell me. I'm sure your news
Will be as welcome as our friend himself.
OLD SLAVE:
Orestes is dead. That is all.
ELECTRA:
Orestes dead! This is the death of *me*!
CLYTEMNESTRA:
What, what are your saying, sir? Don't listen to her.          675
OLD SLAVE:
I'll say it again: Orestes has been killed.
ELECTRA:
Killed? Oh god! What can I live for now?
CLYTEMNESTRA:
You keep out of the way! Don't mind about her.
I must have the truth, sir. *How* was he killed?
OLD SLAVE:
They sent me to tell the truth, and I'll tell it all.          680
Orestes went to Delphi, to compete in the great

Panhellenic festival, the Pythian Games.
The first event was the foot-race. As soon as he heard
The herald's loud announcement, Orestes made
685 A magnificent entrance on to the course and took
The spectators' breath away. He finished the race
As well as he started, emerging victorious and bearing
The prize of honour. To cut a long story short,
I've never known a man with such an amazing
690 Run of success. One thing's for sure:
Whatever events the games officials announced,
He walked away with the prizes in every one,
Receiving the acclamation of the crowd
As his name and city were called: Orestes of Argos,
695 Son of Agamemnon, Supreme Commander of Greece.

So far, so good. But when a god is purposing
Mischief, no man can escape, however strong.
Another day Orestes entered the chariot race,
700 Scheduled for sunrise. Of the many other competitors,
One was Achaean, another from Sparta, two were
Charioteers from Libya. Then came Orestes
As number five with a team of Thessalian horses,[40]
Number six an Aetolian with chestnut mares,
705 Seven a man from Magnesia, eight an Aenian
With white horses, nine from god-built Athens,
Lastly a Boeotian to make the full complement of ten.
Lots were drawn, and they all stationed their chariots
710 Where the officials ordered. Then, at the sound
Of the bronze trumpet, they were off, with a loud yell
At the horses and shaking their reins. The whole course
        rang
With the din of clattering chariots. The dust flew up
715 As all in a confused mass struck their teams
With their goads unsparingly, hoping to overtake
The wheels and snorting steeds of the car ahead.
They could feel the horses' breath blasting behind
Their backs, as the foam bespattered their spinning wheels.

Each time Orestes came to the turning point,[41]                           720
He'd almost graze his axle against it, giving rein
To his right-hand trace horse and checking the one on the
    left.
To start with, all the chariots flew safely on.
But then the Aenian driver's unruly colts
Started to bolt just after they rounded the bend                           725
Between the seventh and eighth laps, and then collided
Head on with the Libyan team. Further disasters
Followed, as one car crashed and smashed into
Another, until the whole Crisaean racecourse
Was strewn with the debris of shipwrecked chariots.                        730

Observing this, the Athenian driver craftily
Drew his horses aside and rode at anchor,
Allowing the surge of horses to pass him by
As they swirled around in the middle. Orestes was driving
In last position, holding his horses back
And pinning his hopes on a final spurt. At last,                           735
When he saw he'd only one competitor left,
He sent a sharp yell ringing through the ears
Of his nimble steeds, and off they shot in pursuit.
The drivers drew level, and now they were neck and neck,
Each taking the lead in turns by the shortest of heads.                    740

They were on the last lap! Orestes, unlucky man,
Had survived all the others without mishap to himself
Or his chariot. But then, as his team was rounding the bend,
He slackened his left-hand rein and accidentally
Struck the edge of the pillar. The axle-box                                745
Was shattered in two, and he tumbled over the rail.
The reins got tangled round him, and as he fell
To the ground, his colts dashed wildly across the course.
When the crowd realized the young Orestes was thrown
From his chariot, a loud cry of horror went up.                            750
To follow such successes with such a disaster!
There he was, now forcibly dashed to the ground,
Now kicking his heels to the sky, until the other

Charioteers managed at last to bring
His runaway horses under control and cut
755 Him free, so covered with blood, that none of his comrades
Could have identified his mangled body.
They burned his corpse on a pyre at once. And now
A detail of Phocians is bearing that mighty frame,
Reduced to pitiful dust, in a small bronze urn,
760 So he can be duly interred in his native soil.

That is my story, madam, painful enough
To hear, but for those of us who were there to see it –
Well, *I* was never witness to such a calamity.

CHORUS LEADER:
And so the royal house of Argos
765 Is now, it seems, cut down at the roots.

CLYTEMNESTRA:
O Zeus! Can I call this happy news
Or sad, though good? It must be sad
When I pay so dear to save my life.

OLD SLAVE:
My lady, you're looking distressed. How so?

CLYTEMNESTRA:
770 Motherhood is a strange thing. No wrong
Can make you hate the child you've borne.

OLD SLAVE:
It seems my journey was all in vain.

CLYTEMNESTRA:
775 No, not in vain. How can you say in vain?
You've come to me with *proofs* that he is dead,
Dead, the son born of my own body,
Who tore himself from my nurturing breast for exile
In a foreign land. Once he left this country
He never saw me again. He only accused me
Of killing his father and sent me terrible threats.
780 Sleep never wrapped me up in its soothing mantle,
Night or day. From moment to endless moment,
My life dragged on under the shadow of death.
But now, today, I am free, free from fear,

Fear of him and of her. She was the greater
Menace, sharing my home and constantly sucking          785
My life-blood.[42] Now, I believe, her threats are empty,
And I can enjoy my days in peace.
ELECTRA:
Oh, I am wretched! Now I can well lament,
Orestes, for your sad fate. You're dead, and all
Your mother can do is gloat. Can this be right?        790
CLYTEMNESTRA:
All's right with him – but not with you!
ELECTRA:
Nemesis,[43] hear, and avenge my brother!
CLYTEMNESTRA:
Nemesis has passed the correct sentence.
ELECTRA:
Mock on! Enjoy your moment of triumph.
CLYTEMNESTRA:
Why don't you and Orestes stop me?                     795
ELECTRA:
No stopping you. It's we who are finished.
CLYTEMNESTRA:
Good, sir, if your arrival has really curbed
Her noisy tongue, you deserve a great reward.
OLD SLAVE:
If all is in order, I'd like to take my leave.
CLYTEMNESTRA:
I can't let you go like this. I shouldn't be doing     800
My duty by you or the friend who sent you.
Please come indoors. And leave Electra outside
To moan away for herself – and her poor lost brother!
    [*Exeunt* CLYTEMNESTRA, *her attendant and the* OLD SLAVE
    *into the palace.*]
ELECTRA:
You see? There is maternal grief for you!              805
Her son is dead. What pain she shows, how bitterly
She weeps and wails for him – the wretched woman!
She's gone, laughing in triumph. Oh, Orestes!
Belovèd Orestes, your death has destroyed me too.

I thought you'd live and one day come back home
810   To avenge your father and champion me. Those were
The only hopes left in my heart, and now
You've wrested them all away. Where can I turn?
Without my father and you I'm quite alone.
It's back to my life as a slave to those I hate,
815   Hate the most in the world – my father's murderers!
Tell me, can it be right? Still, I'll never,
Never set foot in that hateful house again.
Here by the gates, I'll sink to the ground and wither
820   My days away unloved. If that annoys them,
Let them come out and kill me. They'd do me a
    kindness.
Life can be only pain. Far better to die.


## LAMENT FOR ELECTRA WITH CHORUS[44]


CHORUS:                                              [*Strophe 1*]
    Oh, *whére* is the líghtning
    Of Zeus? Whére now are the bríght beams
825       Of the sún god? Do they sée this
    And *híde* it regárdless?
ELECTRA:
    *E e aíai*!
CHORUS:
    My *chíld*, why this wéeping?
ELECTRA:
    Woe!
CHORUS:
    Quíet! No despáiring.
ELECTRA:
830       You'll destróy [me].[45]
CHORUS:
    How?
ELECTRA:
    He's góne to the dead, góne without doubt.
    Óffer me no hópe any more.

Lóok at me now wásting away.                                    835
Trámple me no fúrther!


CHORUS:                                          [Antistrophe 1]
Lord Ámphiaráus[46]
Was entángled through a nécklace
To be bróught low by a wóman,
But *nów* in all his pówers
ELECTRA:
E e ío!                                                         840
CHORUS:
He *rúles* down in Hádes.
ELECTRA:
Woe!
CHORUS:
        Súrely, for the múrderers
ELECTRA:
Were destróyed.
CHORUS:
                Yes!
ELECTRA:
I knów it, be sure. Sóon there appeared            845
Óne to exact véngeance for him.
Mý hope is gone, áll that I had
Swépt right away, vánished!


CHORUS:                                             [Strophe 2]
Unháppy gírl: unháppy fáte!
ELECTRA:
I knów it wéll, know it too súrely.                 850
My túrbid life, month áfter mónth
Of crúel paín has taúght me.
CHORUS:
Yés, we have séen your gríef.
ELECTRA:
Léave me, then, léave me, don't
Cómfort me nów, when áll . . .

CHORUS:

855                                        When áll?

ELECTRA:

My hópes are lóst, the ónly relíef that I hád,
Lóst with my nóble bróther.

CHORUS:                                              [Antistrophe 2]

860        Death cómes to áll mankínd alíke.

ELECTRA:

Must *áll* be kílled, trámpled by hórses
And drágged alóng by tángled réins
On a rácecourse, líke Oréstes?

CHORUS:

Whén was a dóom so hársh?

ELECTRA:

865        Hársh indeed! Búried in
Álien éarth, withoút . . .

CHORUS:

*Papaí*!

ELECTRA:

My tóuch to ténd him, réady to láy him to rést,
870        Réady to móurn his pássing.


# SCENE 4[47]

[*Enter* CHRYSOTHEMIS.]

CHRYSOTHEMIS:

Dearest Electra, look! I'm so happy.
I've run in quite undignified haste to tell you.
All your troubles are over. I've wonderful news!

ELECTRA:

875    You? Where could you find a remedy
For pain like mine? No cure exists.

CHRYSOTHEMIS:

Orestes is back! You can take my word.
It's plain as plain, as you see me here.

ELECTRA:

Have you gone crazy? Or are you making

Fun of your own misfortunes and mine?                                    880
CHRYSOTHEMIS:
I swear by our father's sacred hearth,
I'm perfectly serious. Orestes is here.
ELECTRA:
Oh god! Just who on earth has told you
This story? What makes you so terribly sure?
CHRYSOTHEMIS:
It isn't a rumour. Surely my eyes                                        885
Can be trusted. The visible proof is there.
ELECTRA:
The visible proof? What have your eyes seen
To make you so feverishly excited?
CHRYSOTHEMIS:
For god's sake, listen to what I tell you.
Then you can call me sane or crazy.                                      890
ELECTRA:
All right, tell me, if it gives you any pleasure.
CHRYSOTHEMIS:
This is what I actually saw, Electra.
When I arrived at the family burial vault,
I noticed some fresh libations of milk spilling
Over the side of the mound, and our father's grave                      895
Wreathed with garlands of every kind of flower.
The sight gave me a shock and I glanced around
To assure myself that no one was there to watch.
The place appeared to be perfectly quiet and still,
So I crept up nearer the grave. There on the edge,                      900
I spotted a lock of hair, newly cut off.
As soon as my eyes fell on it, a familiar face
Flashed in front of my mind. This had to be a sign,
A sign of our dear beloved brother Orestes.
As I took it up, tears of happiness sprang                              905
To my eyes, though I managed to keep a reverent silence.

I know it now, as I was sure at the time,
This loving tribute can only have come from him.
Who else could do it, apart from you and from me?

910 I didn't, I'm perfectly certain. Neither did you.
You can't leave the house to go to the temple
Without getting into trouble. And Mother could never
915 Do it unnoticed, nor would she ever want to.
No, these offerings must have come from Orestes.
Now, my dear, take heart! Fortune never
Stands still for ever. Ours has been cruel till now.
Today perhaps will mark a change for the better.

ELECTRA:
920 What a fool you are! I pity you.

CHRYSOTHEMIS:
Pity me? Aren't you pleased by my news?

ELECTRA:
You're simply dreaming. You haven't the first idea.

CHRYSOTHEMIS:
Surely I know what I saw with my own eyes?

ELECTRA:
He's dead, dear girl! Don't look to *him*
925 To rescue us now. Our hopes are gone.

CHRYSOTHEMIS:
Oh, no! Who told you that?

ELECTRA:
A man who was with him when he died.

CHRYSOTHEMIS:
Where's the man now? I'm so bewildered!

ELECTRA:
Indoors with Mother – a welcome guest!

CHRYSOTHEMIS:
930 Oh god! Then who on earth could have laid
All those offerings on Father's grave?

ELECTRA:
If you ask me, they're for Orestes. Probably
Gifts that someone put there in his memory.

CHRYSOTHEMIS:
And there was I, joyfully rushing along
935 To break the marvellous news, without the slightest
Idea of our tragic plight. Now that I've come,
I find our troubles are even worse than before!

ELECTRA:
That's how it is. But if you'll listen to me,
You can help to lighten our load of suffering.
CHRYSOTHEMIS:
By bringing the dead to life again?                        940
ELECTRA:
No, no! I'm not as stupid as that.
CHRYSOTHEMIS:
What do you want, then, that *I* can promise?
ELECTRA:
You must have the courage to do as I tell you.
CHRYSOTHEMIS:
I shan't say no, if it's any *use*.
ELECTRA:
Remember, sister: no pain, no gain.                        945
CHRYSOTHEMIS:
All right, I'll help as best as I can.
ELECTRA:
Very well, listen. This is how I've decided.
When it comes to friends, you know as well as I
That we haven't one left. Death has swept them all
Away, and the two of us are now on our own.               950
So long as I still had word that our brother Orestes
Was alive and well, I went on hoping that he
Would one day come to avenge his father's murder.
But now that he's gone for good, I'm looking to *you*.     955
You mustn't flinch. Your sister needs your help
To kill Aegisthus – the man who perpetrated
Our father's murder. No secrets between us now.
Where will inaction get you? What can you still
Look forward to? Only resentment in being deprived
Of your father's heritage. Only the pain of growing       960
Old without the blessings of love or marriage.
Those joys are nothing more than a forlorn hope.
Aegisthus isn't foolish enough to allow
A son of yours – or a son of mine – to grow               965
To manhood and so to ensure his own destruction.
No, if you'll fall in with my proposal,

First you will merit praise for filial devotion
From your murdered father below and your brother too.
970 Second, the freedom which is your birthright will be
Acknowledged forever after, and you'll achieve
The marriage that you deserve – everyone looks
To make a good match.

                              Then think of what people will say,
If you follow my plan. What glory you'll win for yourself
975 And for me! When our fellow-townsmen or strangers see us,
They'll all acclaim us with words of praise like these:
'Just take a look at those two sisters, friends.
They rescued their father's house. They gallantly shed
The blood of their foes, who were standing proud at the time,
980 Without a thought for their own dear lives. Such women
Deserve our love, deserve our admiration,
Deserve our honour on festal and public occasions
For their great courage.' That's how the world will describe us.
985 In life and death our glory shall never fade.

Chrysothemis, please say yes. Work with me to serve
Our father, to please our brother. Save me and yourself
From all our misery. Always remember this:
It shames a noble nature to live in shame.
CHORUS LEADER:
990 In cases like this, a little forethought
Can help both sides in the argument.
CHRYSOTHEMIS:
Yes, women, if Electra had any sense at all,
She wouldn't have thrown all caution to the winds
995 Before giving tongue. What are you trying to do?
Why are you putting on this audacious front
And calling on me to follow? Don't you see?
You're not a man, but a woman. You haven't the strength
To conquer your foes. Their star is rising daily,
1000 While our fortunes are ebbing away to nothing.
Who could plot to murder a man as strong
As Aegisthus and then emerge from the fray unscathed?

Be careful. If anyone hears us talking like this,
We can only make a bad situation worse.
Your plan won't set us free, nor does it help                    1005
To win renown, but die an inglorious death.
Moreover, dying isn't so terrible, only
Wanting to die under torture, but staying alive.
Please, please think calmly before you destroy us both
And plunge the house into ruin and desolation.                   1010
For myself, I promise not to give you away,
But I want no part in your plan. As for you,
Do show some sense, late in the day as it is.
You're powerless. They're on top. Give in.

CHORUS LEADER:
Do listen. The most precious of human                            1015
Gifts are forethought and common sense.

ELECTRA:
Exactly what I expected! I always knew
That you'd reject my proposal out of hand.
Well, it's over to me. I must act alone.
I cannot allow this task to be left undone.                      1020

CHRYSOTHEMIS:
Electra!
I wish your resolution had been as strong
When Father was being killed. You'd have thwarted the crime!

ELECTRA:
The strength was there, but I was less wise then.

CHRYSOTHEMIS:
Why can't you stay 'less wise' now and for good?

ELECTRA:
Don't lecture me. You're not prepared to help.                   1025

CHRYSOTHEMIS:
I'm not, as this attempt is bound to fail.

ELECTRA:
I envy you your 'sense', but loathe your cowardice.

CHRYSOTHEMIS:
I shan't reproach you when you say I'm right.

ELECTRA:
*I* say you're right? That's inconceivable.

CHRYSOTHEMIS:

1030 There's plenty of time to run. We'll wait and see.

ELECTRA:

You're not prepared to help, so go!

CHRYSOTHEMIS:

I am. *You*'re not prepared to *learn*.

ELECTRA:

Run off and tell on me to Mother!

CHRYSOTHEMIS:

I couldn't hate you as much as that.

ELECTRA:

1035 You're letting your sister badly down, you know.

CHRYSOTHEMIS:

Not letting you down, just thinking for your good.

ELECTRA:

Must I adopt your scale of values, then?

CHRYSOTHEMIS:

When you are sensible, *you* can guide us both.

ELECTRA:

To speak so plausibly, and be so wrong!

CHRYSOTHEMIS:

1040 You've named the illness that you suffer from.

ELECTRA:

Will you deny my argument is right?

CHRYSOTHEMIS:

You can be right and do a lot of harm.

ELECTRA:

These principles of life won't work for *me*.

CHRYSOTHEMIS:

Well, if you *do* this, you'll agree with me.

ELECTRA:

1045 Of course, I'll do it. *You* won't scare me off.

CHRYSOTHEMIS:

You really mean that? You won't think again?

ELECTRA:

*Wrong* thinking's what I hate most in the world.

CHRYSOTHEMIS:

I might as well be talking to a wall!

ELECTRA:
My mind was made up many moons ago.[48]                    1049
CHRYSOTHEMIS:
Well, if you think there's any sense in what               1055
You're doing, you think that way. When trouble strikes
And you can't escape, you'll say my advice was right.

    [*Exit* CHRYSOTHEMIS *into the palace.*]


# CHORAL SONG 2[49]


CHORUS:
    Oh, *whére* is wísdom?                    [*Strophe* 1]
    Do but líft your eyes úpward.
    See the bírds[50] and gaze with wónder;          1060
    How they lóve their own begétters,
    With what cáre they tend their óffspring.
    Can we nót be as wíse as théy are?
    Zéus, O lórd of the líghtning flásh,
    Jústice,[51] góddess who dwélls belów,
    Sóon must sín be requíted!                        1065
    *Óh*, holy vóice from men to Hádes,
    Shout alóud my cries of sórrow
    And besíege the kings of Árgos
    In the gráve with my grím repróaches.


    They *múst* take nótice            [*Antistrophe* 1]   1070
    Of the plágue that grips the hóusehold,
    Of the wár between their chíldren,
    How Eléctra hates her síster
    And all hópe of peace is dýing;
    How betráyed in her lónely strúggle,
    Stórm-tossed, ánguished and fúll of téars,        1075
    Níghtingále-like, wórld without énd,
    She móurns the fáte of her fáther.
    *Deáth* shall not daúnt her into shrínking;
    She'll forgó the joy of súnlight

1080      To convíct the pair of Fúries,[52]
          Ever trúe to her nóble fáther.


          Goodness never can stoop to                    [Strophe 2]
          Shame its fame and lead a lífe of wrong, to die
          Namelessly, O my child.
1085      You máde your chóice. Téars for yóu
          Paved the path to glory.
          You turned your back on ignoble ways
          To win for yourself two excellent names,
          A náme for wísdóm, a náme for góodnéss.


1090      Live to tower above them;                    [Antistrophe 2]
          Trounce your foes in might and wealth, as you for now
          Grovel beneath their feet.
          The fáte which stíll dógs your dáys
          Belies your noble nature;
1095      And yet you've championed the highest laws
          Of héaven,[53] to wín that náme of all námes,
          The náme that Zéus lóves, the náme of réverénce.


# SCENE 5[54]

[*Enter* ORESTES *and* PYLADES *from a side entrance with*
ATTENDANTS *carrying a small urn.*]

ORESTES:
Women, please tell us, were our directions
Correct, and are we on the right road?
CHORUS LEADER:
1100   Tell us where you're hoping to be.
ORESTES:
We're trying to find Aegisthus' house.
CHORUS LEADER:
They've guided you to the right place, then.
ORESTES:
Please could someone announce our arrival?
We are expected.

CHORUS LEADER [*pointing to* ELECTRA]:
This person here is the next of kin.                          1105
ORESTES:
Woman, please go indoors and tell them
That men from Phocis are looking for Aegisthus.
ELECTRA:
O heaven help me! You've not arrived
With visible proof of the rumour we heard?
ORESTES:
I don't know what you were told. Old Strophius              1110
Sent us. Our business concerns Orestes.
ELECTRA:
What is it, sir? You make me tremble.
ORESTES:
We're here to deliver this little urn.
It holds the small remains of his body.
ELECTRA:
Oh god! It's true, it must be him –                          1115
This tiny urn, in front of my eyes!
ORESTES:
If you are shedding tears for Orestes'
Accident, this urn contains his body.
ELECTRA:
Good sir, I beg you, if this vessel
Really contains him, please let me hold it.                  1120
I need to weep and wail for myself
And my whole house as well as these ashes.
ORESTES [*to* ATTENDANTS]:⁵⁵
Take it across and let her have it,
Whoever she is. She can't be an enemy.
Some friend, maybe, or one of the family.                    1125
ELECTRA [*taking the urn in her hands*]:
Orestes! All that's left to remind me of the life
That I loved best in the world, home to me now.
How far from those fine hopes in which I let
You go! You were a strong and lovely boy.
But what are my arms enfolding now? Nothing.                 1130
If only I could have died before these hands

Stole you away and sent you abroad to save
Your life. You'd have been killed that very day
1135 And won your rightful place in your father's grave.
But now, such a way to die! Far from home,
Exiled in a foreign land, and I not there.
My loving hands were never given the chance
To wash or dress your body or lift your poor
1140 Ashes out of the pyre as you deserved.
Strangers performed those rites for you, and now
Your tiny weight has come home in a tiny urn.
Oh, what a waste, the tender care I lavished
Upon you! My labour of love all gone for nothing!
You were never your mother's child. You were mine.
I was your only nurse, not one of the servants,
And I was the one you always called your sister.
Now your death has blotted my efforts out
1150 In a single day. The storm has swept through the forest
And left a barren waste. We're all of us gone:
Father, you, now I. While our enemies laugh!
That fraud of a mother of ours is crazy with joy.
How often you sent ahead those secret messages,
1155 Promising to come yourself to take revenge!
But no, the evil spirit that haunts us both
Has taken all that away and sent me back,
Instead of the living form I loved so much,
An urn of ashes, an insubstantial shade.
1160 Ah me, me!
You poor, poor ashes! What a way,
What a way to come home! How you've destroyed me,
Yes, destroyed me, Orestes, my darling brother.
1165 So let me come into this little house of yours,
Nothingness into nothing, and live with you in the earth.
There was a time when all that we had, we shared.
So now I long to die and to share your grave.
1170 If I can die, I shall be rid of my pain.
CHORUS LEADER:
Do remember, Electra, your father was mortal.
So was Orestes. We *all* are bound to die.

You mustn't grieve overmuch.
ORESTES:
Oh, what can I say?
I'm lost for words, but I have to speak!                            1175
ELECTRA:
Why are you so distressed? Explain.
ORESTES:
Are you indeed the princess Electra?
ELECTRA:
Wretched as you find me, yes, I am.
ORESTES:
Oh, how I feel for your pitiful plight!
ELECTRA:
Good sir, you cannot be grieving for *me*.                          1180
ORESTES:
A life so wrecked! It's vile, barbaric . . .
ELECTRA:
Those ugly words fit no one but me.
ORESTES:
Without a husband, so cruelly treated!
ELECTRA:
Why are you staring at me so sadly?
ORESTES:
I never knew how wretched I was myself.                             1185
ELECTRA:
Yourself? What have I said to show you that?
ORESTES:
To see you suffering all this pain and grief!
ELECTRA:
What you can *see* is one small part of my pain.
ORESTES:
What could be worse to see than I see now?
ELECTRA:
I have to make my home in a murderers' den.                         1190
ORESTES:
Whose murderers? What are you talking about?
ELECTRA:
My father's murderers, who force me to be their slave.

ORESTES:
Who on earth could treat you like that?
ELECTRA:
My so-called mother – more like a monster.
ORESTES:
1195 Does she subject you to violence – or hardship?
ELECTRA:
Violence, hardship, every kind of abuse.
ORESTES:
Does nobody come to your aid or try to prevent it?
ELECTRA:
There was only one – and you've just shown me his ashes.
ORESTES:
Poor woman, how the sight of you stirs my pity!
ELECTRA:
1200 No one has ever offered me pity before.
ORESTES:
Only I can share the pain of your suffering.
ELECTRA:
Who are you? Surely not some kinsman of mine?
ORESTES:
I'll tell you, if these women can keep a secret.
ELECTRA:
They won't give you away. They're loyal friends.
ORESTES:
1205 Let go of this urn, and I'll tell you all.
ELECTRA:
No, no, sir, you cannot do this to me!
ORESTES:
It will be all right. Just do as I say.
ELECTRA:
He's all I have. Please, please don't take him away.
ORESTES:
I must!
ELECTRA:
          Oh god! Orestes,
1210 They won't allow me to give you burial.

ORESTES:
Don't use such words! You're wrong to be weeping.
ELECTRA:
Wrong to weep for my brother who's dead?
ORESTES:
You haven't the right to call him that.
ELECTRA:
No right even to mourn for the dead?
ORESTES:
Mourn anyone you should. But this isn't yours.                1215
ELECTRA:
It is, if it holds Orestes' body.
ORESTES:
It isn't Orestes – except in fiction.
ELECTRA:
Where *is* my unhappy brother's grave, then?
ORESTES:
Nowhere. The living don't belong in a grave.
ELECTRA:
My boy, what are you saying?
ORESTES:
                                        Only the truth.        1220
ELECTRA:
He's alive?
ORESTES:
            Yes, if *I* am alive.
ELECTRA:
*You* are *Orestes*?
ORESTES:
                    Look at this ring
With our father's seal. Do you believe me now?
ELECTRA:
The sun's come out!
ORESTES:
                    It's shining bright!
ELECTRA:
Is this your voice?

ORESTES:
1225                    I am here at last.
ELECTRA:
Is it you in my arms?
ORESTES:
                    Hold me forever.
ELECTRA:
Women of Argos, my dearest friends,
Here is Orestes! It all was a trick:
First he was dead, and now he's alive!
CHORUS LEADER:
1230   Yes, my dear, we can see. Your happiness
Fills our eyes with tears of joy.


ELECTRA:                                              [Strophe]
        O róyal prínce!⁵⁶
        Orestés, the són of that kíng I lóved,
        You have at lást retúrned.
        You've foúnd, you've seén, you've toúched
1235      The síster whóm you lóst.
ORESTES:
Yes, I am here. But do keep silence now and wait.
ELECTRA:
        Why shóuld I?
ORESTES:
It's better so. Someone might hear us from indoors.
ELECTRA:
        I swear, yés, I swéar, Ártemis⁵⁷ bé my stréngth,
1240      I'll never stóop to féar my old fóes agáin,
        Those stáy-at-hómes, those spáre wéights
        On éarth's flóor, those wómenfólk!
ORESTES:
Be careful, now. The spirit of war can still be strong
In women. Your own experience should tell you that.
ELECTRA:
1245      Áh, for shame! Ónce agáin
        You bring it báck to mínd,

Hátred which cánnot be clóuded,
Néver to be bánished from the fámily,
The évil that wón't forget.                                              1250

ORESTES:
I know that too. But now is not the time to speak
Of what we've suffered, only when occasion serves.


ELECTRA:                                                      [*Antistrophe*]
The whóle of tíme,
Yes, each dáy that dáwns and each hóur, will sérve
To sing their crímes alóud.                                              1255
I've hád to waít so lóng,
And nów my líps are frée.

ORESTES:
Yes, they are free. And so make sure they stay as free.

ELECTRA:
Make súre? How?

ORESTES:
Contain your happiness until the moment comes.

ELECTRA:
Orestés, my príde! You have appéared at lást.                           1260
Could I be sílent nów on this glórious dáy?
My éyes have séen your déar fáce
Beyónd thóught, beyónd hópe.

ORESTES:
You only saw me when the call came from the gods.
I could not show my face until they gave the word.

ELECTRA:
Jóy and new jóy you gíve.                                                1265
I am so trúly bléssed.
Wé are the fávoured nów.
Gód has brought you hóme and I can crý in triumph,
'Thís is a sígn from héaven!'                                            1270

ORESTES:
I hate to stem this flood of happiness, but I'm
Afraid you're being drowned beneath a tide of joy.

ELECTRA:

> Oréstes, áh,                                              [*Epode*]
> At long lást you've cóme,
> You chose that lóvely róad,
> The róad that léd to mé hére.

1275
> You've séen me strícken by gríef, so pléase . . .

ORESTES:

> Whát are you ásking?

ELECTRA:

> Pléase don't éver léave mé.
> Your fáce gives mé such jóy. I néed you álwáys.

ORESTES:

> I'd kill the man who'd keep the two of us apart.

ELECTRA:

> You méan that?

ORESTES:

1280
>                          Don't doubt me.

ELECTRA:

> Darling brother,
> I've heard the voice I never even
> Hoped to hear. And so, poor me,
> How could my brimming heart be voiceless, or my
>    cries

1285
> Still be gagged? But now I feel you in my arms.
> I'm gazing on your precious face.
> No pain could ever wash it from my memory.

ORESTES:

Enough of words,[58] Electra. No need to explain
1290 How vile our mother is, or how Aegisthus
Is draining our father's wealth by extravagance and waste.
Talking could make us miss the crucial moment.
Here is the question that needs an answer *now*:
Where should we show our presence or wait in ambush,
1295 If our mission's going to wipe the smile off their faces?
You're looking too happy. When the two of us go inside,
Our mother mustn't suspect what's going on.
Treat the false report of my death as though

It were true, and keep the tears flowing. Joy and laughter
Will be in order when freedom follows success.                    1300
ELECTRA:
Dearest Orestes, your wishes are all my own.
This joy of mine is due entirely to you,
Not to myself. No gain could be great enough
To warrant my causing you the slightest worry.                    1305
That would be throwing away the luck we have.
You understand the position, surely: Aegisthus
Is not at home, but Mother is in the palace.
Don't be afraid she'll see my face lit up                          1310
With smiles. My hatred for her has been so long
Ingrained in my heart, and now I've seen you back,
I'm so intensely happy, I can't stop crying.
How could I? Today you returned and I saw you dead,
And today I see you alive. It has been amazing.                   1315
I shouldn't think it a miracle any more
If Father came back to life. I'd believe my eyes.
No coming home was ever like this! So give me
Whatever orders you will. If I'd been left
All by myself, you know I'd have either fought                     1320
And lived like a hero, or else have died like a hero.
ORESTES [*near the palace entrance*]:
Quiet now! Someone is coming out of doors.
ELECTRA [*putting on an act*]:
Walk in, good sirs. I assure you, what you are bringing
Will not be refused, though it may not give much pleasure.        1325
    [*Enter* OLD SLAVE *from the palace.*]
OLD SLAVE:
You crazy fools![59] Have you no care for your lives,
Or are you completely witless? Don't you realize
You're on the verge of the greatest danger? No,
You're right in the lion's den. If I hadn't been                   1330
Standing on guard in the porchway there, your plan
Would have been inside these doors before yourselves.
Thank goodness *I* was about! Now stop this endless                1335
Talking and all these cries of insatiable joy
And come on in. At such times any delay

Is disastrous. The moment's come to be shot of your task.

ORESTES:
How does the land lie there indoors?

OLD SLAVE:
1340 All's well. No one will know it's you.

ORESTES:
You gave them the news of my death, I take it?

OLD SLAVE:
As far as they are concerned, you're finished.

ORESTES:
What have they said? Are they pleased about it?

OLD SLAVE:
You'll know in due course. For the moment, everything
1345 There looks good – even what's not so good.

ELECTRA:
Who is this man, Orestes? I beg you to tell me.

ORESTES:
Don't you realize?

ELECTRA:
                                I've no idea.

ORESTES:
Don't you remember handing me to him?

ELECTRA:
Whom do you mean?

ORESTES:
                                The man who smuggled me
1350 Out to Phocis – as *you* arranged.

ELECTRA:
Is he the only person I found
That I could trust when Father was killed?

ORESTES:
It is. No further questions, please!

ELECTRA:
Oh glorious day![60] It's you, the only preserver
1355 Of King Agamemnon's house! How have you come here?
Are you truly the man who rescued Orestes
And me from all our troubles? Oh, bless those dear
Beloved hands, those feet, my faithful servants!

How could I fail to know you all that time,
Here but never giving yourself away?
Your words were daggers, however lovely the truth.                    1360
Welcome, Father! Father is how I see you.
Welcome home! There's nobody in the world
I've hated and loved so much in a single day.

OLD SLAVE:
Enough for now, I think. There will be plenty
Of circling nights and as many days to tell you                       1365
All that has passed, Electra, since you were parted.
Now! Orestes and Pylades, are you ready?
The time for action is now. Clytemnestra's
Alone and none of the men are at home – now!
Remember, if you delay, you'll have much stronger                     1370
Opponents to fight, and there'll be more of them.

ORESTES:
Pylades, the time for talking is over.
Let's now salute our ancestral gods[61]
Whose statues guard the palace porch,
And move inside at once.                                              1375
    [*Exeunt* ORESTES, PYLADES, *the* OLD SLAVE *and* ATTEN-
    DANTS *into the palace, taking the urn with them.*]

ELECTRA:
O Lord Apollo,[62] graciously hear their prayers
And mine besides. Many a time I have stood
In supplication before your holy altar
And offered there such gifts as I could afford.
So now, Lycean Apollo, with what I have,
I pray, beseech and supplicate your godhead.                          1380
Vouchsafe to aid us in this enterprise
And show to all mankind what recompense
The gods bestow on sinful wickedness.
    [*Exit* ELECTRA *into the palace.*]

# CHORAL SONG 3[63]

CHORUS:
Lóok at the fire swéeping the bush,                    [*Strophe*]
1385   The god of wár and strífe whose foul bréath is blóod!
They're stríding thróugh the cóurt and nów they're ón the
    tráil,
Those Fury dógs of déath who hunt múrder dówn
And deal críme for críme.
So nót for lóng, not lóng the dréam
1390   In mý divíning héart shall línger póised in áir.

Wátch as he moves pácing the floor                    [*Antistrophe*]
With wily tréad, that chámpion to avénge the déad.
He spíes his fáther's thróne insíde the áncient háll.
His fingers gríp the swórd of new-whétted blóod.
1395   Now look thére! The gód
Of ámbush, Hérmes, shróuds his guíle
In níght and léads him tó his góal. The gáme's afóot!

# CLOSING SCENE[64]

[*Re-enter* ELECTRA *from the palace.*]
ELECTRA:
Dearest women, the men are at work.
Soon it will all be over.
Don't move, keep silent!
CHORUS LEADER:
1400   Tell us! What are they doing?
ELECTRA:
*She* is dressing the urn,
And they are standing behind her.
CHORUS LEADER:
And you? Why have you rushed outside?
ELECTRA:
I'm keeping guard. Aegisthus
Mustn't surprise us as he walks in.

CLYTEMNESTRA [*off*]:
*Io! Aiai*!
My house is empty of friends,
And all possessed by destroyers![65]                                    1405
ELECTRA:
Listen, a cry indoors! Did you héar, my friends?
CHORUS:
    I héard a sóund crúel to hear,
    And félt a trémbling cóldnéss!
CLYTEMNESTRA:
*Oimoi!* Aegisthus! Where are you?
ELECTRA:
Another cry, there!
CLYTEMNESTRA:
My son, my son! Have mercy on your mother!                              1410
ELECTRA:
You had no mercy on him,
Nor on his father before him.
CHORUS:
City of Argos, O house of Atreus! Now
The destiny dogging your days is waning fast.
CLYTEMNESTRA:
O *moí*! I am struck!
ELECTRA:
Strike her a second blow, if you have the strength!                     1415
CLYTEMNESTRA:
O *moí*! Again!
ELECTRA:
I wish Aegisthus were lying beside you!
CHORUS:
    The déadly cúrse is nów at wórk –
    Éye for éye, tóoth for tóoth.
    The déad belów are rísing úp to life,                               1420
    And nów the óld sláin
    Súck their kíllers' blóod drý.
    [*Re-enter* ORESTES *and* PYLADES *from the palace.*]
CHORUS LEADER:
Here they come. That dripping hand is red

With blood from a sacrifice to the god of war.
I cannot condemn it.

ELECTRA:
Orestes, how has it gone?

ORESTES:
All is well, indoors,

1425 If Apollo prophesied well.[66]

ELECTRA:
Is that vile woman dead?

ORESTES:
You've nothing further to fear.
Your mother's spite shall never hurt you again.

CHORUS LEADER:
Stop! I can see Aegisthus coming.

ELECTRA:
Get back, Orestes!

ORESTES:
                              Where can you see the man?

1430

ELECTRA:
We've got him now. There he is,
Blithely walking into the city.

CHORUS LEADER:
Back to the inner porchway as fast as you can!
The first round's won. Make sure of the second.

ORESTES:
We shall, never fear.

ELECTRA:
                              Off with you, then!

1435

ORESTES:
I'm gone.

ELECTRA:
        *I* can look after everything here.
        [*Exeunt* ORESTES *and* PYLADES *into the palace.*]

CHORUS:
Cáreful nów! Póur a féw
Géntle wórds dówn his éars.
That víllain mústn't bé allówed to guéss

1440 He's rúshing héadlong

Into jústice's ámbúsh.

[*Enter* AEGISTHUS *from a side entrance.*]

AEGISTHUS:

They tell me messengers have arrived from Phocis
With news of Orestes' death in a chariot crash.
Does anyone know where they are? [*Pause.*]
You there, *you* can tell me. Yes, you!                    1445
You used to be so outspoken. You're the person
Most affected and ought to be able to say.

ELECTRA:

Of course I know. I must. I am his next of kin.

AEGISTHUS:

Where are the messengers, then? Don't waste my time.       1450

ELECTRA:

Indoors with the mistress. They've won their way to her
    heart.[67]

AEGISTHUS:

Has he really been killed? Was that what they actually said?

ELECTRA:

Not only said it. They've brought the proof.

AEGISTHUS:

Can I see him, then, with my own eyes?

ELECTRA:

You can indeed – it's hardly a pretty sight.               1455

AEGISTHUS:

What welcome tidings to give me! Unusual for you.

ELECTRA:

You're welcome to them – if they are truly welcome.

AEGISTHUS:

Open the doors! I want the whole of the people
Here in Mycenae and Argos to see for themselves.
If any among them was foolish enough to put               1460
His hopes in Orestes, now he can see his corpse
And learn to strain at the leash no longer. He won't
Need whipping by *me* to teach him how to behave.

ELECTRA:

Now look, I'm playing my part. I've shown
The sense at last to oblige my masters.                    1465

[*Enter* ORESTES *and* PYLADES *from the palace, with*
CLYTEMNESTRA's *body covered.*][68]

AEGISTHUS:
O Zeus! This sign portends the anger of heaven.
No gloating, though.[69] Remove the shroud from his face.
Kinship requires some mourning, even of me.

ORESTES:
1470  Lift it yourself. This body belongs to you,
Not me. Take a final look and say your farewells.

AEGISTHUS:
Good, I'll do as you say. Electra,
Call Clytemnestra, if she's at home.

ORESTES [*as* AEGISTHUS *lifts the cover from the body*]:
No need to look. She's here already.

AEGISTHUS:
Oh god! What's this?

ORESTES:
                              Who are you frightened of?
1475  Don't you know who it is?
              [ORESTES *and* PYLADES *draw their swords.*]

AEGISTHUS:
I'm caught in a trap. Who are you men?

ORESTES:
Don't you realize you've been exchanging
Words while alive with a man who's dead?

AEGISTHUS:
1480  My god! I read your riddle. You must be Orestes!

ORESTES:
Fooled for so long, such a clever prophet as you?

AEGISTHUS:
I'm at your mercy, then. Please! Allow me a word –
Just one!

ELECTRA:
              No, Orestes, for god's sake,
Don't give him the chance to argue with you.
1485  When a man's been caught and is doomed to die,
What can he gain by a moment's delay?[70]
Kill him at once; kill him, and then

Throw out his corpse for the dogs and birds[71] to bury
Out of our sight. No other payment
For all I've suffered could be enough for *me*.                    1490
ORESTES:
Inside, then, quickly! Move!
The talking's over. Your time is up.
AEGISTHUS:
Inside? If what you're doing is right,
Why do you have to do it in the dark?
Kill me here now!
ORESTES:
                    Don't give orders to me.
Move to where you murdered my father.                    1495
I mean you to die on the very same spot.
AEGISTHUS:
The curse of Pelops' house![72] This palace has seen
Enough destruction already. Must there be more?[73]
ORESTES:
*Your* destruction at least. Trust *me* for that.
AEGISTHUS:
Your father wasn't so clever at telling the future.                    1500
ORESTES:
Stop bandying words. You're wasting time. Now move!
AEGISTHUS:
Lead on.
ORESTES:
          You first.
AEGISTHUS:
                    Afraid I'll escape?
ORESTES:
No, I'd rather you didn't enjoy
Your execution, but died in agony.
All who presume to defy the law                    1505
Ought to be punished at once like this –
Kill them! Crime would not be so rife.[74]

     [*Exeunt* AEGISTHUS, ORESTES *and* PYLADES *into the
     palace.*]

CHORUS [*to* ELECTRA]:
    O seed of Atreus, how much you have suffered!
    But now this attack has forced you out
1510  Into freedom. You've come to the ending.[75]
    [*Exeunt* ELECTRA *into the palace and the* CHORUS *down a side entrance.*]

# PHILOCTETES

# Preface to *Philoctetes*

## THE TRADITION

The story, taken by Sophocles from Homer and the Epic Cycle, was that Philoctetes, an archer who had inherited the unerring bow and arrows of Heracles, led seven ships to the Trojan War, but on the way was bitten in the foot by a snake and consequently abandoned on Lemnos by the leaders of the Greek expedition. After the siege of Troy had run for nine years, the Greeks received a prophecy that Troy would never fall unless Philoctetes with Heracles' bow could be brought there to sack the city. Odysseus and Diomedes (or, in some versions, one of the two) were therefore sent to fetch him, and he went.

This myth was the subject of earlier tragedies by Aeschylus and Euripides, as well as by Sophocles, but only this play survives.

## SYNOPSIS

Odysseus comes to Lemnos with Neoptolemus, the young son of the recently dead Achilles, and persuades him to practise a trick on Philoctetes, through which he can capture the hero's bow and arrows and lure him to Troy. The plot hinges on Neoptolemus' innate reluctance to use deception and on the growing relationship of trust between him and the wild, embittered Philoctetes. Odysseus' plan looks as if it will succeed, particularly when Philoctetes suffers an overwhelming attack of pain in his wounded foot and Neoptolemus has won possession of Heracles' bow. But Neoptolemus' compassion and integrity override the

Greek interest, and a stalemate is reached. After returning the
bow to Philoctetes, Neoptolemus makes a last attempt to persuade the hero, but to no avail. Philoctetes only leaves Lemnos
for Troy when commanded to do so by his patron god, Heracles.

## INTERPRETATION

*Philoctetes* is the only play in this volume that can be precisely
dated. We know it was first performed in 409 BC, when Sophocles
was already in his late eighties. The treatment of political issues
might have been inspired by the short-lived oligarchic revolution
that took place at Athens in 411; the piece has also been linked
with the return of the infamous Alcibiades during the same year.[1]
However that may be, the themes explored in this great piece go
well beyond the circumstances of its time.

Sophocles made two important innovations in his dramatic
treatment of the Philoctetes myth. The first was the replacement
of Diomedes by Neoptolemus as Odysseus' main instrument in
the plan to bring Philoctetes to Troy. The second was the use of
a chorus of Greek sailors to replace the chorus of Lemnians who
featured in the earlier plays by Aeschylus and Euripides. This
decision enabled Sophocles, among other things, to turn Lemnos
into an uninhabited island and so to emphasize his hero's desperate isolation in a hostile environment.

A brief consideration of the three main characters and their
interrelationships may help to highlight some of the issues in a
drama with a complex moral texture. This is the only surviving
play by Sophocles to contain no female roles. We are in a man's
world.

Philoctetes himself is a figure in the heroic mould of Sophocles'
Heracles and Ajax, but he is probably the most powerfully compelling of the three. His ownership of Heracles' inescapable bow
and arrows invests him with a strange, almost supernatural quality, while his lameness and loneliness, his wild and ragged appearance and consuming bitterness, make him intensely human.
Sophocles brings him vividly alive in his first suspicious confrontation with Neoptolemus and his crew, and then in his detailed

description of the life he has had to live on Lemnos. His warm response to the youthful Neoptolemus and the trust he places in him are a touching feature of the drama; the presentation of him later on in the throes of an attack of pain is even more memorably terrifying than that of Heracles' onstage agony in *Women of Trachis*. All this commands our sympathy as a modern audience. What may be less easy for us to identify with is Philoctetes' uncompromising stance in refusing to come to terms with his enemies, even when he is offered the prospect of the highest honour together with a cure for his diseased foot. In his implacable hostility to Odysseus and the Atridae – a keynote theme – he reminds us disturbingly of Ajax. We may say that he conforms to the normal Greek ethic of doing harm to one's enemies, but the moral position is complicated because Philoctetes' enemies, like those of Ajax, are his former allies and comrades-in-arms. This dilemma is symbolized by the fact that he cannot be cured of his disease *unless* he agrees to go to Troy. Here Sophocles prompts a mixture of responses: we *want* Philoctetes to go to Troy, but not at the cost of his dignity and integrity.

Philoctetes' arch-adversary, Odysseus, is very different from the character encountered in *Ajax*. Here there is no humility or generosity of spirit. Paramount are his commitment to the Greek cause at Troy and his insistence on the use of deception to lure Philoctetes there. For him the end justifies the means, and words count for more than deeds. 'Piety', which in this play seems to include truth to oneself no less than reverence to the gods, can take second place. Odysseus embodies the theme of deception, which plays such an important part in the drama, particularly in the False Merchant scene, when truth and falsehood seem inextricably intertwined. Yet, although Philoctetes does eventually sail to Troy, it is not the result of Odysseus' subtle machinations. These are presented as coming to nothing, and their author's rapid and undignified final exit shows him thoroughly routed and discomfited. We are bound to question his cynical manipulation of Neoptolemus as his pawn in the game.

Why does Odysseus' moral seduction of the young and impressionable Neoptolemus ultimately fail after what looks like a promising start? One reason is that the youth's *physis* – his

natural make-up as the son of the great warrior Achilles – is
fundamentally opposed to deception. Here Sophocles seems to
be exploring how far people can be impelled to actions which
are contrary to their basic natures. But other forces are also at
work. One is *philia*, a sense of kinship (not necessarily based on
ties of blood) and mutual responsibility. As Neoptolemus goes
through with his deception of Philoctetes, Sophocles portrays the
growth of a relationship analogous to that of father and son.
Philoctetes instinctively warms to the natural decency of a youth
who, on his side, has never known his father, and seems fasci-
nated by this strange, wild outcast with a special power symbolized by his ownership of Heracles' bow. The bond between
the two is sealed when Philoctetes allows Neoptolemus, for one
brief but very significant moment, to hold and then to return the
precious weapon.

The other human force that ruins Odysseus' stratagem is
simple pity or compassion, the emotion that impels Achilles, at
the end of Homer's *Iliad*, to forgo his destructive anger and
return the body of Hector to the Trojan warrior's father, King
Priam. The sight and sound of Philoctetes' excruciating pain from
the wound in his foot moves Neoptolemus to a point where he
feels he can no longer keep up his deception, but must confess to
his suffering friend what his real intentions are. That confession
marks the crisis and turning point of the play's action. Odysseus'
clever scheme to trap Philoctetes is in tatters. The claims of
political expediency have not been able to override the values of
friendship and compassion.

The audience now waits in suspense to see how the plot will
be resolved – not merely the problem of Philoctetes' going to
Troy, but also the issue of the torn relationship between him
and Neoptolemus. An exciting phase follows, during which
Philoctetes is shown in confrontation with Odysseus himself.
Neoptolemus now has charge of the bow, and it looks as if
Philoctetes will be left behind on Lemnos to die, since he no
longer has any means of sustaining his life there. But then
Neoptolemus decides to return the bow to Philoctetes, and their
relationship is restored. He makes one final attempt to persuade
his friend to come to Troy, where healing and glory await him.

But Philoctetes is still too uncompromising to come to terms with the enemies who once abandoned him so cruelly. We are back to square one. All Neoptolemus can do, in terms of their mended friendship, is to take Philoctetes, still sick from his incurable wound, back to his home in Greece, and to risk the destruction of his own people.

But the myth said Philoctetes *did* go to Troy. In a puzzling but beautiful closing scene, Sophocles introduces an epiphany of the deified Heracles, the original owner of Philoctetes' bow, to declare 'the counsels of Zeus'. These demand the healing of Philoctetes' wound and Troy's fall at the hands of the hero and Neoptolemus, working in cooperation. Heracles finally asserts 'piety' as an ultimate human value. Scholars have seen an ironical point to this (see note 52), but Sophocles also seems to be suggesting a perspective that transcends the claims of the state or the heroic code and envisages a pattern and purpose in the unexpected turns of mortal life. (The poet may be expressing a similar vision in 'Zeus' at the end of *Women of Trachis*.) At all events, Philoctetes accepts the divine will without demur. There is a strange and moving tranquillity about his farewell to Lemnos. All the bitterness is gone. He seems mentally healed, and even the harsh environment of his wild island appears transformed in the atmosphere of acceptance and reconciliation.

## STAGING

Aristotle[2] says that Sophocles introduced 'scene-painting', which seems to imply some dressing of the *skênê* with painted flats. In this play it is probable that the central entrance of the *skênê* represented and served as one of the two mouths to Philoctetes' cave and that other stylized scenery suggested the drama's unusual setting. There must have been some way for Odysseus to make his sudden 'jack-in-the-box' entrances at 974 and 1293, rather than down one of the *eisodoi*, where he could have been visible too early (see Preface to *Ajax*, note 7; also *Ajax*, notes 2, 69). Heracles can be imagined appearing at a higher level, either on the roof of the stage building or in the *mêchanê*, the crane device commonly used for the deus ex machina. One of the *eisodoi* must be assumed to have led to and from the shore, and the other to the interior of the island, from which Philoctetes makes his first entrance at 219.

## CASTING

The first actor would have played Philoctetes, the second Neoptolemus, while the third combines the roles of Odysseus, the false Merchant and Heracles. The voice associated with Odysseus could have added a sinister note to the delivery of the Merchant, his instrument. It might also have contributed to the transforming impact of Heracles' epiphany.

## DRAMATIC TECHNIQUE

Besides raising profound questions about universal human values, *Philoctetes* is also a superbly crafted and moving piece of drama. How does Sophocles succeed in sustaining his audience's interest in one single situation and manipulating its emotional responses in a theatrical experience? His technique in this play was strikingly original.

The poet's skilful use of *rhesis* and *stichomythia* speaks for itself. Some critics have emphasized the element of surprise, the use of 'delayed exits' and of 'significant actions' involving gestures or patterns of movement which are 'mirrored' at important points in the play by way of deliberate repetition or contrast.[3] Others have commented on the unusually realistic detail and shrewd characterization. The discussion that follows focuses on two issues which have often been treated as problematic and also involve an element of calculated ambiguity.

As already indicated, the resolution of the plot and of the issues explored in the play occurs in the closing scene, when Heracles declares 'the counsels of Zeus' as to what must be. Of course, Sophocles' audience would have *known* that Philoctetes went to Troy, as the one unalterable mythological datum. But the play

represents the failure of deception, force and persuasion to get
him there. In fact, he has started on his way back to Greece only
sixty-three lines before the end. The closing scene, however,
should not be regarded as an appendage of miraculous intervention, tacked on because the poet had to get his hero to Troy
somehow or other. It is carefully prepared for by the mention
of prophecies at various points (191–200, 610–13, 839–42,
1326–41), each of them hinting at what is going to happen but
none, except the last, revealing the whole truth. The idea is also
planted early on (191–200), and confirmed in the end (1326–41),
that Philoctetes' wound and consequent suffering are part of a
divine plan for the capture of Troy. Although prophecies do not
play as conspicuous a part in this play as oracles do in *Women
of Trachis*, the divine dimension is there, subtly and in the background.

Moreover, the audience's expectations are constantly manipulated to keep them guessing. There is a certain vagueness as to
whether Odysseus' plot is directed at Philoctetes himself coming
to Troy or merely at the capture of his unerring bow and arrows.
The latter seems to be the primary aim of his original briefing to
Neoptolemus; but the story he asks Neoptolemus to tell about
his quarrel with the Greeks must presumably be directed at
Philoctetes' asking to be taken on board Neoptolemus' ship and,
once on it, conveyed not to his home in Greece but to Troy. This
vagueness can only be sensed during performance at a subliminal
level, as the audience's main interest must be in *how* Philoctetes,
given the bow and his implacable hostility to the Greek generals,
will be got to Troy. However, it contributes to the feeling of
mystery and suspense, and is a point Sophocles exploits in two
specific places (836–42 and 1054–60, where see notes 33, 38).

A similar flexibility may be seen in the poet's use of his Chorus.
Ostensibly, they are members of Neoptolemus' crew and under
his orders. They know they have landed in Lemnos on a dangerous mission. But whose side are they on – Odysseus' or
Philoctetes'? The answer is: whatever Sophocles chooses at any
particular moment. He allows the sailors' stance to vary as a way
of reflecting the complexity of the issues he is exploring.

Thus in their entrance song they contribute to the build-up

towards Philoctetes' first appearance and help to establish him
as a figure who needs wary handling. They also strike the keynote
of pity for the suffering hero as they anticipate some of the details
in his way of life on the island, which Philoctetes will later
describe himself. During the long Scene 2, when Neoptolemus
wins Philoctetes' confidence, they perform two short (metrically
corresponding) dance-songs: the first reinforces their captain's
false story about his quarrel with the Atridae, while the second
backs Philoctetes' appeal to be taken home. Are they simply
playing a conspiratorial role in these interventions? I would
rather see them picking up and intensifying the mood of the
preceding long speeches through the different media of song and
dance.

The Chorus' one 'number' when they are left alone onstage in
the very centre of the play certainly does not present them in a
conspiratorial role. Once again human sympathy and empathy
are the keynotes, as the sailors recapitulate the details of
Philoctetes' hardships as he has recounted them – hardships now
to be ended when the son of a great hero returns him to his native
land, where Heracles burned on a blazing pyre in his apotheosis.
The last stanza seems quite inconsistent with a part in a plot to
take Philoctetes to Troy. The explanation must surely be that
Sophocles wants his Chorus (and so his audience) to identify at
that point with Philoctetes in his imagined reversal of fortune
and in the joy attendant on that prospect. The sailors' empathy
with Philoctetes' suffering anticipates Neoptolemus' crucial compassion, which, in the following scene, makes him unable to go
through with Odysseus' plan, while their note of joy in the final
stanza is in magnificent contrast with the horror very soon to be
witnessed in the 'pain scene'. Lastly, the ode reaches a grand
climax in the reference to Heracles, the god who gave Philoctetes
his bow and is later to make a surprise epiphany.

At 827, when Philoctetes has collapsed unconscious, the
Chorus sings a brief song of prayer for healing to the god of
sleep, but then, by an exceptionally abrupt transition, the sailors
snap back into a conspiratorial role. They urge Neoptolemus
to use his opportunity and act at once, obviously by leaving
the sleeping Philoctetes alone and going off with the bow.

When Neoptolemus grandiloquently tells them that the god has declared Philoctetes himself must come to Troy, they respond, 'Surely *the god* will provide for it.' Here the Chorus is used to foster the ambiguity already observed in Odysseus' plan – though it is, in the end, a god who settles the matter.

Finally, when it comes to Philoctetes' great lament (1081ff.), the Chorus is no longer required to sympathize with him, but rather to urge his coming to Troy as an alternative to dying on Lemnos. The hero's rejection of their pleas and reaffirmation of his unrelenting hatred for Odysseus presage his subsequent rejection of Neoptolemus' last attempt to persuade him in the following scene.

Thus Sophocles' consummate skill and control over his dramatic medium can be seen in this play particularly in his repeated introduction of prophecies to prepare for his ending, in his manipulation of the audience's expectations with regard to the plot's mechanics, and in his flexible use of the Chorus in the continuum of action and feeling.

# NOTES

1.    A. M. Bowie, in *Greek Tragedy and the Historian* (Oxford 1997), pp. 56–62.
2.    Aristotle, *Poetics*, chap. 4.
3.    On significant actions, see references to *Philoctetes* in O. Taplin, *Greek Tragedy in Action* (London 1978).

# Characters

[*Scene: Before a cave on Lemnos, a desert island.*]

# SCENE 1¹

[*Enter* ODYSSEUS *and* NEOPTOLEMUS, *followed by a sailor.*]

ODYSSEUS:
Here at last, here on the shore of Lemnos!
Not a path, not a single house, to be seen on the island.
Now, Neoptolemus, true-born son of Achilles,
Greatest of all the Greeks, it was here that I once
Put ashore the Malian, Pocas' son, Philoctetes,                     5
Acting upon the orders of my superiors.
The gnawing wound in his foot was oozing with pus.
We couldn't pour a libation or offer sacrifice
Undisturbed.² His animal shouts and yells
Were constantly filling the camp with sounds of ill omen.          10
That story needn't detain us now, however.
This isn't the moment for long discussion. He mustn't
Realize I am here. It would wreck the ingenious
Plan I think will ensure his speedy capture.
Now for your part in the business. I need your help.               15
I want you to look for a cave with a double entrance,
Allowing a man two places to sit in the sun
During winter, and also providing a tunnel through which
A cooling breeze can allow him to sleep in summer.
A little below, on the left, you may discover                      20

A spring of water – assuming it's not dried up.
Approach there quietly, please, and show with your hand
If the place is still his home or he's moved away.
Then you can listen, while I explain the rest
25 Of my plan, and so we'll be able to act in concert.
NEOPTOLEMUS:
Odysseus, sir! No need to look very far.
I think I see the kind of cave you've described.
ODYSSEUS:
Above or below you? I can't tell from here.[3]
NEOPTOLEMUS:
High up. No sound of anyone moving about.
ODYSSEUS:
30 Make sure he isn't lying inside asleep.
NEOPTOLEMUS:
The shelter's empty. There isn't a soul in sight.
ODYSSEUS:
Can you find any sign of its being inhabited?
NEOPTOLEMUS:
Yes, a mattress of crushed leaves. Someone must sleep here.
ODYSSEUS:
What else can you see? Is the whole place otherwise bare?
NEOPTOLEMUS:
35 Just a rough-made wooden cup – it's hardly the work
Of an expert craftsman – and twigs for kindling a fire.
ODYSSEUS:
Those have to be Philoctetes' household goods.
NEOPTOLEMUS:
Oh, no! Here's something else – rags hanging out
To dry in the sun, all stained with revolting pus!
ODYSSEUS:
40 The man lives here, beyond any doubt, and he can't
Be far away. With a foot still badly sore
From that old affliction, he couldn't walk any distance.
No, he must have gone out in search of food,
Or perhaps he knows of some painkilling herb.
45 Order your man away to keep a lookout.
He must not pounce on me by surprise. He'd sooner
Get hold of me than capture the whole Greek army.

[*Exit sailor.*]

NEOPTOLEMUS:
Very well, he's going. The track will be carefully watched.
Now tell me more, sir. What do you want me to do?

ODYSSEUS:
Son of Achilles, this mission calls on you                          50
To prove your worth – not just in physical prowess.
My plan may strike you as odd – you won't have heard it
Before – but do remember you're here to serve.

NEOPTOLEMUS:
What are your orders, then?

ODYSSEUS:
                                          Your role is to trick
Philoctetes into believing a yarn you'll spin him.               55
He'll ask you who you are and where you come from.
Say you're Achilles' son, don't lie about that.
You are homeward bound and have left the Grecian task force
After a blazing quarrel. They'd fetched you away
From home with solemn entreaties, as this was the only          60
Means they had of capturing Troy. But when
You arrived and rightfully claimed your father's arms,
They refused to award them to you and gave them instead
To Odysseus. Yes, you can be as rude as you like                65
About *me*. I shan't take it amiss. But if
You fail, you'll cause distress to the whole of Greece.
Unless you capture Philoctetes' bow
And arrows, you won't be able to flatten Troy.

Now let me explain why you can safely meet                       70
This man and secure his trust, when I can not.
You didn't sail with the main expedition. You weren't
Committed by oath or forced into taking part.
But every one of these charges applies to me.
If he sights me while the bow's in his own possession,           75
I'm finished and you'll be finished for being with me.
Those weapons can't be resisted. Our task must be
To contrive a way for you to steal them from him.

I know, my boy, it isn't part of your nature
80  To tell untruths or resort to double-dealing.
But victory's a prize worth gaining. Bring yourself
To do it. We'll prove our honesty later on.
Now, for a few hours, put yourself in my hands
And forgo your scruples. Then, for the rest of time,
85  Be called the most god-fearing[4] man in the world!
NEOPTOLEMUS:
You know, Odysseus, if ever I find advice
Distasteful, I'm most reluctant to carry it out.
You're right, sir. Double-dealing is not my nature,
Neither, they tell me, was it my father's way.
90  I'm quite prepared to capture the man by force,
Without resorting to tricks. With only one foot,
He'll be no match for a band as large as ours.
However, they've sent me to help you, and I've no wish
To be called a traitor. But sir, I'd rather fail
95  In a noble action than win an ignoble victory.
ODYSSEUS:
So like your father! Yes, in my own young days,
I too had a busy hand and an idle tongue.
But life has taught me better, and now I see
It's words, not deeds, that shape the course of events.
NEOPTOLEMUS:
100  What, then, are my orders? Nothing but telling lies?
ODYSSEUS:
I say you must use deception to trap Philoctetes.
NEOPTOLEMUS:
Why use deception and not persuasion?
ODYSSEUS:
He won't be persuaded, and cannot be forced.
NEOPTOLEMUS:
Has he some fearful power he banks on?
ODYSSEUS:
105  Deadly arrows, which never miss.
NEOPTOLEMUS:
So I dare not even approach the man?

ODYSSEUS:
Unless, as I say, you use deception.

NEOPTOLEMUS:
Don't you believe that telling lies is shameful?

ODYSSEUS:
Not if our lying leads to success.

NEOPTOLEMUS:
But how could I look him straight in the eye? 110

ODYSSEUS:
You can't have qualms if you're looking to gain.

NEOPTOLEMUS:
What gain to *me* is his coming to Troy?

ODYSSEUS:
It's only his arrows can capture Troy.

NEOPTOLEMUS:
You said that *I* was the man who'd sack it.

ODYSSEUS:
Not without them, or they without you. 115

NEOPTOLEMUS:
If that is the case, they'd be well worth catching.

ODYSSEUS:
Exactly. Get them – and win two prizes.

NEOPTOLEMUS:
What prizes? Tell me, and I could give my assent.

ODYSSEUS:
They'll call you clever, as well as a hero.

NEOPTOLEMUS:
Very well. Confound my scruples, I'll do it! 120

ODYSSEUS:
Now do you remember the plan I suggested?

NEOPTOLEMUS:
Of course, sir, now that I've once agreed.

ODYSSEUS:
You stay behind, then, here and await his return,
While I go off – he mustn't observe me with you –
And order our lookout down to the ship. If you 125
Appear to be over-running the proper time,

I'll send him back, disguised as a merchant captain,
So Philoctetes won't know that he's in with us.
He'll tell an elaborate tale, and after that,
130  My boy, you'll have to play the business by ear.
I'm away to the ship and handing over to you.
And may we be guided by Hermes, god of deception,
Who gives safe conduct, and by my constant patron,
Athena, guardian of cities, whose name is Victory.[5]

     [*Exit* ODYSSEUS.]


# ENTRY OF THE CHORUS[6]


[*Enter* CHORUS *of sailors.*]

CHORUS:
135       Commander, I'm a stranger here on foreign soil.   [*Strophe 1*]
     The man's bound to suspect me. What's my tale, sir?
     Tell me now.
     Skill and judgement shine in a king,
     Shine in those whom Zeus has endowed with sceptred
140       Sway divine and a prince's rule.
     So you, young master, have been bequeathed
     Power supreme by your ancestors. Say to me
     Hów I néed to sérve you.

NEOPTOLEMUS:
     First you may wish to inspect where he lives
145       On the edge of this island. At present it's safe;
     You may look without fear. But after he comes
     Back home from his foray, he could be a danger.
     So watch till I wave you forward, and try
     To follow the needs of the moment.


CHORUS:
150       My prince, you know I've always been
          concerned               [*Antistrophe 1*]
     To keep a particular eye on what concerns *you*.
     Tell me, sir,
     What kind of shelter he has for his home.

Where's he roaming now? It would be as well, sir,
For me to know of his whereabouts.                                      155
He must not pounce on me unawares.
Where is he walking, or where is he resting?
Abroád, or únder cóver?

NEOPTOLEMUS:
Look, this is his house, with its two ways in,                          160
His lair in the rock.

CHORUS:
Where is the luckless owner himself, then?

NEOPTOLEMUS:
Close nearby. It's apparent to me
That he's ploughing a trail in a search for food.
This is how they say Philoctetes succeeds
In remaining alive, shooting the beasts                                 165
With his arrows, despite his terrible pain,
While nobody comes
To comfort or cure his affliction.


CHORUS:
How I pity his dismal plight!                    [Strophe 2]
No one there to look after him,                                         170
No companion with kindly eyes,
Wretched, always so lonely.
He's sick, sick with a cruel sore,
And each trivial, trifling need
Drives him frántic and mad. Hów in the world,                          175
              hów to abíde such páin?
Oh you deceitful gods!
Oh, how wretched the fall of men
Blessed too kindly by fortune!


Take this son of a noble house,                  [Antistrophe 2]   180
Maybe second to none in birth,
Wanting every comfort in life,
All alone without neighbours,
None but the spotted or shaggy wild
Beasts. He's tortured by hunger's pangs,                                185

Rácked with the shóoting pain, hárdships that no héaling
    or cáre can cúre.
Only a far-off voice,
Babbling Echo, responds to his harsh
Cries and long lamentations.

190

NEOPTOLEMUS:
His dreadful fate's no wonder to me.[7]
If I have an inkling, his sufferings first
Were sent by the gods, when he entered the shrine
Of cruel Chryse, who dealt him his wound.
So what he endures now, far from his friends,
Must also be due to the will of some god:
He may not aim those god-given shafts,
Which none can resist, at the towers of Troy,
Till the time has come when the prophet declares
Those arrows will prove her destruction.

195

200

    [A cry offstage.]

CHORUS:
Be sílent, my són![8]                                    [Strophe 3]

NEOPTOLEMUS:
                    What ís it?

CHORUS:
                            Quíet! I héard a crý.
Súrely it sóunds like a man tróubled by gréat pain.
Over here, or could it be there? [Another cry.]
So near, so clear, it is true!
Someone's coming, painfully limping [groan]
Along this way. I can hear it,
That distant agonized groaning.
Tortured creature! His sighs are all too plain.

205

210

Now lísten, my bóy!                                      [Antistrophe 3]

NEOPTOLEMUS:
                    Please téll me.

CHORUS:
                            Tíme to bé prepáred.
The mán's not fár from his home, clóse to arríving.
That's no shepherd in from the fields,

With a merry tune on his pipe. [*Cry*.]
There! that anguished shout in the distance.                    215
His pain has caused him to stumble,
Or else he's sighted our vessel,
Anchored off this unfriendly, empty shore.


# SCENE 2

[*Enter* PHILOCTETES.]⁹
PHILOCTETES:
[*In surprise*:] Ah! Strangers!
Who are you? Sailors, this place you've just put into              220
Hasn't a decent harbour. Nobody lives here.
What land do you come from? Tell me, I want to know.
What people? Greeks, I'd guess from the clothes you're
      wearing.
How welcome to me if you were! I want to hear
You speak your language. Don't be frightened and shrink          225
Away because of my wild appearance. No,
Pity a miserable wretch – alone, abandoned,
Severely injured, without a friend to help.
I think you have come as friends. Say something to me. [*Pause*.]
Oh, answer me, *please*! You cannot refuse me that.               230
I'll answer *you*.
NEOPTOLEMUS:
                    Very well, sir. First of all, then,
Yes, we are Greeks. There is your question answered.
PHILOCTETES:
Greek! That beautiful sound! At last, at last
To hear the greeting words of a man like you!                    235
What's brought you in to land, my boy, right here?
What need or venture? What kind and gracious wind?
Explain it all. I must know who you are.
NEOPTOLEMUS:
The island of Scyros is my birthplace, sir,
And I'm homeward bound. My name is Neoptolemus,                  240
And I'm the son of Achilles. There, that's all.

PHILOCTETES:

The son of a friend so dear, dear like your island!

Old Lycomedes must have brought you up.

What mission brings you to Lemnos? Where have you come
    from?

NEOPTOLEMUS:

245  Just now, in fact, I'm sailing from Troy.

PHILOCTETES:

From Troy? You weren't on board with us

When the expedition first set out.

NEOPTOLEMUS:

Were *you* involved in this troublesome war?

PHILOCTETES:

My boy! You don't know whom you're facing?

NEOPTOLEMUS:

250  How *can* I know someone I've never seen?

PHILOCTETES:

Not even my name? You haven't heard speak

Of the frightful fate still blighting my life?

NEOPTOLEMUS:

All your questions mean nothing to me.

PHILOCTETES:

How wretched I am, and how the gods must hate me!

255  Not even a rumour about my plight has yet

Got through to my home or anywhere else in Greece.

No, the men who wickedly cast me out

Have hushed it up in delight, while my disease

Is in full bloom and still continues to grow.

260  Listen, my boy! Listen, son of Achilles,

I'll tell you who I am. You may perhaps

Have heard of the man who wields the bow of Heracles,

Philoctetes, Poeas' son. I am that man.

I'm here because the two Greek generals, backed

265  By Odysseus, shamefully flung me ashore, alone

And abandoned, to waste away with a raging wound,

Struck down by the savage bite of a deadly snake.

With that for company, son, they marooned me here

And left me to rot on my own. (The fleet had sailed

From the isle of Chryse, and this was their first port of call.)     270
Then once, to their joy, they'd seen me asleep on the shore
After a stormy passage, they laid me inside
A rocky cave and left, tossing me out
A few beggarly rags, with a small amount of available
Food to keep me alive and avoid pollution.                            275

How do you think I felt, my boy, when I woke
From sleep and pulled myself up – to find them gone?
Imagine the tears I shed and my cries of lament
When I saw the ships which I was leading to Troy
Had all disappeared and there wasn't a man in sight,                  280
No one to lend me a hand, no one to help
Look after my painful wound. As I looked around me,
All I could find to sustain my life was pain,
Pain and distress, my boy – no shortage of *them*!

So time dragged on, season following season.                          285
I always had to tend for myself, alone
In that bare, cramped shelter. My body's demands for food
Were catered for by this bow, which brought to earth
Any doves on the wing. Whatever my arrows shot,
I'd have the effort of crawling along myself                          290
And dragging my wretched foot behind me to find it.
Whenever I needed water to drink, or else
Some wood to break up during the winter frosts,
I'd creep out once again and manage that too.
But then, to light my fire, I'd have to lure                          295
A spark from its lair by scraping stones together.
And that just keeps me alive. Fire and shelter
Supply my wants – except a cure for my sickness.

Now, my boy, let me tell you about the island.                        300
No sailor will ever land here, if he can help it.
There's nowhere safe he can anchor his ship, no port
In which he can trade for profit or find a welcome.
No sensible man would steer a course for this place.
He might, perhaps, put in because he is forced to –                   305

It happens now and again in a long lifetime.
Such people, when they arrive, my boy, will *say*
They're sorry for me. They might feel sorry enough
To give me a scrap of food or something to wear.
310  But when I raise the question of taking me home,
Nobody wants to do it. No, I've now
Been rotting away for nine whole years, in hunger
And misery, feeding my greedy, insatiable wound.
That's what Atreus' sons and the forceful Odysseus[10]
315  Have done to me, boy. I pray the Olympian gods
Will make them suffer the like, in payment for *me*!
CHORUS LEADER:
Son of Poeas, I think I also
Pity you, like your other visitors.
NEOPTOLEMUS:
I too can testify to the truth
320  Of your story. I know how bad the sons
Of Atreus and forceful Odysseus are.
PHILOCTETES:
Have *you* a complaint to bring against
Those curséd villains, some grounds for resentment?
NEOPTOLEMUS:
I wish my arm could express my fury
325  And make Mycenae and Sparta know
That Scyros too has courageous sons!
PHILOCTETES:
Well said, my boy! Explain to me why
You feel so bitterly angry with them.
NEOPTOLEMUS:
Philoctetes, I'll tell you – with great reluctance –
330  How they insulted me there at Troy.
When fate decreed Achilles must die . . .[11]
PHILOCTETES:
No, no! Please stop for a moment. I must
Know first: is great Achilles dead?
NEOPTOLEMUS:
Yes, he is dead – not killed by a man
335  But a god. He was shot, they say, by Apollo.

PHILOCTETES:
At least his killer was noble too!
My boy, I'm not sure whether to hear
Your grievances first, or to mourn for him.
NEOPTOLEMUS:
My unhappy friend, I believe your own
Troubles are more than enough for one.                          340
PHILOCTETES:
You're right. We'd better return to your
Concerns. Now tell me how they insulted you.
NEOPTOLEMUS:
They came for me[12] in a ship bedecked with garlands,
The great Odysseus and Phoenix, my father's tutor.
The message they brought – it may have been true or false –    345
Was this: Fate ruled that, since my father was dead,
No one but I should take the towers of Troy.
When I heard this news from their lips, I wasn't going
To wait for long, but eager to sail at once.
I wanted above all else to see my father                        350
Before he was buried – I'd never seen him alive.
But the splendid promise gave me an added inducement:
That I should be going to capture the Trojan citadel!

My voyage was now on its second day, when a fair wind
Brought me into Sigeum, a harbour of cruel                       355
Memories. As soon as I landed, the whole of the army
Gathered round in a circle to greet me, swearing
They saw the lost Achilles alive again.
But no, he was lying dead. Bereaved as I was,
When I'd paid my due of tears, without delay                    360
I approached the sons of Atreus, naturally thinking
They were my friends, and asked for my father's arms
With everything else he'd left. The answer they gave me
Was shameless beyond belief: 'Son of Achilles,
We'll let you take the whole of your father's possessions –     365
Except for his arms, which now belong to another,
Odysseus.' With tears in my eyes, I at once sprang up
In a furious rage and gave full vent to my feelings:

'You wretches!' I cried, 'have you dared to give my arms
370   To somebody else, without consulting *me*?'
Odysseus, who chanced to be standing by, then said,
'Yes, boy! This award of theirs is perfectly fair.
I rescued those arms when I rescued their owner's body.'
That made me lose my temper and instantly load him
375   With every kind of abuse. I pulled no punches.
That *he* should deprive me of arms which were properly mine!
At this point, stung by the taunts he'd heard, Odysseus,
Not an irascible man as a rule, replied,
'You weren't there on the field when you should have been. I
        was.
380   I'll teach you to speak so boldly, boy. You'll never,
Never return with those arms to your isle of Scyros!'
With suchlike insults ringing inside my head,
I'm sailing for home, deprived of what ought to be mine
384   By that son of a bitch, that villain of villains, Odysseus.
That's my story[13] in full. Heaven bless, as I do,
390   Every man who detests the sons of Atreus!
CHORUS:
        O mountain goddess,[14] nurturing Earth,                     [*Strophe*]
        Mother great of mighty Zeus,
        Whose shrine is by Pactolus' river, rich in gold![15]
395       In Troy, tóo, my lády, I invóked your náme,
        When thóse proud Atrídae
        Insúlted my máster,
        When they surréndered his fáther's arms to Laértes' són,
400       Those áwesome árms. So now héar our práyer,
        O blest Cýbele, héar, whose great thróne's adórned
        With bull-sláying líons.
PHILOCTETES:[16]
The anger that has brought you to me here,
My friends, must be a sign that I can trust you.
405   Your story chimes with my own. It's just what I'd
Expect of Atreus' sons and Odysseus too.
I know he'd use his tongue to forward any
Evil scheme or villainous action, if that
Was likely to serve his wicked ends. I'm not

Surprised by this. But it's odd that the greater Ajax[17]                410
Could bear to watch this outrage, if he was there.
NEOPTOLEMUS:
He never lived to see it, sir.
If he had, they wouldn't have dared to rob me.
PHILOCTETES:
Ajax! Truly? Is he dead too?
NEOPTOLEMUS:
I have to tell you he's now no more.                                     415
PHILOCTETES:
I'm sorry. But Diomedes and Sisyphus'
Spawn,[18] whom Laertes bought, will *never*
Die. *They* should not have been born!
NEOPTOLEMUS:
They'll live, be certain of that. What's worse,
Their stock is high in the Argive camp.                                  420
PHILOCTETES:
Well, then, what of my good old friend
Nestor of Pylos? He used to block
Their schemes, at least, with his wise advice.
NEOPTOLEMUS:
Nestor's fortunes are low. He has lost
His son and chief support, Antilochus.                                   425
PHILOCTETES:
Another good man! Ajax and he
Were the last I'd have wished to hear were dead.
Well, well! What *are* we to think, when these
Are gone and Odysseus is still alive?
*His* name, not theirs, should be on the death roll.                     430
NEOPTOLEMUS:
He's a clever trickster, but even the cleverest
Schemes, Philoctetes, can be frustrated.
PHILOCTETES:
For god's sake, wasn't Patroclus there?
He was your father's closest friend.
NEOPTOLEMUS:
Dead too. To put the truth in a nutshell:                                435
War always chooses the better men

To make his victims, never the worse.
PHILOCTETES:
I'm with you there. And speaking of bad men,
What of that clever but worthless rogue
440 With the gift of the gab – what's happened to him?
NEOPTOLEMUS:
Whom can you mean apart from Odysseus?
PHILOCTETES:
No, not him! Thersites his name was.
He'd always go on talking when everyone
Told him to stop. Is *he* alive, do you know?
NEOPTOLEMUS:
445 I never saw him myself, but heard he was.
PHILOCTETES:
He would be! Nobody bad has ever died.
The gods protect such people and take delight
In keeping crooks and criminals out of Hades,[19]
450 While always sending the honest and decent down.
What sense can we make of this? Can we be content
When we scan the divine and find the gods are evil?
NEOPTOLEMUS:
To speak for myself, Philoctetes, son of Poeas,
From this day on I'll give the widest possible
455 Berth to the land of Troy and the sons of Atreus.
Where baseness counts for more than noble worth
And honour loses out while cowardice wins,
I want no more to do with men like these.
No, craggy Scyros will be good enough
460 For me in future. I'll be delighted to live there.

Now I'll be off to my ship. Goodbye, Philoctetes,
I wish you all of the best. I hope the gods
Will answer your prayer and grant a cure for your wound.
    [*To the sailors*]: Let's all be going. As soon as the god
    allows us
465 A favouring wind, we can put to sea at once.
PHILOCTETES:
Already, son? You're leaving?

NEOPTOLEMUS:
                                    Yes, we must
Be close to our ship the moment the wind sets fair.
PHILOCTETES:
Oh please, my boy! In your father's and mother's name,
By all you love and treasure at home, I humbly
Implore you, please don't leave me here on my own,                    470
Abandoned like this, living in all these horrors,
As you can see for yourself or have heard me tell.
Find me a corner somehow. I won't be an easy
Cargo to have on board, I know. But still,
Put up with me, please! A noble nature will hate
What's mean and take a pride in acting with honour.                   475
They'll say unpleasant things if you let me down;
But if you agree, my son, and bring me alive
To Malis, you'll win the prize of the highest glory!
Please! It won't be more than a few hours' trouble.                   480
Make the effort. Stow me wherever you like –
In the hold, the prow or the stern – just where I'll be
Least likely to give annoyance to others on board.
Say yes, my boy! By Zeus, the god of suppliants,
Listen! I kneel before you, although, alas,                           485
I'm only a feeble cripple. Don't abandon me
Here alone, where nobody ever comes.
No, either bring me safely as far as your home
In Scyros, or else to Calchodon's place in Euboea.
From there it's only an easy crossing to Oeta,                        490
To Trachis' heights and Spercheüs' beautiful stream.
And so you can show me again to my own dear father –
Though I've been long afraid I shall find him gone.
When people arrived, I often used to send him
Imploring messages, hoping he might be able                           495
To come in a ship of his own and fetch me home.
But either he's dead, or else my messengers couldn't
Be bothered with *me* – it was natural enough, I suppose –
And wanted to hurry on with their homeward voyage.
Now *you* can take me on board and also bear                          500

My news. It's you who must save me, you who must show me
Pity. I warn you! The life of man is haunted
503 By doubt and danger. Our luck is constantly changing![20]
CHORUS:
507     Show pity, royal sir.[21] His cruel                    [Antistrophe]
        Pain is past strength to bear.
        I pray such suffering never falls to friend of mine.
510     If you detést those hárd princes of Gréece, my lórd,
        Let théir crimes be cóunted
        To this man's advántage.
        Let me convéy him hóme to where he lóngs to bé.
515     Our shíp is swíft and its equípment góod.
        Aboard nów, at ónce! We must néeds escápe
        The gods' wráth to cóme.

NEOPTOLEMUS:
Look, men! You may feel easy enough just now,
520 But when you've lived with his wound and found it all
Too much, you could be tempted to change your tune.
CHORUS LEADER:
I'll not let him down. I promise I'll never
Give you cause to reproach me with that.
NEOPTOLEMUS:
Well, it would be disgraceful if I fell short
525 Of you in helping a stranger in time of need.
All right, let's sail if you wish. He can leave at once.
The ship, for sure, will hardly refuse to take him!
I only pray that the gods will bring us safely
Away from this island to where we want to go.
PHILOCTETES:
530 The day I dreamed of! Oh you kind, kind man!
Dear sailors, I wish my actions could show you all
How grateful I am, how much I'm in your debt.
Let's leave, my son – though first let's bid a last
Farewell to my cheerless dwelling. I want you to know
535 How I've stayed alive and kept my spirits up.
Anyone else, I think, would have shied away
From merely seeing what I have had to endure.
I've had no choice but to be content with hardship.

CHORUS LEADER:
Wait, sirs, what's this? Two men are coming towards us.
One belongs to your crew, the other's a stranger.                540
Don't go inside until you've heard their news.
    [*Enter* NEOPTOLEMUS' *lookout, disguised as a* MERCHANT
    *with another sailor.*][22]
MERCHANT:
Son of Achilles, I asked my companion here,
Who was keeping guard on your ship with two other men,
To show me where I might be able to find you.
Our paths have unexpectedly crossed, you see,                    545
As chance has brought me to anchor here off Lemnos.
I'm a merchant captain, trading in wine, and sailing
From Troy with a small ship's company back to my island
Home, Peparethos. After the sailors told me
They all belonged to your crew, I thought I shouldn't            550
Continue my voyage before I'd had a personal
Word with *you*. No doubt you'll reward me for it.
I don't suppose you know your own situation:
The Greeks have got new plans for you – not merely               555
Plans, they're putting them into action fast.
NEOPTOLEMUS:
Well, sir, this is extremely thoughtful of you.
I'll be at fault if I don't remember your kindness.
Tell me, what's this action you're talking about –
This sinister plot the Greeks are hatching against me?          560
MERCHANT:
A ship is now on its way in pursuit of you,
With aged Phoenix and Theseus' sons[23] on board.
NEOPTOLEMUS:
To bring me back by force, or by persuasion?
MERCHANT:
Can't say. I'm simply telling you what I heard.
NEOPTOLEMUS:
Would Phoenix and his companions be so keen                     565
To help the kings of Greece on a mission like this?
MERCHANT:
The mission is under way, I can assure you.

NEOPTOLEMUS:

Why wasn't Odysseus ready to sail and bring
The message himself? Was he afraid of something?

MERCHANT:

570   Oh, he and Diomedes[24] were off to collect
Another person when I was leaving harbour.

NEOPTOLEMUS:

Who *was* this person Odysseus himself was after?

MERCHANT:

A man called – listen! Just tell me first, who's that
Over there? You'd better keep your voice right down.

NEOPTOLEMUS:

575   That's Philoctetes, the famous bowman, sir.

MERCHANT:

Ask me no more. Get away from here
Yourself, and sail as soon as you can!

PHILOCTETES:

Son! What's he saying? What shady deal
Is that seaman up to concerning me?

NEOPTOLEMUS:

580   I don't know yet. He must make his point
In the open – to you, to me and the crew.

MERCHANT:

Neoptolemus, sir, don't get me into trouble
With all the army for talking out of turn.
I do a lot of business with them and need
Their custom badly. I'm only a poor man, sir.

NEOPTOLEMUS:

585   Well, *I* want nothing to do with them. This man
Is a special friend, because he hates the Atridae.
You've come as a friend to *me*, so don't conceal
From us one single detail of what you've heard.

MERCHANT:

Now watch what you're doing, boy.

NEOPTOLEMUS:

                                    Just as I always have.

MERCHANT:

I'll hold you responsible.

NEOPTOLEMUS:
                    Fine, but out with the truth!                    590
MERCHANT:
Very well. This man is the one they're after, the two
I've mentioned, the son of Tydeus and forceful Odysseus.
They've sworn a solemn oath to bring him to Troy,
Whether it's through persuasion or by brute strength.
Odysseus said so clearly before the whole                            595
Achaean assembly. He himself was a great deal
Surer than Diomedes that they'd succeed.
NEOPTOLEMUS:
What made the Atridae, after all this time,
So very concerned about Philoctetes here –
The man they'd marooned on Lemnos years before?                      600
Did they suddenly miss his presence? Or was it the force
Of nemesis from the gods for evil deeds?
MERCHANT:
I can explain the whole of this – you probably
Haven't heard it yourself. There was a high-born
Seer, a son of Priam in fact, whose name                             605
Was Helenus. One night this crafty fellow, Odysseus,
The man whom everyone likes to curse and revile,
Went out on his own and captured the prophet – a prize
Whom he brought in chains and proudly displayed to the
     Greeks.
Helenus prophesied all they wanted to know,                          610
Including this: they never would capture Troy,
If they couldn't persuade Philoctetes to leave this island
Where now he's living and come with them to the mainland.
As soon as Odysseus heard the prophet's warning,
He gave his promise at once to fetch the man                         615
And produce him before the Greeks. Most likely, he thought,
He'd come of his own accord; otherwise, perforce.
'If I fail in my mission,' he said, 'you may cut my head off!'
That's the story, my boy. So hurry's the word                        620
For yourself – and anyone else you care about.
PHILOCTETES:
No, no! You mean to say that poisonous devil

Swore to get *me* to Troy by means of persuasion?'
He'd sooner persuade me to leave the land of the dead
625  When I'm gone and return to life like his cheat of a father!²⁵
MERCHANT:
*I* wouldn't know about that. Well, I'll be off
To my ship – and pray the god will be with you both.
     [*Exit* MERCHANT.]
PHILOCTETES:
I can't believe it! To think, my son, that Odysseus
Could ever expect to practise his tongue on *me*
630  And bring me ashore to parade me before the Greeks!
He shan't. I'd rather obey my bitterest foe,
The deadly snake which turned me into a cripple.
But there's nothing he wouldn't promise or have the face
To perform. And now I know he'll be coming here.
635  Come on, my boy, let's move. We must put a good stretch
Of sea between ourselves and Odysseus' ship.
Off on our way! Speedy action in time
Brings sleep and respite once the effort is over.
NEOPTOLEMUS:
Good. We'll slip the cable as soon
640  As the headwind drops. It's now against us.
PHILOCTETES:
It's always departure time when you're running from danger.
NEOPTOLEMUS:
I know. But the weather's against them too.
PHILOCTETES:
Pirates feel no contrary winds
When theft and plunder are there for the taking.
NEOPTOLEMUS:
645  All right, let's go, when you've found what you need
Or would specially like to take from your cave.
PHILOCTETES:
There *are* some things, though I haven't much.
NEOPTOLEMUS:
What things that we cannot provide on board?
PHILOCTETES:
There's a certain herb which I always use
650  To soothe my wound and relieve the pain.

NEOPTOLEMUS:
Well, fetch it. What else do you want to take?
PHILOCTETES:
I might have mislaid a few of my arrows.
I wouldn't want anyone else to find them.
    [*Pause.*]
NEOPTOLEMUS:
Is that the famous bow[26] in your hand?
PHILOCTETES:
It is – the very one that I'm holding.                    655
NEOPTOLEMUS:
Would you let me take a closer look
And touch it, with reverence, as for a god?
PHILOCTETES:
You, my son, may do it, and anything else
Which lies in my power to do you good.
NEOPTOLEMUS:
I dearly want to – but only if                            660
It is truly right. Otherwise, better not.
PHILOCTETES:
Your words show fear of the gods. It is surely right,
My boy, since you alone have granted me life,
To enjoy the light of the sun, to see Mt Oeta's
Country, my aged father and friends. You've raised me     665
Beyond my enemies' reach when I lay at their feet.
Yes, I'll allow you to hold this precious bow –
And now to give it me back, and proudly boast
That because of your goodness you were the only person
Who ever touched it. I won it myself by kindness.         670
NEOPTOLEMUS:
How glad I am to have met you and won your friendship!
A man who responds to kindness as you have done
Must surely become a friend beyond all price.
Now go inside.
PHILOCTETES:
                Yes, you must come in too.
With my ailing foot, I need you close beside me.          675
    [PHILOCTETES *and* NEOPTOLEMUS *enter the cave.*]

# CHORAL SONG[27]

CHORUS:
          I never saw it, only heard the story told,          [*Strophe 1*]
          Heard how Ixion[28] whirled on a wheel of fire.
          The man who assaulted the gods' queen
          Zeus the almighty enchained
680      Deép belów in hársh bónds.
          Yét my eárs have not heard, éyes have not seen súffering
             like thís man's.
          How can poor Philoctetes' pain be equalled?
          He scórned áll violence, néver róbbed a sóul,
          Lived in peace with his fellow men,
685      All to earn this endless death!
          To be sure, wónder I múst,
          Hów when he héars the béating bréakers,
          As he síts alone in sórrow,
          Could he béar to weep and súffer
690      Such a life of tórment?

          Alone! No one with whom to pass the time
             of day,          [*Antistrophe 1*]
          No one who dwells close by and could share his pain,
          To whom he could cry in his anguish,
          Cry to an echoing heart,
695      'Gnáwing, bléeding, crúel wóund!'
          Nó one thére to apply hérbs which could be sóothing to
             that sóre foot,
          Cool the burning flux from the oozing snakebite
          And bríng néeded hélp when wríthing páin attácked,
700      Wresting aid from the nurturing earth.
          And then he'd creep from place to place,
          To and fro, límping alóng,
          Líke a chíld with no núrse besíde him,
          To a pláce where comfort waíted
705      And his wánts could find fulfílment
          When the páin subsíded.

Hóly Éarth could not féed him with fresh córn
   crops;                                                    [*Strophe 2*]
Nó hard gróund he could make frúitful, like us mórtals.
Thére was nóthing to eat, ónly a féw birds                             710
Shot dówn from the ský with his bów and flýing árrows.
Oh, what a wretched life!
Tén long yéars, and not ónce to enjoy drínking a cúp of                715
  wíne,
Still searching where to light on a standing pool
And struggling to get there.

Nów to encóunter the young són of a great héro! [*Antistrophe 2*]
Nów his lífe can attain háppiness and gréatness.                       720
Sóon he'll sáil in a ship, áfter so mány
Long yéars maróoned on this ísland, báck to Mális,
Haunt of the dancing nymphs;                                           725
Sée Sperchéüs' dear bánks, where the strong wárrior
  Héraclés[29]
Rose up to join the gods in a blaze of fire
On high above Oeta!

# SCENE 3[30]

[NEOPTOLEMUS *and* PHILOCTETES *re-enter from the cave.*
PHILOCTETES *suddenly stops.*]
NEOPTOLEMUS:
Come on, keep going. Why have you suddenly                             730
Gone so silent? Has something stunned you?
PHILOCTETES  [*utters four groans*[31] *of gathering intensity*].
NEOPTOLEMUS:
What is it?
PHILOCTETES:
Nothing to bother about. Go on, my son.
NEOPTOLEMUS:
You're not in pain from the wound in your foot?
PHILOCTETES:
No, no. I think that it's easing now.                                  735

O gods!

NEOPTOLEMUS:
What's making you call so loudly upon the gods?

PHILOCTETES:
I pray they'll come to my rescue and bring relief!
    [*Four more groans of pain.*]

NEOPTOLEMUS:
740   What's happened? Cannot you say one word?
Explain! Something is clearly wrong.

PHILOCTETES:
I'm done for, boy. I can't conceal it
From all of you any more. Oh, oh! It's driving,
Piercing me through! Ah, the pain, the pain!
745   I'm done for, boy. It's gnawing me, boy. Oh god!
It's gnawing, gnawing, gnawing, gnawing!
For god's sake, where's your sword, boy? Take it,
Take it! Cut this wretched foot off!
Shear it away – quickly! Don't spare my life,
750   Go on, my son!

NEOPTOLEMUS:
What new attack is this?
What's making you groan and howl so loudly?

PHILOCTETES:
You know, my boy!

NEOPTOLEMUS:
                    What is it?

PHILOCTETES:
                              You know, my son!

NEOPTOLEMUS:
I don't. Tell me!

PHILOCTETES:
                  You *must* know! [*Another howl of pain.*]

NEOPTOLEMUS:
755   Yes, your wound – it's a terrible load to carry.

PHILOCTETES:
It can't be described. Still, you can show me pity.

NEOPTOLEMUS:
What can I do?[32]

PHILOCTETES:
        Don't leave me because you are frightened.
The torturer comes and goes and will let me alone,
Perhaps, when he's done his worst.
NEOPTOLEMUS:
                        Poor Philoctetes!
Poor man, I can see you've been through hell.                    760
Shall I hold your arm and help you up?
PHILOCTETES:
No, no, don't touch me. Take this bow of mine,
As you asked to do just now. Look after it
And keep it safe until this present seizure                      765
Of pain subsides. You'll see, as soon as it starts
To go, I'll fall asleep, and only then
Will it stop completely. After that you must let me
Sleep in peace. If *they* come during that time,
I charge you in heaven's name, they mustn't persuade             770
Or force or trick you into letting them have
These weapons. Or else, at a single blow, you'll kill
Yourself and me, who've thrown myself on your mercy.
NEOPTOLEMUS:
Never fear. I'll take good care. No one will hold
This bow but you or myself. So hand it over
And then let's trust to our luck.
PHILOCTETES:
                    There, take it, son,           775
And say a prayer to the gods to avert their jealousy.
Pray that this bow will never bring you the trouble
It brought to me and the hero who owned it before me.
NEOPTOLEMUS:
O gods, fulfil this prayer for us both, and grant
A following wind and an easy voyage to wherever                  780
Our journey takes us now, with the god's approval.
PHILOCTETES:
My son, I fear that your prayer will not be answered.
The blood is oozing again from deep inside,
In great red drops. I feel there is worse to come.
    [*Cry of pain.*]

785   Oh, curse you, foot! Can't you leave me alone?
      It's creeping up.
      Here it is coming – now! Oh! Oh!
      Now you know what it's like. Don't run away.
790        [*Another howl.*]
      Damn you, Odysseus, I wish this pain could shoot
      Right through your body and grip you!
           [*Three increasingly loud sounds of pain.*]
      Agamemnon and Menelaus, I wish you both
      Could feel this foul disease instead of me
795   For as long as I have!
           [*Two sharp cries.*]
      Death, death, I call on you to my aid
      Like this every day. Why can you never come?
      My boy, you are nobly born. Seize my body
      And burn me in the volcano, the holy fire
800   Of Lemnos. Be true to your nature. I brought myself
      To do the same for Heracles, son of Zeus,
      The hero who gave me the arms you now are guarding.
      What do you say, my son? Oh, speak!
805   Why are you dumb? You seem to be lost, boy!
      NEOPTOLEMUS:
      Your pain! I felt it before, and I feel it now.
      PHILOCTETES:
      You must take it bravely, my boy. These fits are sharp
      When they first arrive, but they go away as fast.
      Don't leave me here on my own, I beg you.
      NEOPTOLEMUS:
      Don't worry, we'll stay.
      PHILOCTETES:
                              You truly will?
      NEOPTOLEMUS:
810   ·                                              We'll stay.
      PHILOCTETES:
      I shan't ask you to swear an oath, my son.
      NEOPTOLEMUS:
      I'm bound already and may not travel without you.

PHILOCTETES:
Your hand on it, then.
NEOPTOLEMUS [*offers his hand*]:
                    You have it, I promise to stay.
    [PHILOCTETES *looks up to the sky in fresh delirium.*]
PHILOCTETES:
There! Now! Take me there!
NEOPTOLEMUS:
                        Where do you mean?
PHILOCTETES:
                                        Up there!

NEOPTOLEMUS:
Delirious again? Why are you looking up at the sky?                    815
PHILOCTETES:
Let me go, let me go!
NEOPTOLEMUS:
                    Go where?
PHILOCTETES:
                            Just let me go!
NEOPTOLEMUS:
I won't.
PHILOCTETES:
        You'll kill me. Take your hand away!
NEOPTOLEMUS [*releases his hand*]:
All right, if it makes you feel any better.
PHILOCTETES:
O Earth, receive me! Cover me as I am!
This fearful pain – I can stand no longer! [*He collapses.*]                    820
NEOPTOLEMUS:
It won't be a moment, I think, before he falls
Asleep. You see, he's turning on to his back.
Yes, the sweat is bathing the whole of his body.
A vein has burst and a murky stream of blood
Has broken out from the heel of his foot. Come,                    825
Let's leave him in peace, my friends. He must have sleep.

CHORUS:[33]

Sleep, who knows nothing of pain or anguish,              [*Strophe*]
Come with your gentle breezes,
830    Lord of richest, richest blessing!
Shelter his eyes with tranquil dream-light,
Gleam that pervades them now.
Spirit of healing, come!

Young master, where do you stand, sir?
What's the next step?
Tell us how you're thinking.
835    Look, he is quietly sleeping.
What's the point in our waiting?
Occasion rules, and stays for no man.
If you are quíck to móve,
You must wín the príze.

NEOPTOLEMUS [*boldly*]:

Yes, it is true he hears nothing, but I see further than you can.
840    The bow has been captured in vain, if we sail without
Philoctetes.
His is the crown,[34] it is he whom the god has declared we must
bring there.
Shame and disgrace if we boast of failure compounded by
falsehood.

CHORUS:

Surely, young master, the god will provide
for it.                                                   [*Antistrophe*]
When you reply to us next time,
845    Please, I beg you, sir, speak quietly.
Speak in a whisper, sir. In sickness
Sleepers will hardly sleep.
Sight is alive and well.

No, *that* must be your object.
Take it quietly,
850    Take it while he's sleeping,
Try your best to achieve it.
You know well what the man's like.

If you have changed your plan of action,
He won't be eásy. I seé
A black stórm ahéad!

Son, the breezes are blowing fair.                    [Epode]
Now the man is sightless, completely helpless,
Stretched on the ground in the dark,
Powerless in hand and in foot, over anything,
Weak as a fluttering ghost in the underworld.         860
Consíder, wére your gránd wórds
So tímely? If mý advíce
Is sound, go for the plan, my son,
Which savours least of danger.

NEOPTOLEMUS:
Hold your tongues, men, and keep your wits about you.  865
Philoctetes' eyes are moving. He's raising his head.

PHILOCTETES:
To wake, and see the sun, and find my friends
Still watching here – beyond all hope or belief!
My son, I'd never have dared to say that you
Could bear to wait, still pitying my great pain,      870
Still standing by to give me your support.
Those hero generals, the sons of Atreus, never
Managed to face the horror as you have done.
But you, my boy, have a noble nature – true
To your father, Achilles. You've made light of it all –  875
My frightening screams and the filthy stench from my wound.
And now it seems I'm allowed to forget this plague
And relax for a few brief moments. Please, my boy,
Please lift me and set me up on my feet yourself.
And then, as soon as I've recovered my strength,     880
We'll go on board and delay our voyage no longer.

NEOPTOLEMUS:
How glad I am to see you so unexpectedly
Free from pain, eyes open, and still alive.
As you lay asleep, you might have been dead, to judge
By your symptoms after that devastating attack.      885
Here is my hand. Now rise to your feet. Or if

You prefer, these men will lift you. They won't object
To the trouble, since you and I have agreed we're going.
PHILOCTETES:
Thank you, my son. You help me, as you suggest.
890  Don't bother these men. I wouldn't want them upset
By the noxious smell, while that can still be avoided.
Living on board with me will be trouble enough.
NEOPTOLEMUS:
Very well, hold on and get to your feet.
PHILOCTETES:
There now! I always manage it somehow.
      [NEOPTOLEMUS *turns away*.]
NEOPTOLEMUS:
895  Oh god! What shall I do – do now?
PHILOCTETES:
What is it, my son? What on earth are you saying?
NEOPTOLEMUS:
I'm torn apart, and cannot say how!
PHILOCTETES:
You torn? Over what? Don't speak like that.
NEOPTOLEMUS:
That's how I feel at this moment.
PHILOCTETES:
                       Don't say
900  My wound has filled you with such disgust,
You're not prepared to take me on board.
NEOPTOLEMUS:
Disgust is the word – when a man betrays
His own true nature and acts against it!
PHILOCTETES:
But you are helping a man of honour.
In every one of your words and actions
905  You're being true to your noble father.
NEOPTOLEMUS:
Base! That's how the world will regard me.
The thought's been dogging me all along.
PHILOCTETES:
Not base in your acts – but I wonder about your words.

NEOPTOLEMUS:
Zeus, what shall I do? Prove false twice over –
Telling those shameful lies and now concealing
The truth?
PHILOCTETES:
                    Unless I was born a fool,                              910
The man will sail and leave me behind.
NEOPTOLEMUS:
Not leave you behind. I'll take you. But you'll
Regret it. That's why I am so distressed.
PHILOCTETES:
Son, what do you mean? I don't understand.
NEOPTOLEMUS:
Here is the truth. You must sail to Troy                                  915
And join the Greeks on their mission.
PHILOCTETES:
The Greeks! On their mission?
NEOPTOLEMUS:
                                        Don't protest till you know . . .
PHILOCTETES:
Know what? Just how do you mean to treat me?
NEOPTOLEMUS:
To rescue you, first, from this wretched plight,
Then once we are there, to ravage the plains
Of Troy with you at my side.                                             920
PHILOCTETES:
Can this be true? Do you really mean it?
NEOPTOLEMUS:
I have no choice. You mustn't be angry.
PHILOCTETES:
I'm utterly lost, betrayed! You stranger,
What have you done to me? Give me my bow back – quickly!
NEOPTOLEMUS:
I can't. I have to obey my masters.
Right and interest alike demand it.                                       925
PHILOCTETES:
You all-destroying devil! You masterpiece
Of loathsome craftiness! What have you done to me?

How you've deceived me! Wretch, do you feel no shame
930  When you face the man who threw himself on your mercy?
By taking my bow you've taken away my life.
Return it, I beg you. Return it, son, I implore you.
In the name of your father's gods, don't rob me of life.
Oh, heaven help me! He won't even speak to me now.
935  He's looking away and will never hand it back.

You coves and jutting headlands,[35] mountain beasts
Who shared my wild existence, jagged rocks,
You, my familiar neighbours, are all I have.
To you alone I can cry my loud laments.
940  Hear what wrong the son of Achilles has done me!
He swore he would take me home, but he's sweeping me off
To Troy. He gave his right hand's pledge to his word,
But now he has stolen my sacred bow, the bow
Of Heracles, son of Zeus, and means to parade it
945  Before the Greeks. He's marching me off by force,
As though he'd captured a strong man. Can't he see
He's killing a corpse, the shadow of smoke, the merest
Ghost? He couldn't have caught me in my full powers,
And he's only achieved it now by a cowardly trick.
*Me* the victim of fraud! So what shall I do?
950  Give it back. It's not too late to be true to yourself.
What do you say? Silence? Then that's the end.

It's back inside once more to my mansion of rock
With its double entrance, weaponless, there to starve.
Alone in my tunnelled chamber, I'll wither away.
955  That bow won't shoot any birds or mountain beasts
To keep me alive. I'll die, and I myself
Will provide a feast for the creatures I used to feed on.
The beasts I formerly hunted will hunt me now.
Blood for blood, I shall pay the price that I owe them,
960  Because of a man who seemed to be free from guile.
I curse you – no, not yet. I must know first
If you'll change your mind. You won't? Then die in misery!

CHORUS LEADER:
Now, sir, what shall we do? It depends on you.
Should we sail as we are, or listen to this man's pleas?
NEOPTOLEMUS:
It depends on me? I only know he moves me                    965
With terrible pity – I've felt it right from the start.
PHILOCTETES:
In god's name, *show* your pity, my son. You mustn't
Incur the reproach of men for deceiving *me*.
NEOPTOLEMUS:
Oh, what shall I do? I wish I had never left
My home in Scyros! This conflict is torture to me.          970
PHILOCTETES:
*You* are not bad, I'm sure. But wicked men
Have taught you this base behaviour. Leave it to others
And sail. But first return my weapons to *me*.
NEOPTOLEMUS:
What shall we do, men?
      [ODYSSEUS *suddenly appears, followed by two soldiers.*]
ODYSSEUS:
                    Traitor!³⁶ What are you up to?
Back! And hand those weapons over to *me*.                   975
PHILOCTETES:
Who is it? Could that be Odysseus' voice?
ODYSSEUS:
Yes, Odysseus' – it's I, as you see.
PHILOCTETES:
I'm sold and betrayed! So *he* was the man
Who set this trap and has stolen my weapons.
ODYSSEUS:
Yes, it was I, none else. I admit it.                        980
PHILOCTETES:
Quickly! My bow back, son!
ODYSSEUS:
                    He'll never
Do that, however he feels. What's more, you must come
With the bow yourself, or they'll take you away by force.

PHILOCTETES:
By force? You vile, audacious scoundrel!
*Me?* Will these men take me by force?

ODYSSEUS:
985  Yes, if you don't come quietly.

PHILOCTETES:
O land of Lemnos and the fiery power that dwells
In your volcano, is this to be borne?
Will *he* remove me from you by force?

ODYSSEUS:
It's Zeus, I tell you, Zeus who rules this island,
990  Zeus who's determined it. And I'm his servant.

PHILOCTETES:
The pretexts you'll invent, you odious man!
You shelter behind the gods and make them liars.

ODYSSEUS:
No, they reveal the truth. Now come!

PHILOCTETES:
I refuse.

ODYSSEUS:
          I say you must. Obey!

PHILOCTETES:
995  Oh, help me, gods! It's clear my father's son
Was born not to be free but live a slave.

ODYSSEUS:
No, born to vie with heroes, and with them
To capture Troy and bury its towers in the earth.

PHILOCTETES:
Never, whatever hardships I have to face –
1000  So long as this island's cliffs have not caved in.
          [*He starts to move.*]

ODYSSEUS:
What are you trying to do?

PHILOCTETES:
                          To throw myself over
At once, and shatter my head on the rocks below!

ODYSSEUS:
Stop him, you two! Grab hold of his arms!

[PHILOCTETES *is overpowered.*]

PHILOCTETES:

Poor hands, you have been deprived of your own dear bow
And now are powerless. This man has entrapped you both.          1005
Odysseus, your unwholesome, cravenly mind
Has crept up on me again and tracked me down.
You've hidden behind this boy, whom I never knew,
Who was far too good for you, though not for me,
Whose only thought was to carry out his instructions.          1010
But he's already showing remorse for the wrong
He has done in failing himself and making me suffer.
Your evil influence, always spying in corners,
Skilfully taught him, despite his nature, against
His wishes, to practise cunning in doing wrong.          1015
And now, you wretch, you mean to truss my body
And take me away from this shore, where you marooned me,
A friendless, desolate outcast, a living corpse.

Curse you, Odysseus! How often I've made that prayer!
But the gods will never grant me what I desire.          1020
Life is a joy to you, but a pain to me
When I contemplate my wretched, tortured existence,
Mocked by you and the sons of Atreus, the pair
Of generals whose bidding you are performing now.
It's strange. You had to be kidnapped, forced into joining          1025
Their expedition to Troy, while I went freely
With seven ships of my own. Yet I was the one
With the wretched luck to be dishonoured and ditched
By them, as you claim, though they would say it was you.

So why are you taking me now and carting me off?
What for? I'm nothing to you, I've long been dead.          1030
How, you bane of the gods, am I no longer
A stinking cripple? How, if I come on board,
Will you burn your victims or go on pouring libations?
That was your specious pretext for throwing me out.
Perish the lot of you! Perish you surely will          1035
For the injuries done to me, if the gods have any

Concern for justice. I know they have. You'd never
Have crossed the sea in quest of a mouldering wretch,
Unless some spur from heaven were goading you on.
1040    Now, O land of my fathers, watchful gods,
I pray for vengeance, vengeance, late though it be,
On them all, if you can feel any pity for me.
My life is indeed to be pitied, though I'd believe
My sickness was gone, if once I could see them dead.

CHORUS LEADER:
1045    Harsh words from a harsh man. Clearly,
Odysseus, he won't surrender.

ODYSSEUS:[37]
There's much that I could say in reply to his speech,
If time permitted. One thing only for now.
You know I'll play the part the moment calls for,
1050    And if you're looking for just and noble men,
You'll find my pious scruples[38] are second to none.
However, on all occasions, I like to win –
Except over you. And now, for you, I'm willing
To stand aside. Release him, men. Hands off.
1055    Allow him to stay. Now that we have these arms,
We don't need you. Teucer, an excellent marksman,
Is there at Troy, and I think I also can manage
Your bow as well as you and shoot as straight.
1060    So why should we want your help? Goodbye, Philoctetes.
Enjoy your strolls round Lemnos. We must now
Be off on our way. Perhaps your treasured prize
Will bring the honour to me which should have been
    yours.

PHILOCTETES:
Oh, what in the world can I do? Will you
Show off my arms in front of the Greeks?

ODYSSEUS:
1065    No more retorts from you. I'm going.

PHILOCTETES:
Son of Achilles! What? No final word
To me from you? Will you leave like this?

ODYSSEUS:
Make haste and don't look back. Never mind
Your noble instincts. You'll spoil our luck.
    [*Exit* ODYSSEUS.]
PHILOCTETES:
You too, my friends? Will you desert me                        1070
And show no pity?
CHORUS LEADER:
                    This lad's our captain.
What he says goes for us no less.
NEOPTOLEMUS:
The chief will call me too inclined to pity,
But stay behind if Philoctetes would like it.                 1075
The crew will need some time to hoist the sails,
And then we'll have to offer the usual prayers.
Meanwhile, he might begin to think a little
Better of us. I'll after Odysseus, then.
As soon as we call you, quickly follow down.                  1080
    [*Exit* NEOPTOLEMUS.]


# LAMENT[39]


PHILOCTETES:
    O my home in the hollow rock,            [*Strophe 1*]
    Home to heat and the winter's frost,
    So, alas! I was not to leave,
    Never destined to say farewell.
    No, you'll witness my dying.                              1085
    *Ó moí moí moí!*
    Cave which echoed my cries of pain,
    Long condemned to endure my wound,
    What shall now be my daily portion?
    Where shall I find some hope,                             1090
    Hope of providing the food for my nourishment?
    You birds, once so shy,
    Fly as you will in the whistling breezes!
    My power to harm you is all gone.

CHORUS:

1095        You only have yourself to blame, unhappy man.
           Nothing has struck you with force irresistible.
           Where was your better judgement?
           Fáte would have been kínder, but you
1100       Chóse to accépt a wórse life.


PHILOCTETES:

           Wretched, wretched I surely am,                    *[Antistrophe 1]*
           Crúshed and broken by toil and pain.
           No one ever again to come,
           No one ever to share my home,
1105       While I wither and die here.
           *Aíaí, aíaí!*
           Never more to bring home my food,
           Never using my sturdy hands
1110       To wing arrows towards their targets.
           No, I was caught unawares,
           Trapped by the treacherous words of an enemy.
           Could I but see you too,
           Cráfty contriver, enduring for ever
1115       The endless torture that wracks me!

CHORUS:

           The góds impósed this fáte upón you. Whát trapped yóu
           Was not any cunning of mine. You should level
           Your curses and hate at others.
           Mý care and concérn is that you
           Shoúld not rejéct my fríendship.


PHILOCTETES:

           *Oímoi, moí!* I can seé him nów                    *[Strophe 2]*
           Sitting there on the grey sea's edge,
1125       Mocking me, while he fondles
           My whole means of life in his hands,
           Wields what no man wielded before.
           Trusty bow, so dear to my heart,
           Forcibly wrested from loving hands,
1130       Suŕely, I think, if you have any feeling,

You loók in gríef on póor mé,
Heracles' heir, whom you'll serve
Never again to provide for his sustenance.
Anóther mán hólds you nów,                              1135
A designing, ingenious schemer.
Your gáze is on shámeful deceit,
The cruel face of my bitterest foe,
Foé who devised ínfinite wrong,
Sprúng from the most shámeful of ácts agaínst me.

CHORUS:
True men always will plead their causes justly.        1140
Yet once they've spoken, they say no more,
Curb their spite and withdraw their sting.
Our young master was chosen.
Under Odysseus' orders he came,
Helping friends and doing his public duty.             1145

PHILOCTETES:
Yoú winged bírds whom I úsed to húnt,    [Antistrophe 2]
Tribes of beasts who with glaring eyes
Stalk the mountains of Lemnos,
No more need you run from my cave
In flight. Gone is the strength of my hands,           1150
Gone the arrows I shot to kill.
Oh, how wretched this new-found life!
Come as you will, for this place is no longer
A pláce of dréad for yóu, béasts.
Now you can take revenge.                               1155
Now you can feast till you've glutted your maws on my
Fóul, spótted, quívering flésh.
My departure is certain before long.
What élse can still kéep me alive?
Who coúld survive sólely on air,                        1160
Ónce he has lost pówer to gain
Fóod from the earth, gíver of lífe to mórtals?

CHORUS:
Look, man! Won't you respect a kindly stranger?
Can't you see I'm eager to help?

1165       Listen, listen, you truly can
           Break away from this sickness.
           Shame to feed your flesh to the fiend!
           Indeed, none could endure such endless hardship.


PHILOCTETES:
           That old reminder yet again!                     [Epode]
1170       Kínd you've been, déeply kind.
           Still it fills my soul with pain.
           You've done enough. Why kill me now?
CHORUS:
           What dó you méan?
PHILOCTETES:
                               How cán you hópe
1175       That you'll táke me to the háteful land of Tróy, man?
CHORUS:
           It will bé the best thing fór you.
PHILOCTETES:
           You must léave me now at ónce, then.
CHORUS:
           Very wéll, very wéll, I shall dó as you sáy.
           I'll raise no objection.
           Let's make our way shoreward,
1180       Dówn to the ship, báck to our bénches.
PHILOCTETES:
           Pléase do not go. Zéus is above.
           Hé will not let . . .
CHORUS:
                               Quíet, I say!
PHILOCTETES:
                                             Saílors, waít!
           Wait in the name of god!
CHORUS:
1185                               What now?
PHILOCTETES:
           Aiaí, aiaí!
           My fate, my fate! I am utterly lost!
           Oh fóot, fóot! Can I tréat you nów?

How to manage the pain to come?
Sailors, return to me! Back, I implore you!                    1190

CHORUS:
Now whát, sír, do you wánt us to dó?
All these changes of mind confuse us.

PHILOCTETES:
You mustn't be angry.
A man crazy with raging pain
Often says what he doesn't mean.                              1195

CHORUS:
Cóme with us, thén, poor mán, as we téll you.

PHILOCTETES:
I'll never agree to it, never, believe me.
Not if the lord of the fire and the lightning
Comes to set me ablaze with his thunderbolts!
Troy can go hang and the crowd of them there                 1200
Who cruelly hardened their hearts to reject me
Becáuse of my fóot. Nów,
Sailors, one favour, one only – please grant it me!

CHORUS:
What are you asking?

PHILOCTETES:
                              A sword, if you have one.
Pass me a sword or an axe, any weapon!                        1205

CHORUS:
What violent act are you hoping to do, sir?

PHILOCTETES:
To sever my head and my limbs from my body.
It's déath, déath that I séek now.

CHORUS:
Why?

PHILOCTETES:
                    To lóok for my fáthér.                     1210

CHORUS:
Whére, whére?

PHILOCTETES:
                    In the únderwórld.
Súrely hé no lónger líves.

O my city, my father's home,
If only I could see you,
Wretched man that I am,
1215   I who left the river I love
And went to help the Greeks whom I hate!
1217   I'm nothing, I now am nothing.
[*He retires to his cave.*]


# SCENE 4

[*Re-enter* NEOPTOLEMUS, *still with* PHILOCTETES' *bow,
followed by* ODYSSEUS.][40]

ODYSSEUS:
1222   Please tell me why you're coming back!
What's all this frantic haste for, man?
NEOPTOLEMUS:
To undo the wrongs that I did before.
ODYSSEUS:
1225   I don't understand. What wrong have you done?
NEOPTOLEMUS:
I listened to you and the whole Greek army.
ODYSSEUS:
What wicked action did that entail?
NEOPTOLEMUS:
Guile and deceit to entrap a man.
ODYSSEUS:
For god's sake, whom? What crazy idea . . .
NEOPTOLEMUS:
1230   Not crazy at all. To give Philoctetes . . .
ODYSSEUS:
What do you mean to do? I'm frightened.
NEOPTOLEMUS:
To restore this bow I stole to its proper . . .
ODYSSEUS:
What! Are you going to give it back?
NEOPTOLEMUS:
Yes, it was shameful and wrong to take it.

ODYSSEUS:
For heaven's sake, are you joking with me?          1235
NEOPTOLEMUS:
If telling the truth is a joke, I am.
ODYSSEUS:
Look here, Neoptolemus! What do you mean?
NEOPTOLEMUS:
Have I got to repeat it three times over?
ODYSSEUS:
I wish I needn't have heard it once.
NEOPTOLEMUS:
Well, it's all that I have to say.                 1240
ODYSSEUS:
Be careful! You may quite well be prevented . . .
NEOPTOLEMUS:
Tell me, Odysseus, who will prevent me?
ODYSSEUS:
The whole Greek army, myself included.
NEOPTOLEMUS:
A foolish remark for a clever man!
ODYSSEUS:
Your words and actions are no less foolish.        1245
NEOPTOLEMUS:
I'd rather my actions were right than wise.
ODYSSEUS:
How *can* it be right to throw away
What my wise planning has helped you win?
NEOPTOLEMUS:
I made a mistake, a shameful mistake,
And I now must try to retrieve it.
ODYSSEUS:
Aren't you afraid of the Greeks?                   1250
NEOPTOLEMUS:
I'm not, with right on my side.
ODYSSEUS:
Then aren't you afraid of *me*?
NEOPTOLEMUS:
Your threats won't make any difference.

ODYSSEUS:
So now we are fighting *you*,
And not the Trojans.

NEOPTOLEMUS:
                        I'm happy with that.

ODYSSEUS:
1255  You see my hand on the hilt of my sword?

NEOPTOLEMUS:
Two can play at that game. [*He draws his sword.*] Look! I'm
    ready to fight.

ODYSSEUS:
I can't be bothered with you.[41] I'm off
To report to the whole Greek force. They'll get their own back!
    [*Exit.*]

NEOPTOLEMUS:
Wisely done! If you stay that way in future,
1260  You might succeed in steering clear of trouble.
    [*He turns towards the cave.*]
Hey! Philoctetes, sir! I'm calling *you*.
Please come out of your cave. Come on!
    [PHILOCTETES *re-emerges.*]

PHILOCTETES:
Now! What's all this noise and commotion?
Why are you calling me out? Sailors,
What do you want?
    [*Sees* NEOPTOLEMUS.]
1265                    Oh god, it's you!
Not here to add new trouble to old?

NEOPTOLEMUS:
No, no. Please listen to what I've come to say.

PHILOCTETES:
You make me scared. I listened to you before.
Your words were splendid, but I suffered for it.

NEOPTOLEMUS:
1270  Can't a man be allowed to change his mind?

PHILOCTETES:
That's just the way you talked when you stole my bow
And arrows – convincing you were, but a snake in the grass.

NEOPTOLEMUS:
Truly, I'm not so now. I want you to tell me
How you've decided: to stay on Lemnos and face
It out, or to sail with us?

PHILOCTETES:
                    Stop, you needn't        1275
Bother to say any more. It will all be pointless.

NEOPTOLEMUS:
Your mind's made up?

PHILOCTETES:
                More firmly than I can say.

NEOPTOLEMUS:
Oh, how I wish you might have listened to my
Persuasions! But if I'm only wasting my breath,
I'd better give up.

PHILOCTETES:
              Yes, anything now will be useless.   1280
How *can* you ever expect to win me round?
You've taken my bow, you've stolen my means of life
By a gross deception, and then you come to read me
A lecture – you, the son of the noble Achilles,
But now my bitterest foe. To hell with you all –
The Atridae first, then with Laertes' son,       1285
And finally you!

NEOPTOLEMUS:
          No need to curse any further.
Here are your bow and arrows. Take them back.

PHILOCTETES:
What? Are you playing another trick?

NEOPTOLEMUS:
                       I'm not.
I swear it in holy awe of Zeus supreme.

PHILOCTETES:
These are most welcome words, if you're telling the truth.   1290

NEOPTOLEMUS:
My actions will prove me true. Put out your hand.
These weapons belong to you. Take hold of them now.
    [*Re-enter* ODYSSEUS.][42]

ODYSSEUS:
But I forbid it – the gods will bear me witness –
In the name of the sons of Atreus and all the army!

PHILOCTETES:
1295  My son, whose voice was that? Did I hear Odysseus?

ODYSSEUS:
Yes, you did! And you see him close at hand.
I'll force you to come with me to the plain of Troy,
Whether Achilles' son approves or not.

PHILOCTETES:
It'll be to your cost, if this arrow flies to its mark.

NEOPTOLEMUS:
1300  Don't shoot, for heaven's sake!

PHILOCTETES:
Dear son, let go my hand!

NEOPTOLEMUS:
I won't let go.
          [*Exit* ODYSSEUS.]

PHILOCTETES:
                    Too late! Why have you stopped me
Using my weapons to kill my hated foe?

NEOPTOLEMUS:
It would do no credit either to you or to me.

PHILOCTETES:
1305  Well, one thing's certain: these military chiefs,
These blustering spokesmen may be bold in their speech,
But when it comes to a fight, they're arrant cowards.

NEOPTOLEMUS:
All right. At least you have your bow, and there's no more
Reason for you to blame or be angry with *me*.

PHILOCTETES:
1310  That's so. You've proved the stock you're made of, boy.
Your father wasn't a cheat like Sisyphus.[43] No,
You're the son of Achilles, known as the greatest hero
Among the living and now in the underworld.

NEOPTOLEMUS:
Philoctetes, I'm touched to hear you praising my father
1315  And praising me. Now listen to what I want you

To do. All men are bound to endure with patience
The various chances of life which heaven brings.
But if they cling to trouble that's self-inflicted,
As you are doing, they don't deserve any pity
Or understanding. You've grown too brutal. You won't          1320
Accept advice, and if somebody out of kindness
Makes a suggestion, you hate him as though he were
Your implacable foe. But still, I'm going to speak,
And I call on Zeus, god of oaths, to bear me witness.
Mark what I say, and carefully take it to heart.[44]          1325

The painful sickness you have is sent from heaven.
You disturbed the goddess Chryse's watcher,[45] the secret
Inmate guarding her roofless shrine, the snake.
And while the same sun mounts the sky in the east            1330
And sinks in the west, you'll never obtain relief
From your sickness until you come to the plain of Troy
Of your own volition. There you will meet Asclepius'
Sons, who will cure your wound. And then, with the help
Of the bow and me, you'll bring the citadel down.            1335

How do I know all this? Let me tell you now.
Among the prisoners we hold at Troy is an excellent
Seer, Helenus, son of Priam. He tells us
Clearly that all these things must be. What's more,
Troy is bound to be captured this very summer.               1340
He offers to let us kill him, if he's proved false.

Now that you know this, surely you must agree,
And gladly. You have so much to gain. First,
To come into healing hands, and then to be judged            1345
The foremost hero of Greece, by taking Troy,
The city of sorrows, and winning the highest glory.
PHILOCTETES:
Life is so cruel! Why must I stay alive
On earth and not be allowed to go to Hades?
What *am* I to do? How can I reject the words                1350
Of advice this boy has offered me out of kindness?

But must I yield, then? How, oh how, if I do,
Could I show myself in public? Who would speak to me?
How could my eyes which have witnessed all I've suffered
1355 Bear to see Philoctetes out in Troy,
Joining the sons of Atreus, his own destroyers,
There with Odysseus, their cursed agent in evil?
Resentment of all their past ill-treatment worries me
Less than how I foresee I must be treated
1360 By them in the future. Minds which generate evil
School men's hearts to evil in all that follows.

*You* surprise me, too: you shouldn't be going
To Troy yourself and ought to be keeping me
Away from the place. Those generals did you an outrage
1365 In robbing you of your father's arms. Will you
Still fight on their side and force me to do the same?
You can't, my son. No, take me back to my home,
As you swore to do. Stay in Scyros yourself,
And leave those rotten men to a rotten death.
That way you'll earn my father's thanks and my own
1370 Twice over. And further, you won't by helping scoundrels
Allow the world to think you a scoundrel too.

NEOPTOLEMUS:
You're right, I suppose. But still I want you to put
Your faith in the gods and in what I've told you. Sail
1375 From Lemnos with me. You know that I am your friend.

PHILOCTETES:
What! Sail to Troy? And face Agamemnon,
My deadliest foe, with this wretched foot?

NEOPTOLEMUS:
No, no! Face men who will soothe the pain
In that oozing limb and cure your malady.

PHILOCTETES:
1380 Shocking counsel! What are you saying?

NEOPTOLEMUS:
What I see will be best in the end for us both.

PHILOCTETES:
For us both? Do you feel no shame before god?

NEOPTOLEMUS:
Can a man feel shame when he's helping his friends?
PHILOCTETES:
Helping the sons of Atreus, or me?
NEOPTOLEMUS:
You, of course, as I am your friend,
And all that I urge is urged in friendship.                    1385
PHILOCTETES:
How, when you want to betray me to *them*?
NEOPTOLEMUS:
Dear man, how proud your suffering's made you!
PHILOCTETES:
This nagging will be my ruin, I know.
NEOPTOLEMUS:
Ruin you? I? You don't understand!
PHILOCTETES:
Not understand those generals marooned me?            1390
NEOPTOLEMUS:
Yes, they did. But what if they now
Restore you to health?
PHILOCTETES:
                         They'll never restore me,
Not if it means my agreeing to go to Troy.⁴⁶
NEOPTOLEMUS:
Oh, what can *I* do now? Persuasion's failed.
You won't agree to anything I say.
It's time I finished arguing, while you                         1395
Must go on living as you are, unhealed.
PHILOCTETES:
Just let me suffer what I have to suffer. [*Pause.*]
Neoptolemus, look!
You promised me on oath to take me home.
Fulfil that promise to me now, my son.
Don't dilly-dally or mention the name of Troy           1400
Again. I've heard it bandied often enough.


NEOPTOLEMUS:
Óff at ónce, then,⁴⁷ íf you sáy so.

PHILOCTETES:
                            Nóbly spóken, like a mán!

NEOPTOLEMUS:
Walk, your hand upon my shoulder.[48]

PHILOCTETES:
                            Yes, with all the strength I have.

NEOPTOLEMUS:
Won't the Greeks be angry? I'll be killed for this.

PHILOCTETES:
                            Don't worry, son.

NEOPTOLEMUS:
Why, suppose they try to lay my country waste?

PHILOCTETES:
1405                                      I shall be there.

NEOPTOLEMUS:
What will you do to help me, then?

PHILOCTETES:
                            I'll use the bow of Heracles!

NEOPTOLEMUS:
How do you mean?

PHILOCTETES:
                    They won't come near you.

NEOPTOLEMUS:
                    Kiss the soil, and come away!

## CLOSING SCENE[49]

[HERACLES *appears above.*][50]

HERACLES:
    Not yet! You must listen to *my* commands,[51]
1410  Philoctetes, before you part from this island.
    It is Heracles' voice that you hear, his face
    That you see. And for your dear sake I have left
    My abode in the sky.
1415  I have left it to tell you the counsels of Zeus
    And to halt your course on the voyage you plan.
    Give ear to my solemn pronouncement.
  First I shall say how fortune dealt with me:

After the many labours I performed,
I won eternal glory, as you see.
The same, be sure, is owed to you: through all                 1420
This suffering to glorify your life.
You'll go with Neoptolemus to Troy,
Where first your painful wound will soon be healed.
Then, chosen for your prowess from the host,
You'll use my bow and arrows to bring down                     1425
Paris, the cause of all this bitter strife.
When you've sacked Troy, the army will present
You with the prize of valour, and you'll bear
Your spoils back to your home on Oeta's heights                1430
To show your father Poeas. Do not fail,
Whatever spoils the army grants to you,
To lay a portion on my pyre in tribute
To my bow. Now, Neoptolemus,
My words concern you too. You'll not take Troy
Without his aid, nor he without your help.                     1435
No, each one guard the other, like two lions
Prowling the bush together. [to PHILOCTETES:] I shall send
Asclepius to heal your wounds in Troy.
The citadel must be captured by my bow
A second time.⁵² But when you lay the land
To waste, remember this: show piety                            1440
Towards the gods, since nothing ranks so high
With Zeus. For piety does not die with men.
Men live or die, but piety cannot perish.⁵³
PHILOCTETES:
    O voice that I longed so dearly to hear,
    You are with me at last,
    I shall not disobey what you bid me do.                     1445
NEOPTOLEMUS:
    I too accept the will of the gods.
HERACLES:
    No waiting here, then. Straight into action!
    Time presses, and look!                                    1450
    The wind has veered and is set fair.
        [*Exit* HERACLES.]

PHILOCTETES:
　　Come now, let me greet this land[54] as I go.
　　Farewell, my cave, who shared in my watch.
　　Farewell, you nymphs of the watery meads.
1455　Farewell, deep boom of the waves on the cape.
　　Farewell, the driving spray that so often
　　Drenched my head in the depths of the rock.
　　Farewell to the mount of Hermes, which often
　　Returned me the sound of my own lone voice
1460　As I howled and groaned in the storm of my pain.
　　And now, you springs and Lycian Apollo's
　　Fountain,[55] I leave you, now I must leave you,
　　You whom I never thought to abandon.
　　So farewell, seagirt island of Lemnos,
1465　And send me forth on a perfect voyage,
　　To where I am summoned by mighty Fate,
　　By the will of my friends and the power supreme
　　Who has brought these things to fulfilment.
　　　[*Exeunt* PHILOCTETES *and* NEOPTOLEMUS *to the shore.*]
CHORUS:
　　Sailors all, let us follow together
1470　And pray to the nymphs of the ocean to come
　　And guide us homeward in safety.
　　　[*The* CHORUS *follows.*]

# Notes

## WOMEN OF TRACHIS

1. *Trachis*: Trachis was a city in northern Greece, not far to the west of Thermopylae. It was ruled by King Ceyx (not named in the play), at whose house Heracles and Deïanira are staying in exile from Tiryns (39–40).

2. *Scene 1*: Deïanira's monologue provides a quiet, but uneasy, opening to a play of violent passions. Its keynote is her fear: first of marriage with the multiform river god, then for the absent Heracles. The introduction of the Nurse and Hyllus establishes Heracles' return as the theme that will drive the plot, and the mention of the mysterious tablets (46, 76–81) sounds a note of impending crisis.

3. *An old saying ... his death*: 'Call no man happy until he is dead' is a famous Greek maxim, commonly attributed to the Athenian statesman Solon. The historian Herodotus (1.32, 86–7) tells the story of how Solon spoke these words to Croesus, the extremely wealthy king of Lydia, who was at first confident of his prosperity and inclined to ignore them. Years later, however, Croesus was defeated by the Persian king and about to be burned on a pyre (like Heracles at the end of this play), when he recalled the warning Solon had given him. He was rescued from death by the gods (again like Heracles, though in his case only temporarily), who sent a storm to quench the flames. Deïanira's quotation thus has a special resonance in the context of the Heracles story. It also asserts the important theme of the mutability of human fortune at the very outset of the play.

4. *shimmering*: Sophocles uses a rather unusual adjective *aiolos*, applied here and at 834 to a serpent and to night (shimmering with stars) at 94 and 132. The word seems to combine the

ideas of variegation and rapid motion, another instance of the 'mutability' theme.

5. *Enter Nurse from palace*: She probably enters at this point (or perhaps at 40), so that she can appear to hear what Deïanira says and to be responding to her mistress when she speaks herself. An example of a 'dovetailed' entrance (see Preface p. 12).

6. *Iphitus*: The son of Eurytus, king of Oechalia. The story of his killing is told at 270ff.

7. *Lydian woman*: Queen Omphale, whom Heracles had to serve for a year (252–3) to obtain purification for the murder of Iphitus.

8. *Euboea*: A long island in the Aegean Sea, lying off the coasts of Attica, Boeotia and Locris. The precise location of Oechalia (75) is uncertain.

9. *Choral entrance song*: In Strophe I the Chorus of young Trachinian women adopts the form of a prayer-hymn to call on Helios, the sun god, to reveal Heracles' whereabouts. In the two antistrophes, they voice their sympathy for the anxious Deïanira. In 129–31 the imagery articulates the cycle of change in human life, a theme reinforced hopefully in the epode: sorrow and anxiety yield to joy, and Zeus would not neglect one of his own sons. The change motif is echoed in a remarkable rhythmical effect in the structure of 116–21 (= 126–31): the sequence of heavy and light syllables places the distinctive 'choriamb' ♩ ♫ ♩ at the *end* of the first three lines, but then transposes it to the *beginning* of the second three lines. The translation aims to bring this out, as shown by the placing of stress marks.

10. *O Sun ... cradle of flame*: In nature's alternations, Night is both the mother and the destroyer of Day. The Chorus' opening words, like Deïanira's, are charged with deeper layers of significance. The Sun to which it appeals is still under the control of Night. Furthermore, the word translated by 'spoiled' can also mean 'killed'; the play tells the story of Heracles killed and laid to rest in flames. For 'shimmering' see note 4.

11. *To eastward ... straddling continents*: The translation takes the Chorus to be referring to the extremities of the Mediterranean world: the Pontus (Black Sea) to the east and the so-called Pillars of Hercules (Straits of Gibraltar) to the far west. In the latter, Heracles is imagined as a giant grasping the pillars that 'straddle' the continents. This interpretation also accords with the daily passage of the sun.

12. *Hades*: The Greek underworld and home of the dead.

13. *Deïanira re-enters from the palace*: Probably another 'dovetailed' entrance which contributes to the smooth flow of the drama.

14. *King Zeus ... distress*: Zeus, already named at 19 as Heracles' father, is now linked to the theme of suffering as part of the texture of human life.

15. *For who beheld ... own sons?* The Chorus' optimism is belied by the play's action, but not by its implicit conclusion in Heracles' apotheosis.

16. *Scene 2*: The play's situation and themes are absorbingly developed in the next long sequence. First Deïanira shares her anxiety with the Chorus and heightens the sense of impending crisis by describing the tablet Heracles left behind before his last journey. Excitement follows in the Messenger's announcement of Heracles' forthcoming return after a victory abroad, and the Chorus responds in an ecstatic dance-song with powerful (and ironic) overtones of marriage ritual. This culminates in the processional entry of the captive women, led by Lichas, with Heracles' concubine, the beautiful princess Iole, prominent among them. The ensuing scene shows Deïanira being caught in a web of deception by Lichas' garbled account of Heracles' activities during his fifteen-month absence and by his feigned ignorance regarding the identity of Iole, to whom Deïanira seems strangely drawn. The withdrawal of the procession into the house marks the beginning of Deïanira's un-deception. By the end of the episode, she has learned the truth about Iole and apparently accepted it with a degree of equanimity. Here Sophocles makes excellent use of his third actor to mount a dramatic triangular scene with his two messengers in stichomythic confrontation, one of them prepared to lie to spare Deïanira's feelings, the other determined to tell the truth at all costs. The theme of knowledge is brilliantly explored: is blissful ignorance to be preferred to painful enlightenment?

17. *ancient tablet*: The theme of oracles in written form is repeated (compare 46, 76–81). The substance of this tablet is disclosed in 166–9, and its source in the words of the 'talking' oak at Dodona (in northern Greece, where Zeus had an oracle) in 171–3. Heracles himself refers to it (1165–73) when he perceives its full significance.

18. *twin priestesses*: Known as the Doves, who interpreted the sounds emitted by the oak in the rustling of its branches.

19. *No more ill-omened words*: The idea that ordinary words are omens with power to affect the future favourably or adversely

is rooted deep in the ancient Greek consciousness. Related to dramatic irony, it plays an important part in the dynamic of Aeschylus' and Sophocles' tragedies.

20. *O Zeus ... Oeta's / Heights*: Deïanira's cry of joy (the only one she utters in the whole play) ironically contains the first of numerous references to Oeta, the highest mountain in Malis, and the mythical scene of Heracles' funeral pyre. There is archeological evidence for a cult of Heracles on Oeta in pre-classical times.

21. *song of joy*: This jubilant 'number' for the Chorus unites the praise of several gods and contains echoes of the form of worship appropriate to each: Apollo (209) and Artemis (214), to whom the paean is raised; the nymphs in the local region of Malis (215); and Bacchus / Dionysus, god of revelry (220), who is normally worshipped in a dithyramb. There is also the suggestion of a wedding ritual (208), which will ostensibly reunite Deïanira with Heracles, but the chorus' words are realized ironically in the arrival of Heracles' new bride, Iole, destined to be the mother of a 'foul fiend', in Greek 'Erinys', a spirit of vengeance (893–5). The agitated 'dochmiac' rhythm (see *Electra* note 62) used in several metrical phrases contributes to the excitement.

22. *pipe*: The instrument called the *aulos*, along with the cry *euhoi* and the ivy crown (219), is associated with the worship of Dionysus.

23. *tribute-bearing soil*: Ground which will yield produce for offerings to Zeus.

24. *Lichas*: The herald's narration is chronologically confused, perhaps reflecting the fact that Lichas is deceiving Deïanira over Heracles' motives for the sack of Oechalia.

25. *Unhappy girl*: There is a wonderful irony in Deïanira's address to her unknown rival, Iole, whose princess-like 'dignity' (312) she instinctively recognizes and feels compassion for. Some in the original audience might have compared Heracles' wife with Clytemnestra in Aeschylus' *Agamemnon*, who addresses her own imported rival, the prophetess Cassandra, far less sympathetically (*Agam.* 1035ff., a passage that contains a reference to Heracles' servitude to Omphale). Iole's failure to reply here (and after 321) is dictated by the 'mute mask' convention, which only allows the three main actors to speak, but it is nicely motivated at 322ff.

26. *No, I beg you*: This remarkable speech, though unexpected, is very much in character for the understanding and compassionate Deïanira, even if we learn later on (531ff.) that her tolerance has

been strained to the limit. It certainly convinces Lichas. Her lines on the irresistible power of Love (441ff.) and its description as a sickness (445, repeated in 491–2) are central to the play's thought, and they apply ironically to Deïanira herself no less than to Heracles.

27. *You can't engage . . . with Love*: But that is just what Deïanira later attempts to do.

28. *But knowing – what's so dreadful in that*: The knowledge that Lichas, under pressure, communicates to Deïanira, will eventually lead to her death. More irony. In 459–60 Sophocles also draws on the tradition of Heracles as a notorious womanizer.

29. *Your husband's prowess . . . defeat*: The theme of Heracles as the 'greatest man in the world' (177) is repeated.

30. *And also carry a gift*: This looks forward to the next scene. There is no reason to suppose that Deïanira has already thought of sending the anointed robe – though the phrase 'fitting response' is an attempt to render the unconsciously ominous use of a Greek verb which could apply to the clinging tunic that destroys Heracles. There might be the slightest tinge of deliberate irony in Deïanira's concluding sentence.

31. *Choral song 1*: This powerful ode takes up the theme of Love from the preceding scene and praises Aphrodite, the goddess of love and sex, who presided over the fight between Heracles and the river god Achelous to win Deïanira. In exciting, fast-moving rhythms (which recall some of the victory odes composed by the poet Pindar in honour of successful athletes) the Chorus describes the battle first mentioned in Deïanira's opening speech (20–25). The brutal physicality of the two contestants is contrasted in the epode with the picture of the lonely Deïanira at 523ff. (where the rhythm changes to a gentle lilt), as she sits on the hillside awaiting the outcome of the fight. So the poetry focuses again on the heroine in preparation for the scene to come. The first, third and seventh lines in the strophe and antistrophe presuppose a sharp instrumental downbeat to launch the rapid rhythm.

32. *the Cyprian goddess*: A regular title for Aphrodite, who rose at her birth from the sea around Cyprus and had her main cult at Paphos.

33. *the Olympian lord . . . Poseidon*: The three most powerful gods are specified as victims of love. There were numerous stories of Zeus' and Poseidon's amours with mortal women, and Hades abducted Persephone.

34. *pounding fists*: Despite the wealth of Heracles' weaponry (511–12), the language here recalls the 'boxing match' imagery of 441.

35. *ladder-like*: The reference is to a special hold in the *pankration*, where the wrestler jumped onto his opponent's back and knotted his arms and legs round him.

36. *For me . . . watched there*: The Greek text here is corrupt, but it may recall Deïanira's words in 22–3, as the translation attempts to do. 528 is similarly uncertain.

37. *Scene 3*: Deïanira is now, after all, unwilling to share Heracles with Iole. In the longest of her seven big speeches, she outlines to the Chorus her plan to regain Heracles' love by a charm based on the blood of the centaur Nessus, whom Heracles had killed long previously in circumstances described in a vivid narration. Deïanira has now elected to resort to magic to fight Love (see note 27), and the Chorus naively approves. The seal is set on Heracles' (and her own) fate when she hands to Lichas the sealed casket containing the poisoned robe. At this point her tone is optimistic, as she imagines Heracles glamorously attired in public for the grand sacrifice at Cenaeum, which will, ironically, entail his own death.

38. *contrived*: The word in Greek has a sinister ring.

39. *extra item of freight*: In making Deïanira use this kind of language about Iole, Sophocles may have been thinking of Clytemnestra's words about Cassandra in Aeschylus (*Agamemnon* 1446–7), after she has murdered her husband.

40. *centaur*: A mythical creature, part man and part horse, associated with 'days gone by' (555).

41. *Hydra of Lerna*: Heracles' second labour was to destroy this monster, a poisonous multi-headed water-snake living in the marshes of Lerna near Argos. After killing it, he dipped his arrows in the Hydra's blood, which made the wounds they inflicted incurable.

42. *You'll only know . . . you try*: This is crucial advice, as it confirms Deïanira's plan to send the anointed robe. She, in her characteristic diffidence, is bound to consult the Chorus (586–7) while their youth, established early on (144ff.), accounts for their simplicity in encouraging such a dangerous experiment.

43. *to clinch the matter*: Another ominous expression (see note 30). Heracles will be held in the poisoned robe's 'clinch' (767–9).

44. *I fear . . . for me*: Moving lines for the conclusion of the scene. Deïanira's optimism seems already clouded by her usual apprehension, and she is perhaps speaking more to herself than to Lichas.

45. *Choral song 2*: The Chorus picks up Deïanira's earlier mood of

hopeful expectation in an ode that looks forward to Heracles' eager return to his wife's arms. They imagine this event attended by strains of music and song, and introduce it by evoking a beautiful local landscape and seascape with strong historical and religious associations. This movement of deluded joy is in ironical contrast (like their dance-song at 205ff.) with the blow that is about to fall – a typical Sophoclean ploy.

46. *O harbours and rocks ... Great Gates*: The Chorus apostrophizes the local inhabitants by invoking the geographical and other features of the area round Trachis. Mt Oeta has already been mentioned twice (200, 437). Thermopylae was renowned for the famous battle there in the Persian Wars, and its hot sulphur springs were associated in myth and cult with Heracles. The Gulf of Malis is surrounded on three sides by land and so can be called a lake. Artemis was worshipped along the eastern coast of Greece and had titles linking her with harbours and marshes. Not far from Thermopylae, at the modern Kallipodi, there was a shrine dating from pre-classical times to Artemis Elaphobolia, the deer-shooter (see 214). The area was also famous as the seat of the ancient Amphictyonic League, a council of different Greek states that concerned itself with cults and sanctuaries. The council took its name, Pylaea, from the pass of Thermopylae, referred to here as 'the Great Gates', near the shrine of Demeter at Anthela, where the council was held.

47. *a weary twelve-month*: Fifteen months, actually (44, 166), but Heracles' servitude had lasted a year.

48. *Melted ... gift*: The irony of the Chorus' lines is extremely sinister, even if the Greek text here is very uncertain.

49. *Scene 4*: The mood now is totally reversed. Deïanira's hopes have been turned to profound fear by what has happened to the wool she used for anointing her present of the robe with the centaur's blood – the experiment she might sensibly have carried out beforehand (see 591). The last of her long speeches is another gripping narrative, balanced and complemented by Hyllus' equally fine account of what resulted when Heracles actually donned the robe. Disaster has now struck, and Hyllus' furious denunciation of his mother for murdering his father leads to her deeply eloquent exit in silence.

50. *Graven ... tablets*: The metaphor links Nessus' instructions with the real tablet of 46 and 156–7. The message on both tablets is misunderstood.

51. *old Chiron*: The divine centaur, known as a healer and great

teacher of heroes, was accidentally shot by Heracles and given an incurable wound.

52. *more of a heart*: Given Deïanira's gentle and compassionate nature, this line is deeply ironical – the more so, if her characterization was an innovation of Sophocles.

53. *The crowd broke silence*: This must mean the silence religiously kept at a sacrifice if it was not to be interrupted by ill-omened cries. See *Philoctetes* note 2.

54. *the very greatest . . . in the world*: Compare 177, 488–9.

55. *Choral song 3*: The play's centre of gravity is at last shifting towards Heracles himself. In the first pair of strophes, the women of Trachis perceive the truth behind the oracle that the present time will win the hero rest from his labours: his rest is to be death, through the centaur Nessus' vengeful contriving, in the grip of the Hydra's poison. In the second pair, the Chorus bemoans Deïanira's plight. Her and her husband's joint tragedy is the manifest work of Cyprian Aphrodite, the gods' silent handmaid (860).

56. *twelfth long year*: The Chorus must be referring to the oracle mentioned by Deïanira in 76ff., which relates to Heracles' absence of fifteen months (44). The mention here of twelve years can only refer to the time when the prophecy was uttered at Dodona (171ff., 1167ff.). The introduction of this further detail is typical of Sophocles' technique (also seen in *Philoctetes*) of *gradually* revealing the gods' purposes.

57. *Scene 5*: The Nurse announces Deïanira's suicide in an exchange with the Chorus that probably includes singing as well as speech (see note 59). She then poignantly describes the death in the last compelling narrative speech of the play. No less moving is her account of Hyllus' grief in the knowledge, acquired too late, that he has unfairly denounced his mother – a crucial point of continuity with what is to come.

58. *cry of lamentation*: Sophocles uses offstage cries to telling effect in the course of his drama (compare *Ajax* 333, *Electra* 77, *Philoctetes* 201).

59. *What passion . . . violent act*: These lines (and 893–5) were probably sung by the whole Chorus (in lyric metre intensifying the emotion), while their Leader spoke the other verses in iambic dialogue with the Nurse.

60. *foul fiend*: See note 21.

61. *And for . . . fatherless*: This translates an uncertain restoration of a corrupt line.

62. *My bed*: There is a special poignancy in Deïanira's killing herself
    on the bed she had shared with Heracles and expected to have
    to share (metaphorically, at least) with Iole as well (538–40).

63. *stabbed . . . two-edged sword*: In two other Sophocles tragedies
    (*Antigone* and *Oedipus Rex*), women kill themselves by hanging
    from a noose; so Deïanira's employment of a man's weapon, a
    sword, is peculiarly shocking. Some critics have been conscious
    of a phallic connotation in this detail, but Deïanira drives the
    sword into her side and so links her death to Heracles, to whose
    sides the poisoned robe is clinging (768ff., 1083).

64. *Close to her side*: The side again. Hyllus embraces his mother's
    dead body almost like a lover. He later touches and lifts Heracles
    on his litter (1020, 1025), another link between the two deaths.

65. *You cannot / Count . . . today*: The Nurse's final utterance recalls
    Deïanira's opening words (1–3).

66. *Choral song 4*: The rhythm of the first very short pair of strophes
    (three lines each) is like the drumbeat of a funeral march, as the
    Chorus links the combined tragedies of Deïanira and Heracles.
    Strophe 2 follows the pattern of an 'escape prayer'; the women
    shrink from the sight they must soon witness and long to be far
    away. The antistrophe dovetails with the arrival of the procession
    carrying the dying Heracles onstage. This is the 'return' of the
    great hero, to which the dynamic of the plot so far has been
    tending.

67. *Closing scene*: At last the conquering hero has returned, but
    borne home prostrate on a litter and shortly to die. The drama
    now shows Heracles moving through a demonstration of violent
    pain and rage to some understanding of the gods' purpose for
    him. At the end he is carried off to the pyre on Mt Oeta, from
    where he is (implicitly) to be transported to Olympus as a god
    whom mortals worship in cult. This long single movement is
    skilfully varied in a structure that uses the different resources of
    sound and tone existing in the three different 'modes of utterance'.

68. *Oimoi*: Hyllus' grief-stricken cry starts this opening section (to
    1002) in anapaestic mode.

69. *Old Man*: This character seems to be some kind of doctor in
    attendance.

70. *O Zeus*: Heracles' first words are to call on his father.

71. *E! E!*: Heracles now launches into a sung sequence of lyric
    phrases, interrupted by a run (probably spoken) of five dactylic
    hexameters. This structure is repeated in an antistrophe (1023–
    43) after five intervening hexameters for the Old Man and Hyllus.

72.  *Pallas Athena*: The goddess was Heracles' special helper, as she
     is Odysseus' in *Philoctetes* (134).

73.  *I shudder to hear*: The dialogue returns to normal metrical mode.

74.  *How many burning labours*: In this long rhetorical speech, Her-
     acles compares his present suffering with the hardships he
     endured on his various heroic exploits, including (in the latter
     part of the speech) some of the famous twelve labours he per-
     formed at the behest of Eurystheus, king of Tiryns. (The reader
     who wishes to follow these up is referred to a classical diction-
     ary.) The recital is dramatically interrupted by the horrific
     moment when Heracles throws off his coverings and exposes his
     body with the poisoned robe clinging to it.

75.  *earth-born / Giants*: Heracles fought with the gods in the famous
     battle against the Giants.

76.  *monster dog*: Cerberus.

77.  *I see*: The mention of Nessus (1141) leads to a great moment of
     recognition, after which the atmosphere changes completely from
     the violent bitterness that has dominated Heracles hitherto. He
     takes control of his future with new-found calm.

78.  *Many years ago ... killed the living*: This oracle (typically
     expressed in the form of a paradox) has not been mentioned
     before and completes the picture (see note 56): the centaur, not
     Deïanira, is the ultimate cause of Heracles' death. The same
     paradox occurs in *Ajax* 1026–7 and *Electra* 1417ff.

79.  *Dodona*: See note 17.

80.  *pray for punishment*: Oaths in Greece generally included this
     kind of rider.

81.  *That is the place*: Heracles' instructions for his immolation on
     Mt Oeta would have taken Sophocles' audience into the realm
     of contemporary cult. Interestingly, Heracles gives no orders for
     the disposal of his bones after cremation. The poet may be hinting
     that this will not be necessary, as Heracles will be transferred
     from the mountain-top to Olympus.

82.  *do all the rest*: Hyllus has to be excused from lighting the pyre,
     as this task was performed in the tradition by Philoctetes or his
     father, Poeas.

83.  *No other man ... but you*: This command can be taken as typical
     of Heracles' gross egocentricity, and Hyllus is horrified at the
     thought of the pollution that marriage with Iole would entail.
     No doubt Sophocles is also taking account of the tradition that
     the historical Heraclidae, who conquered the Peloponnese in the
     Dorian invasion, were the descendants of Hyllus and Iole.

84. *Come then*: The concluding section returns to anapaests, as it began.
85. *the end will be joyful*: See Preface p. 10 and note 1.
86. *No man ... to come*: Another ironical hint of the approaching apotheosis. Sophocles likes to refer obliquely to traditional sequels to the stories or cults on which his plays are based. Compare *Electra* 1498, *Philoctetes* 1441.
87. *We have witnessed ... great Zeus*: The Chorus again unites the tragedies of Deïanira and Heracles (compare 947–9). The final line is mysterious and its interpretation much disputed. I agree with those who see it in the light of an implied apotheosis. See Preface p. 8.

# AJAX

1. *Scene 1*: Sophocles gives his drama an arresting start with Odysseus prowling warily around, then suddenly alerted by the ringing voice of Athena. The facts of the night raid on the sheep and of its causes are vividly recounted before the central moment of grisly spectacle when Ajax himself comes out, still in the exaltation of the delirium induced by Athena. The aftermath of his brief appearance introduces the themes of Odysseus' pity, Ajax's arrogance and the mutability of human affairs.
2. *Athena*: It is hard to be certain how the goddess was revealed in the ancient theatre. At the start she is evidently out of Odysseus' vision (15), but the dialogue from 36 on seems to demand closer contact. Perhaps the opening speech was delivered from the roof of the *skênê* or on a platform hoisted above it (certainly used for divine appearances in some later plays). The actor could have disappeared from view during Odysseus' speech at 14ff., to re-enter at ground level towards the end (at 34, say) and then to engage in the stichomythia that follows. For a suggested means of effecting this second entry, see note 69.
3. *Tuscan trumpet call*: There was a tradition that the trumpet was invented by Athena for the Etruscans.
4. *lord of the shield*: In the *Iliad*, Ajax has a huge, tower-like shield, made of seven layers of ox-hide. It symbolized his status as a great warrior.
5. *the two Atridae*: The sons of Atreus, Agamemnon and Menelaus, whom Ajax holds responsible for the award of Achilles' arms to Odysseus. The brothers are normally referred to by this name.

6. *Odysseus*: The tense dialogue, revealing Odysseus' fear of Ajax in his madness, provides a fine build-up to the hero's first striking entrance. In the original, the speeches are in single lines.

7. *whip*: The whip is an inference from the play's title, *Ajax the Whip-Bearer*, in an ancient catalogue of tragedies.

8. *How well ... my side*: In typical Sophoclean irony, Ajax here and in his exit line at 117 perceives Athena as a close ally.

9. *I'm bound to pity him*: Odysseus' surprising compassion prepares the audience for his espousal of Ajax's cause before Agamemnon in the closing scene.

10. *An arrogant word*: This foreshadows the explanation given by the prophet Calchas for Athena's anger with Ajax, as recounted by the Messenger (756–77).

11. *One day ... human life*: A recurrent theme in the play. The final reversal of Ajax's fortunes can be anticipated, even on Athena's lips.

12. *The gods love ... ignoble men*: See Preface p. 65.

13. *Choral entrance song*: This falls into two sections, the first in anapaestic metre, the second in the form of a lyric triad. In 134–71, the Chorus of Salaminian sailors identify themselves with Ajax and recount the rumours about their master's raid on the cattle. In 172–200, now in song, they seek an explanation for Ajax's madness and behaviour, and call on him to quell the laughter and spite of his foes.

14. *If you aim ... this wisdom*: This reflection on the vulnerability of the great to slander, and then on the interdependence of the weak and the powerful, is more appropriate to the fifth-century *polis* than to the individualistic world of Homer's heroes. The metaphor used is drawn from architecture, likewise more reflective of Sophocles' own era: the gaps between the large stones of a defensive wall need to be filled with smaller ones.

15. *Artemis ... bull-enthroned*: Artemis was, among other attributes, the goddess of hunting (see 178) and the mistress of wild animals. She had a cult in Attica, involving the sacrifice of bulls, and this was said to have been introduced from the Tauric Chersonese to the north-east of Greece, where human sacrifice was practised. The reference is relevant to Ajax, who has killed animals believing them to be human beings. Coins show Artemis riding on a bull, hence 'bull-enthroned' as a translation of the goddess's title in the text.

16. *Incensed ... fray*: For Ajax's rejection of all help from the gods, see 763–75.

17. *spawn of Sisyphus' profligate line*: Odysseus. See *Philoctetes* note 18.

18. *Scene 2*: The entrance of Tecmessa (see note 21) introduces a long sequence, which makes use of all three modes of tragic utterance. Tecmessa's account to the Chorus of Ajax's madness and its consequences leads up to his second spectacular appearance, this time in the suicidal depression that has followed his return to reason. The latter part of the scene includes an exchange of long speeches between Ajax and Tecmessa with strong Homeric overtones (see notes 30, 31).

19. *Tecmessa*: In this first section, the Chorus and Tecmessa begin in anapaests, but at 221 the sailors break into singing mode to express the horror and apprehension that Tecmessa's news inspires.

20. *Sailors of Ajax . . . monarch of Athens*: Although the sailors are supposed to come from Salamis, they are of Athenian stock. This points to an Athenian perspective on the Ajax myth. Erechtheus was a mythical king of Athens, said to have been born out of the earth.

21. *daughter of Trojan Teleutas . . . loves with devotion*: Tecmessa is introduced as a Trojan captive of noble birth. She is Ajax's concubine, but she has borne him a child, and the language used here and later (497–500) implies that Ajax has treated her more as a wife than a slave. He has no wife at home.

22. *Danaan kings*: The Greeks are often referred to as Danaans or Achaeans (1234).

23. *Chorus Leader*: The dialogue now reverts to normal iambic mode for a calmer description of Ajax's madness, followed by his return to sanity, as witnessed by Tecmessa and recounted in her great speech (284–330). Ajax's offstage cries and commands at 333ff. build up to the tableau of his second entrance at 346–7.

24. *The hut . . . cattle*: A spectacular moment, probably achieved by the use of the *ekkyklēma* (compare *Electra* 1465).

25. *Ajax*: Ajax's distress and anger against his foes are expressed in a long formal exchange of three strophic pairs: while he himself sings in lyric metres, Tecmessa and the Chorus Leader respond in spoken iambics. Some of Ajax's phrases are composed in the jerky 'dochmiac' rhythm (see *Electra* note 63). The movement's overall effect is far more like opera than a spoken play.

26. *Ajax*: A pair of balancing long speeches for Ajax and Tecmessa. Ajax dwells on his humiliation and explores his options, to conclude that his only noble course must be to find an honourable

death. In her moving reply, Tecmessa pleads his obligations to her and their son, arguing that true nobility consists in loyalty to one's friends.

27. *Aiai*: Ajax plays on this cry of lamentation and its similarity to his own name, *Aias* in Greek. Names are often presented as ominous in Greek tragedy. At this point I would envisage Ajax leaving the *ekkyklêma* and advancing further towards the audience.

28. *My father ... glory*: Ajax refers to an earlier expedition against Troy, led by Heracles, to punish the perfidious King Laomedon. Telamon's prize was the king's daughter, Hesione, referred to again at 1301–3 as the mother of Teucer.

29. *the invincible goddess*: Here Ajax acknowledges that Athena was not his friend after all. Contrast 92, 117.

30. *Tecmessa*: In this speech Sophocles' audience would have been reminded of the famous and beautiful scene in Homer *Iliad* 6, when the Trojan prince Hector bids farewell to his wife, Andromache, and their little son, Astyanax, before returning to battle. Tecmessa's appeal recalls both that of Andromache to her husband to hold back and Hector's reply when he sadly imagines the ill-treatment and mockery that she must face if she is taken into slavery by the Greeks. Homer's Hector, however, shows understanding and compassion, where Tecmessa points to Ajax's harsh insensitivity. Ajax and Hector are linked elsewhere in the play by the theme of Hector's sword (817f., 1026ff.), and the poet's implied comparison here is not to Ajax's advantage.

31. *Ajax*: Children on stage tend to steal the scene, but this speech should not be sentimentalized. It is another reminiscence of the Homeric episode mentioned in note 30. There Hector greets the arrival of Astyanax with a gentle smile, and when the child shrinks in fear as his father puts on his plumed helmet, Hector laughs and takes it off. Though Ajax shows some empathy with Eurysaces in 552–60, he grimly expects *his* son to be unfazed by the welter of carnage indoors and wants him quickly broken into his own 'wild, rough ways'. He lacks Hector's tenderness and sees his child as an extension of himself.

32. *Tecmessa*: In the stichomythic conflict that closes this long scene, culminating in a tense exchange of half-lines, Tecmessa's renewed pleas are rejected by Ajax with arrogant savagery.

33. *Attendants, shut those doors*: This call is probably the cue for the *ekkyklêma* to be withdrawn before Ajax makes his stormy exit.

34. *Exit Ajax . . . hut*: It is not entirely clear how Sophocles intended
the end of this scene to be managed. Ajax evidently returns inside
the *skênê* in a rage. The effect of this exit could be spoiled if
Tecmessa and Eurysaces followed behind him. Equally, Ajax's
next entrance for the solemn and much more reflective beginning
of the Deception Speech at 646 will be less impressive if Tecmessa
has to trail on again in his wake to overhear him, as she clearly
does (653, 684–5). I therefore imagine that she ignores Ajax's
instructions to shut the doors at 578–80 and remains on stage
with Eurysaces, crushed and anxious, during the following choral
song. Mother and child are certainly present in the background
during Choral song 3 (see note 84).

35. *Choral song 1*: A song of despondency, which reflects Ajax's
mood in the previous scene. The address to the sailors' island of
Salamis contrasts the prosperity and security of their homeland
with their protracted homesickness and misery at Troy, now
compounded by their distress over Ajax. The ode also picks up
what Tecmessa has urged about Ajax's parents (506–9) and
Ajax's own shame at the thought of his father (462–5).

36. *Re enter Ajax . . . sword*: Something of a surprise. Ajax left the
stage at 595 in a fury and with desperate intentions, but he now
returns in a much more restrained and tranquil mood.

37. *Ajax*: This consists entirely of the famous Deception Speech, in
which Ajax indicates that he intends after all to live, to bury his
sword and be reconciled with the Atridae. In plot terms, his
departure at the end, supposedly to the shore, is the first ploy in
the sequence building up to the Suicide Speech (815–65), for
which he needs to be alone in the acting area and which therefore
requires the temporary absence of the Chorus from the *orchêstra*.
The immediate consequence is that he leaves the expectation in
the minds of Tecmessa and the Chorus that he will *not* be killing
himself. For the audience, who know better, the poet has planted
some ironical ambiguities in the language (see notes 38, 40, 42).
This great set-piece, however, is more complex than that, and
its interpretation has been endlessly debated. The puzzle lies
essentially in Ajax's philosophical justification of his 'changed'
decision, in terms of time and the mutability of human minds
and relationships – themes relevant to the play as a whole. This
is all the more compelling because his meditation is expressed by
Sophocles in some of the finest poetry in the play. What is more,
the hero now claims to pity Tecmessa (653), admits the need for
*sophrosynê* (677) and acknowledges that enemies can become

friends – all points which anticipate what happens at the end, when Ajax's enemy, the sound-minded Odysseus, out of pity for a valiant man brought low, sides with Teucer in according the hero's body a proper burial. Are we to suppose that Ajax has genuinely acquired a new insight? If he has, it is hard to reconcile with the reassertion in his Suicide Speech of his grim resolution to kill himself and of his vindictive hostility to the Atridae. Perhaps Sophocles is here allowing his hero, uncharacteristically, to articulate a philosophical truth and human attitudes which Ajax himself could only subscribe to, if at all, in the context of a deception. However we read this paradox, the speech certainly serves a crucial function in terms of the immediate plot, and it also has a wider thematic function in relation to the whole play. It is one way in which Ajax's suicide is linked with his burial and so can be seen as pivotal in the drama.

38. *in my tongue*: Ajax only refers to his *speech* – a hint of insincerity?

39. *this sword of mine*: Ajax, of course, needs the sword to kill himself. It is the gift of Hector (662), which he used to slaughter the animals he imagined to be his foes and so destroyed his honour. See note 31 and compare 1026–33. Ajax's use of Hector's sword to kill himself could be Sophocles' invention.

40. *In future . . . sons of Atreus*: There are several ambiguities here. 'In future' could imply 'after I'm dead'. The use of the plural 'we' may suggest a surly compliance. The objects of the verbs 'yield to' and 'revere' should properly be reversed – another possible hint of Ajax's insincerity.

41. *prerogatives*: Literally 'honours' in Greek. Perhaps Sophocles (not Ajax) is here implying a multiplicity of honours which transcend the *timê* of the individual hero.

42. *what my heart . . . to the end*: Obvious ironies, as are the 'journey' in 690 and 'safe and well' in 692.

43. *Exit Ajax*: He can be imagined leaving by one of the *eisodoi*, as though departing for the 'meadows by the shore' (654).

44. *Choral song 2*: The Chorus responds to Ajax's deception by singing a joyful song of expectation. In the form of an invocatory hymn to Pan and Apollo, it echoes the themes of time (714) and reconciliation (718) in Ajax's preceding speech. It is a favourite ploy of Sophocles to create a mood of excited optimism in his Chorus just before a messenger arrives to report disaster.

45. *I thrill with longing*: The Greek uses the word *erôs*, 'passionate desire', and echoes the verb Ajax has used in 685.

46. *Cyllene*: A mountain in Arcadia, the home of Pan.

47. *Crete or Nysa*: Pan is associated with the ecstatic cults of the
    Corybantic priests of Zeus in Crete and of Nysa, the mythical
    mountain of Dionysus, god of revelry and of the Athenian drama
    festivals.

48. *Delos*: The Aegean island birthplace of Apollo and Artemis.

49. *to quench or kindle*: Text, metre and metaphor in the Greek are
    all uncertain, but the translation reflects the general sense that
    everything is subject to change over time.

50. *Scene 4 ... entrance*: Enter the Messenger, but not to announce
    a catastrophe (see note 44). He comes to report the arrival of
    Teucer. Anxiety returns to the Chorus when he reveals Teucer's
    instructions to keep Ajax inside his hut in view of the prophet
    Calchas' warning about Athena's wrath. This is the speech that
    develops the theme of Ajax's *hubris* (see note 10). Plot-wise, it
    motivates the Chorus' and Tecmessa's hasty exit and leaves the
    acting area finally clear for Ajax's suicide. The dramatic tension
    mounts as the scene progresses.

51. *god's help*: The heroes in the *Iliad* are generally helped by the
    gods and do not feel demeaned by it. Homer's Ajax is not so
    helped, and Sophocles exploits this point from the epic tradition
    to emphasize Ajax's self-willed arrogance.

52. *Exeunt ... entrances*: Normally in a Greek tragedy, the chorus
    remains on stage throughout the action until the final exit. This
    exit in mid-play, unparalleled in the extant plays of Sophocles,
    is dramatically necessary for Ajax's suicide, though the breach
    of convention also serves in itself to emphasize the hero's soli-
    tude. For the commonly supposed change of scene at this point,
    see Preface p. 68.

53. *Scene 5 ... Ajax*: This scene consists entirely of Ajax's Suicide
    Speech, another set piece, which balances the earlier Deception
    Speech. It portrays a return to the grimmer Ajax, imperious
    in his instructions, implacably vindictive towards his foes, but
    courageous in his resolve. He can be imagined as emerging from
    the 'trees close by the hut' (982), to which he has returned instead
    of going down to the shore. For the placing and representation
    of this 'grove', see pp. 67–8. Here he can be supposed to have
    planted his sword, point upwards, in the soil, as he explains in
    819–22. The actor could easily have gestured in the sword's
    direction when it was referred to.

54. *slaughterer*: A grim description of the sword. The Greek noun
    *sphageus* is normally applied to a person who butchers or sacri-
    fices an animal by cutting its throat. The associated verb is twice

used earlier on (236, 298–9) to refer to Ajax's assault on the
sheep. The weapon intended to kill Ajax's enemies is now to be
used on himself.

55. *if a man ... reflect*: A sardonic addition. A man such as Ajax
does not usually bother to calculate, he acts!

56. *as you rightly should*: Zeus was Ajax's ancestor (387). The hero
who had claimed that he needed no god's help (768) now calls
on Zeus – as of right – to inform Teucer about his death. His
prayer is, in the event, answered (998–9).

57. *Furies*: Agents of divine retribution. See *Electra* note 19.

58. *Pounce down ... die themselves*: These lines are linguistically
difficult in the original Greek and have been suspected as inauth-
entic, but Ajax's curse needs to have some substance. The translation omits the equivalent of a single line.

59. *visit me now*: The next four lines (855–8) have been omitted as
a virtually certain interpolation and are hardly worth translating.

60. *glorious Athens*: In his last farewell, Ajax greets Athens, the city
that will include him in its hero-cults.

61. *Exit Ajax*: He withdraws into the grove to kill himself by leaping
on his sword (833). The text has skilfully contrived that the
audience can *imagine* this catastrophic event, as is normal in
Greek tragedy with actions hard to simulate convincingly, though
an ancient commentary tells us of an actor named Timotheus
(date unknown) who was renowned for the realism with which
he performed this moment – presumably by a magnificent leap
(834) on his exit. The actor playing Ajax can now move off under
cover and return as Teucer at 974.

62. *Second entrance song ... entrance*: The return of the Chorus
from two directions, still searching for Ajax, gives the play a
fresh start and mirrors Odysseus' search at the very start of
Scene 1. This extraordinary movement inaugurates the second
part of the play, which culminates in Ajax's funeral procession.
It covers the return of the divided Chorus after their fruitless
search for Ajax, Tecmessa's discovery of his body, and the carrying of it on stage to a central position where it can be clearly
visible throughout the remainder of the action. In terms of emotion, the lament expresses the sense of loss felt by Ajax's friends
and so creates a mood that is essentially sympathetic to the dead
hero. In the opening section (866–78) the two halves of the
Chorus enter separately. The opening verses of half-Chorus A
are in a heavy lyric iambic metre, expressive of their plodding
return. Half-Chorus B returns at 872, but responds in the iambic

trimeters of normal dialogue. This might suggest a mixture of song and speech as indicated in the translation. At 879, the Chorus unites again in an *amoibaion*, or exchange, with Tecmessa, who is first heard crying offstage on the discovery of Ajax's corpse. The action and meditation over the body proceed in an elaborately formal strophic structure, with the Chorus singing in lyric metres (including agitated dochmiacs; see *Electra* note 63) and spoken contributions from Tecmessa and the Chorus Leader. Another operatic movement, involving both song and speech, which balances the earlier lament between Ajax, Tecmessa and the Chorus Leader (348–429).

63.  *trees close to the hut*: See pp. 67–8 and Preface note 7. The grove of trees calls to mind a black-figure vase painting, preserved in the Boulogne Museum, by the sixth-century master Exekias. This shows Ajax setting his upturned sword in a mound of earth; he is framed by a tree on one side and his shield to the other.

64.  *Tecmessa . . . trees*: From where Ajax made his exit at 865.

65.  *You must not look at him*: We have to suppose that during the next few lines Tecmessa uses her cloak to help conceal the possible awkwardness of Ajax's body, now represented by a dummy, being carried on by attendants. If all is ready in the concealed area to the side of the *skênê*, this need not take long. By 920, Tecmessa can have moved upstage of the covered corpse and be facing the audience for the rest of her speech. The cloak would serve to make the dummy more convincing, also the business (probably at 1025) when Teucer draws the sword from Ajax's impaled body.

66.  *Cursed be his soul's dark eye*: The Chorus's expectations of Odysseus are later to be belied, as are their hopes of the Atridae's kindness (946ff.)

67.  *His death . . . not theirs*: A further three lines (971–3) of Tecmessa's speech are omitted as another, almost certain interpolation. They spoil the symmetry of her longer iambic speeches at the end of the strophe and antistrophe, and may be translated: 'Mock, then, Odysseus, in your empty pride! / Ajax is merely gone for you and them; / To me his loss brings grief and lamentation.'

68.  *Scene 6*: Teucer, who is from now on to represent Ajax's cause (and is played by the same actor), enters and takes charge of the body and the situation. In a moving speech, he grieves for his dead half-brother and, like Ajax at 462ff., fears the reaction of their father, Telamon. From 1040 the dramatic focus shifts to

NOTES

the burial of Ajax's corpse. Is it to be honoured with proper interment or left exposed on the seashore? The case for the latter is argued by the Spartan king Menelaus and answered by Teucer in a pair of formal debating speeches, followed by a passage of antagonistic stichomythia. At this point Homer's heroic world is forgotten, and we are in the different atmosphere of Athenian politics and forensic life. Many critics have seen this *agôn* as an undignified lowering of the play's tone, but it is thoroughly compelling in performance and carries the dramatic momentum forward in an exciting way. In any case, the scene is brought to a solemn and touching conclusion when Teucer is joined by Tecmessa (now played by a mute actor) and Eurysaces in the ritual tributes to Ajax's body that imply his status as a cult hero (see note 83).

69. *Exit Tecmessa*: A balancing painted flat at the opposite side of the *skênê* from the grove would provide a suitable place for Tecmessa to exit here and re-enter with Eurysaces at 1168. This might also have proved a convenient point for Athena's suggested entrance at ground level at 34 (see note 2).

70. *as though / It came from a god*: See note 56.

71. *bastard son . . . campaigns*: See note 28.

72. *throw me out*: The tradition went that Teucer was later banished by Telamon and founded a new Salamis on Cyprus.

73. *light-catching . . . Hector's*: The Greek adjective for the sword here is *aiolos*. See *Women of Trachis* note 4. The mutability theme is once again asserted in the idea that the gifts of the sword and belt exchanged in friendship and mutual respect by Hector and Ajax in the *Iliad* (7.303–5) have ironically been applied to their mutual destruction (1029–33).

74. *Although . . . the end*: For the paradoxical idea of the dead killing the living, compare *Women of Trachis* 1159–63 and *Electra* 1418–21. During the last few lines, Teucer has drawn Hector's sword from the dummy – helped, no doubt, by Tecmessa's cloak (see note 65) – and he now displays it.

75. *Sailors, compare*: The Oxford text regards the whole passage 1028–39 as an interpolation. The translation omits only 1034–5: 'Did not a vengeful Fury forge the sword, / And Hades, that fierce craftsman, cut the belt?'

76. *he must be . . . seabirds*: Such treatment of the dead, even of one's enemies, would have been fundamentally unacceptable to a fifth-century Greek, as denial of burial implied pollution. Relatives were allowed to bury a traitor's body beyond the frontier

of the aggrieved city-state. This issue of burial is crucial to Sophocles' *Antigone*, and Menelaus' utterances have much in common with those of the Theban king Creon in that play. (See also *Electra* notes 53, 71). Menelaus, though, shows rather less dignity than Creon.

77. *without the backing / Of fear*: Here Sophocles could be playing on Athenian hostility to Sparta (of which Menelaus is king), where there were temples of Fear.

78. *Life goes by turns*: The cycle of change again; but Menelaus' attitude of 'It's now *my* turn to show *hubris*' is thoroughly objectionable, as the Chorus Leader warns (1091–3).

79. *discipline you*: The next two lines (1105–6) are omitted as a probable interpolation which confuses rather than helps the argument: 'You were under orders yourself on this expedition, / Not chief of staff, with Ajax underneath you.'

80. *He was bound / By oath*: This must be the oath sworn by all of Helen's suitors (who included Ajax) to her father, Tyndareus, that they would support her eventual husband (Menelaus) if anyone tried to abduct her. Teucer's argument is specious, and 1112–14 could be another interpolation, but it fits the tone of the scene.

81. *That archer*: Said with a sneer. In Homer, Teucer is the best Greek archer, but there was a common prejudice in historic times against archers, who fought at a distance, compared with hoplites armed with swords, spears and shields.

82. *A story*: The rather cheap stichomythic argument is followed by an exchange of fables, a common form of rhetorical device. Though Teucer's response (1150–58) can hardly be regarded as a fable, it sees the nasty Menelaus off in an entertaining way.

83. *suppliant*: Eurysaces, by clinging to the corpse in supplication, will be protecting it, since anyone forcing him away will be offending Zeus, the god of suppliants. Teucer's speech as a whole carries an important implication: the combined ritual elements of supplication (1172–3), offering (1174–5) and curse (1176–9) are those associated with a cult hero and signify Ajax's establishment as such. He is already in a position to protect his friends and harm his enemies.

84. *Choral song 3*: A beautiful and quiet interlude between the two angry *agônes*, which also contrasts with the excitement of the previous ode (693–718). The sailors return to the hardships and deprivations of war (compare 600–607) and denounce the imaginary man who ever invented it. Their song will have

resonated powerfully with men in the audience who had experienced homesickness and war-weariness in Athenian expeditions abroad. Although the subject matter is irrelevant to the issue of Ajax's burial, the poem helps to reinforce the Athenian perspective, which treats Ajax, by implication, as a cult hero in the climax to the drama. In the final lines, the sailors seem to regard Athens rather than Salamis as their home. The Chorus's performance should be visualized as backed by the symbolic tableau of Tecmessa and the kneeling Eurysaces close to the dead body.

85. *Sunium's lofty heights*: The sailors imagine themselves, on their return voyage to Salamis, passing the promontory on the southernmost tip of Attica, where there was a temple of Athena at the time of this play's performance. The temple of Poseidon, the ruins of which can be seen today, was probably built a little later.

86. *Closing scene*: First comes another *agôn* for Teucer with Agamemnon, balancing the one with Menelaus. Here again the argument turns out to be more lively than edifying and perhaps suggests that, if heroic values can go tragically wrong when taken to extremes, the adversarial character of contemporary Athenian politics represents a meagre kind of replacement. The argument settles nothing, but then, instead of the expected run of stichomythia, Odysseus enters and takes Ajax's case over from Teucer. His calm, persuasive tone contrasts powerfully with the earlier wrangling, and he eventually succeeds with Agamemnon where Teucer has failed. The remainder of the drama concerns the funeral rituals for Ajax and culminates in a solemn processional exit.

87. *some friend to help you*: In Athenian law courts, slaves were not allowed to argue their own cases. Agamemnon is being very insulting.

88. *What of the time*: This story (1273–82) and the duel with Hector (1283–8) are mainly based on incidents in *Iliad* 7 and 15.

89. *your own father, Atreus ... children's flesh*: Atreus' wife had been seduced by his brother Thyestes, and the former took his revenge by murdering Thyestes' children and serving them to their father as meat.

90. *Laomedon's daughter ... special prize*: See note 28.

91. *for you ... favours*: Agamemnon only agrees out of the need to keep Odysseus' support, not because his mind has changed.

92. *Though I can ... the rest*: Teucer accepts Odysseus' offer to take part in the burial, but not in a 'hands-on' way. Ajax's enmity is assumed to persist.

93.  *Now enough*: Here the metre changes to 'marching' anapaests
     in anticipation of the final procession.
94.  *You there . . . his shield*: Teucer's instructions to three different
     groups suggest the use of a number of extras who join with him,
     the Chorus and the mute characters (Tecmessa and Eurysaces)
     in a spectacular final exit, celebrating the community values
     implicit in the Ajax cult.
95.  *When mortals . . . awaits him*: Conventional sentiments, perhaps,
     as often used in Greek tragedy to see the Chorus out of the
     *orchêstra*. But the second and third lines do enshrine the paradox
     of Ajax's rehabilitation after his humiliation, while the first might
     be thought to attest to the insight which the experience of seeing
     and witnessing a tragedy in the theatre can bring.


# ELECTRA

1.   *Scene 1*: Orestes arrives in Argos with his friend Pylades and the
     Old Slave, known in Greek as the *Paidagôgos*, who rescued him
     at the time of Agamemnon's murder and brought him up in
     Phocis. The Old Slave reintroduces his master to his birthplace,
     and Orestes outlines the deception, commanded by Apollo at the
     Delphic oracle, which will enable him to take revenge on his
     father's killers and recover his patrimony. The atmosphere of
     this opening scene is businesslike and positive. The party walks
     fearlessly into the citadel as the sun is rising and the birds are
     starting to sing. Orestes communicates his plan and gives his
     orders with cold, almost military precision. The prospect of
     matricide does not appear to daunt him, and he is perfectly happy
     for a false report of his own death to be issued. When a cry of
     lamentation is heard from inside the palace, which could come
     from his sister Electra, he decides to ignore it. Aeschylus and
     Euripides both contrived a meeting between Orestes and Electra
     before the plot was formulated (Euripides even made Electra
     suggest the murder plans herself). Sophocles raises this possibility
     at the end of this scene only for it to be rejected (see note 14).
     Much of the action to follow depends on this.
2.   *Io*: The daughter of Inachus, the river god who founded the
     Argive people. She was loved by Zeus and turned by him into a
     heifer to escape the jealousy of his wife, Hera, who later tor-
     mented her rival with a stinging gadfly. The reference to this has
     a sinister resonance, the first in the play.

3.  *forum of Apollo*: In the Greek text, Apollo is referred to here as
    'Lycean', as again at 645, 655 and 1379. The meaning of this
    title is uncertain, but Sophocles evidently identified it with *lukos*,
    Greek for 'wolf', in his amplification 'the wolf-killing god'. The
    phrase could have a benign ring, as one of the god's functions
    was to protect the flocks and herds, but it also sounds rather
    menacing. Ambiguity is a characteristic of Apollo (see note 8),
    who, like the Furies, plays a significant role in *Electra*. His altar
    and statue are visible on stage throughout the play (635, 1378).

4.  *Hera*: The wife of Zeus and the patron goddess of Argos. Her
    temple there was one of the most celebrated in ancient times.

5.  *Mycenae*: The stronghold overlooking the plain of Argos, today
    one of the best-known archeological sites in Greece, following
    the excavations of Schliemann and others. In the *Iliad*, Mycenae
    and Argos are two distinct settlements. Sophocles is here
    returning to the Homeric tradition. In the late fifth century BC,
    there was no separate community of Mycenae, and Aeschylus
    had set his *Oresteia* firmly in Argos.

6.  *palace of Atreus*: Atreus was Agamemnon's father, who killed
    the children of his brother Thyestes and served them to him as
    meat. 'Atreus' here translates 'Pelopidae', the descendants of
    Pelops, who was Atreus' own father and is referred to later in
    the play (504ff., 1497). The whole house was under a curse, so
    the description of the palace as 'rich in blood' has a resonance
    beyond the so-called 'Thyestean banquet'.

7.  *Pylades*: The son of Strophius, king of Crisa in Phocis and Agam-
    emnon's brother-in-law, who had given Orestes refuge and
    brought him up. Pylades always appears with Orestes in Greek
    tragedy, and the closeness between the cousins was seen as a
    prototype of Greek male friendship.

8.  *Delphic oracle*: The most famous of all the Greek oracles, where
    Apollo spoke (often ambiguously) through the priestess, the
    Pythia.

9.  *Pythian Games*: Like the Olympics, one of the great inter-city
    athletic festivals, founded in 586 BC and held every four years in
    Sophocles' time. This anachronistic introduction of a contempor-
    ary event into the heroic world would not have worried the poet
    or his audience.

10. *libations*: Drink-offerings of wine or milk, poured on the earth,
    were believed to reach the dead and were one way of ensuring
    their support.

11. *curling locks*: Cutting one's hair was a token of mourning in

ancient Greece, and locks were traditionally offered on the grave mounds of the dead. Compare Electra's dedication of a lock (451).

12. *What harm . . . glorious prize*: The ancient Greeks regarded the report of a person's death as a bad omen, so Orestes is showing a cynical lack of compunction over his proposed ploy to deceive his intended victims.

13. *with men*: Orestes thinks exclusively in male terms – just before a woman's cry is heard.

14. *Listen . . . she laments*: The reaction to Electra's cry offstage raises an interesting point of interpretation. The allocation of these lines in the manuscript tradition has been: 78–9 to the Old Slave, 80–81 to Orestes and 82–5 (four lines in the Greek text) to the Old Slave. That arrangement allows Orestes to raise the question of waiting to listen, only to be recalled to his duty by the Old Slave. In this translation, a different allocation, advocated by some modern critics, has been preferred. (Since speakers were not specified in the earliest texts of Greek plays, there is no problem in principle over this.) I find it more compelling and significant if it is the insensitively businesslike Orestes himself who decides that the cry issuing from the house should be ignored. See Preface p. 131.

15. *Electra's monody*: Electra emerges from the palace to resume her public lamentations for her dead father and invoke the powers of the underworld to avenge his murder and guide her long-absent brother home. In this she is performing what was felt among the ancient Greeks to be a woman's duty: to keep the memory of a murdered man alive by constant lamentation. In this case, it can also be seen as an aggressive action against the usurpers. The heroine's opening 'number' is a formal lament in 'melic anapaests' and intended for some kind of chanted delivery rather than the spoken mode of normal dialogue. The 'aria' reflects both the pathos and the splendour of Electra's isolation.

16. *Ares*: The god of war. Agamemnon had not been killed at Troy, but returned home to be murdered by his wife and her lover.

17. *nightingale*: A mythological reference to Procne, who killed her son Itys in revenge for her husband, Tereus', rape of her sister Philomela and was subsequently transformed to a nightingale. Procne is an often-quoted exemplar of undying grief in Greek poetry.

18. *Hades, Persephone, Hermes below*: Hades is the god of the underworld, who avenges the dead; Persephone is his queen.

Hermes is the messenger of the Olympian gods, but also the god of cunning (1396) and associated with the underworld since he conducts the souls of the dead there.

19. *dread Furies*: Erinyes, or avenging spirits, represented in art as feminine deities, usually winged and carrying snakes or with snakes in their hair. They feature prominently in the myth of Orestes, who was hounded by them for the murder of his mother, an aspect of the traditional aftermath which Sophocles appears in this play to exclude. However, the Furies are mentioned or implied several times in the imagery of *Electra* (276, 490, 1080, also 785–6, 1387) and personify the whole retaliatory and retributive process in a peculiarly sinister way, not least because of the association with Aeschylus' trilogy.

20. *Entry of the Chorus*: Instead of the usual entrance song for the Chorus, Sophocles has his Argive women engage in a lyric dialogue with Electra. They remonstrate with her for her continued lamentations, using various conventional arguments of consolation and reminding her that Orestes is still alive. But Electra is not to be consoled: Orestes has failed to appear, and she must go on chanting lamentations in her resistance to Clytemnestra and Aegisthus. In this long passage, many of the play's ideas are explored in the imagery, not least the theme of retaliation, the tragic implications of which had been explored par excellence in Aeschylus' *Oresteia*. The exchange also poses Electra's moral dilemma in a disturbing way: fidelity to fundamental duties may preclude the moderation the Greeks admired and necessitate the excess they abhorred. The balanced strophic construction is part of the beauty of this movement, as would have been the contrast between the solo voice of the mourner and the chorus of her comforters. The translation has aimed to reflect the varied rhythmical phrasing of the original, though syllabic correspondence is less exact than elsewhere in this volume. There is a specially effective change to a brisker tempo in Strophe 3 (193–200), when the Chorus stops counselling Electra for a moment to recall the night of Agamemnon's murder, the crime that is to be punished in the play's main action.

21. *nightingale . . . Itys*: See note 17.

22. *Niobe*: Like Procne, a paradigm of perpetual grieving. She was the wife of Amphion, king of Thebes, and boasted that, with her six sons and daughters, she was superior to the goddess Leto, who had only produced two children, Apollo and Artemis. She was punished for her presumption when the younger gods she

had insulted shot all her children dead. In her grief she was turned into a rock on Mt Sipylus in Lydia, with a perpetually flowing spring, which was supposed to consist of her tears.

23. *Chrysothemis and Iphianassa*: The names are derived from Homer (*Iliad* 9.145, 287). The former appears in this play, though not in Aeschylus or Euripides, as a telling foil to Electra. We hear no more of the latter, though her name may remind us of the sacrificed sister, Iphigenia.

24. *Crisa*: In Phocis, where Orestes had grown up.

25. *Acheron*: One of the rivers in the underworld.

26. *conscience ... fear of god*: An attempt to translate two Greek moral abstracts, *aidôs* and *eusebeia*. The first is a sense of shame which derives from respect for other human beings; the other is piety or reverence for the gods, which includes the notion of familial duty.

27. *Scene 2*: Electra amplifies her self-justification and describes her treatment as a slave by the usurpers with great vividness and force in her first long speech in normal dialogue form. A transitional interchange with the Chorus Leader on the subject of Orestes' prolonged absence leads to the entrance of Chrysothemis. Electra's uncompromising stance is shown up in even harsher relief by her sister's willingness to settle for a comfortable life and comply with the usurpers' wishes; the motif of conflicting moralities is further dramatized in the contrast between Chrysothemis' utilitarianism and Electra's obedience to a categorical imperative. Each of the sisters, according to her own lights, is the 'wiser' or 'more sensible'. A number in Sophocles' audience would have been reminded of a very similar conflict and contrast in *Antigone* between the heroine and her sister Ismene. During the discussion, Chrysothemis warns Electra of Clytemnestra's and Aegisthus' plan to imprison her in a cave as a way of suppressing her embarrassing outcries. In terms of the plot, this comes to nothing, but the news has the effect of heightening the tension and may, once again, have reminded some in the original audience of Antigone, who *is* walled up in a cave as a punishment (see note 53). The plot receives a genuine nudge forward when Chrysothemis discloses that she is about to take offerings from Clytemnestra to Agamemnon's tomb, to avert the danger foreshadowed in a sinister dream the queen has had about Agamemnon returning to life. Electra excitedly hails the dream as a good omen and persuades her sister to dispose of their mother's libations and to dedicate other offerings from them both.

28. *Furies*: See note 19.

29. *send me out*: The last three lines of Chrysothemis' speech are omitted from the translation as a probable interpolation that interrupts the flow of the argument. They would read: 'I therefore implore you, by our family gods, / Do listen to me. Don't let your folly destroy you; / If you reject me, trouble will bring you back.' If they are authentic, Chrysothemis is continuing to urge caution in the face of Clytemnestra's fear.

30. *butchered his limbs*: The reference is to a practice of mutilation whereby the hands and feet of a murdered man's corpse were cut off and placed under his armpits, to deprive his spirit of the power to rise and take revenge.

31. *Choral song 1*: In the strophe and antistrophe, the Chorus responds in optimistic mood to the news of Clytemnestra's dream and foresees the inexorable march of Justice in the form of a Fury 'with many hands and feet' (translating literally). The epode meditates in much sadder vein, and in phrases of a very different musical character, on the suffering that has afflicted Electra's family through the curse on the house of Pelops (see note 33). The ode as a whole thus associates the relentless onset of retribution with suffering and sorrow, in line with the ambivalence inherent in Sophocles' whole treatment of this myth. We may observe, too, that the reference to Myrtilus 'flung headlong from his chariot' anticipates the reported fate of Orestes in the chariot race to be described in the next episode. The rhythms of the poetry are boldly expressive. There is a striking tension in the opening lines of the strophe and antistrophe, which can be expressed in musical notation as: ♩ ♩ ♩ ♫ ♩ ♩ ♫ ♩. Later in the two stanzas, the adjacent protracted heavy syllables (marked with accents) produce a strong, pounding effect. The epode is based, with variations, on an unusual metrical phrase of the pattern: ♩ ♫ ♪ ♩ ♩ ♩. The repetition of this is beautifully poignant.

32. *That fearsome Fury*: So justice is here personified (see note 19). The feet and hands of 489 and the mention of bronze in 491 suggest an army of warriors on the march.

33. *Pelops*: The son of Tantalus, who competed in a chariot race against Oenomaus, king of Pisa, to win the hand of his daughter Hippodamia. In some versions of the story, Pelops achieved his aim by bribing Oenomaus' charioteer, Myrtilus, to sabotage the king's vehicle. When Myrtilus demanded his reward (or part of it) in the form of a night with Hippodamia, Pelops threw him

from his chariot into the sea. As he fell, Myrtilus called down a curse on Pelops and his descendants, who included Atreus (see note 6), Agamemnon and his family. The translation refers to the curse (511) more explicitly than the Greek original.

34. *Scene 3*: This episode falls into two sections: In 515–659 (Electra and Clytemnestra), Clytemnestra enters. She is presented as a hard, unpleasant woman, frightened of Electra. Sophocles first gives us an *agôn*, or formal debate, consisting of opposing speeches: the mother attempts to justify the murder of Agamemnon by reference to the sacrifice of Iphigenia, and Electra responds. We are conscious here not only of two powerful personalities in conflict but also of the retaliation motif operating at the level of words as well as of actions. Electra herself, as she acknowledges, is degraded in the process no less than her mother (see note 38). At the end of the argument, Clytemnestra makes prayers and offerings to Apollo, asking, almost blasphemously, to be granted continued enjoyment of the fruits of adultery and murder. In 660–822 (the False Messenger scene), as if in ironic answer to Clytemnestra's prayer, the Old Slave arrives and reports the death of Orestes. Sophocles here uses the Messenger Speech convention in a brilliantly novel way to convince Clytemnestra that Orestes is dead and so to prepare for the admission of her murderers into the palace. There is a remarkable double effect: the narrative is so graphic and thrilling in its own right that at one level we respond to it as if it were completely true; at the same time we can relish it in the knowledge that it is all a colossal fiction. The original audience would also have appreciated the echoes of the Homeric chariot race in the funeral games of Patroclus described in *Iliad* 23.262–650. The devastating impact that the speech has on Electra no less than her mother is yet another dimension. Clytemnestra's reaction to the news (766ff.) is a masterstroke of detail: she is allowed a sense of maternal loss, though her feelings of relief inevitably prevail. She makes a gloating exit, motivating a deeply pathetic speech from Electra which shows the heroine at her lowest ebb.

35. *sacrificed / Your sister*: See note 36.

36. *Ask Artemis . . . Iphigenia*: In Aeschylus' *Agamemnon*, Artemis is the patroness of young animals, and her anger is prompted by an omen of two eagles, representing Agamemnon and Menelaus, tearing to pieces a hare with her unborn young; these stand in turn for Troy and for the innocents doomed to die there. The goddess raises a storm with contrary winds, which prevent the

Greek fleet from leaving Aulis (on the eastern coast of mainland Greece in Boeotia, opposite the island of Euboea) until Agamemnon has sacrificed his daughter Iphigenia. Sophocles, drawing on the post-Homeric epic tradition, makes Electra tell the story quite differently: Artemis is now the 'hunter goddess', and Agamemnon has accidentally killed a stag in her sacred grove. She therefore *becalms* the winds, so that the ships are stranded until the sacrifice is performed and she can be appeased. By putting a version of events more favourable to Agamemnon in Electra's mouth, Sophocles seems to be giving her a debating point in the *agôn*, which will allow her to whitewash Agamemnon's sacrifice of his daughter. It might also suggest that Electra's loyalty to her father entails a blunting of sensibility where her innocent sister is concerned.

37. *Blood for blood*: This theme pervades Aeschylus' *Oresteia* and sums up the retributory process, the tragic implications of which Sophocles is exploring in his own way.

38. *Let me assure ... example*: An important speech that reveals both Electra's self-knowledge and her sense of being compelled to respond to her mother's treatment of her in kind (see 221–2).

39. *I swear by Artemis*: Artemis is here invoked by Clytemnestra as the virgin goddess, since Electra has violated the modesty becoming to her maidenhood. But in the mouth of an adulteress, the oath is something of a blasphemy, like her subsequent invocation of Artemis' brother, Apollo, especially at 649–56.

40. *Thessalian horses*: A fine detail, among several others. Thessaly, in northern Greece, with its level plains, was famed for its excellent horse-breeding terrain. The Old Slave gives Orestes the best possible team.

41. *turning point*: This was marked by a stone pillar at each end of the course. Charioteers would drive anti-clockwise and aim to turn with their left-side wheel as close as possible to the pillar.

42. *sucking / My life-blood*: More imagery associated with the Furies, here applied to Electra herself.

43. *Nemesis*: The personified goddess of retribution.

44. *Lament for Electra with Chorus*: In a further intensification of emotion, Electra expresses her grief in a lyric *kommos* with the Chorus, involving song and doubtless some kind of choreographed movement. Here again some powerful and interesting rhythmical effects may be heard, though the metrical analysis is uncertain. The first pair of strophes is composed in 3/4 time, with two beats to be allowed on the italicized syllables marked, while a steadier 2/4 pulse prevails through the second pair.

45. *You'll destroy [me]*: In this line, to preserve rhythm, the Chorus's interjection 'How?' should coincide in delivery with Electra's 'me'.

46. *Lord Amphiaraus*: The Chorus offers a mythological parallel (to Agamemnon's rather than Orestes' death) in the story of the Argive prophet Amphiaraus, who refused to join Oedipus' son, Polynices, in his expedition to gain the throne of Thebes from his brother Eteocles. The seer's wife, Eriphyle, was bribed by Polynices with the gift of a golden necklace to persuade her husband to change his mind. Amphiaraus went to Thebes, but died when the earth was struck by a thunderbolt from Zeus and he was swallowed down to the underworld with his chariot and horses. The Chorus tries to comfort Electra with the thought that Amphiaraus, like Agamemnon, still rules, with all his prophetic powers, among the dead in Hades. Moreover, Eriphyle was killed in revenge by her son Alcmaeon. Electra can fairly reply (846–8) that Agamemnon no longer has a son living to avenge him.

47. *Scene 4*: As though to twist the knife in Electra's wound, Chrysothemis re-enters in joyful excitement to report news of offerings on Agamemnon's tomb. Orestes must be back! The irony is perfect: where the Old Slave's speech gave evidence of a falsehood that was believed, Chrysothemis offers evidence of a truth that Electra rejects. Chrysothemis' deflation is exquisitely portrayed. Assuming that Orestes can never be there to help them, Electra now comes up with a recklessly unrealistic and (to Greek eyes) unwomanly proposal. She asks for her sister's aid in killing Aegisthus. Her fantasy of future glory for them both, expressed in a splendid flight of rhetoric, marks a shift of moral ground; filial duty and devotion are no longer the sole issue. In practical terms, the idea is reckless and absurd, as Chrysothemis, supported by the Chorus Leader, points out. Has Electra been so unhinged by her grief as to be losing her sanity? We may well wonder. In another powerful stichomythic exchange, centred essentially on the question of whether 'the right' is to be determined by principles or practicalities, Chrysothemis tries to reason with Electra, but their two viewpoints are irreconcilably opposed. Chrysothemis then disappears from the play.

48. *many moons ago*: Five lines follow in the Greek text which may well have been interpolated from one of Sophocles' lost plays. Certainly the end of the scene runs better without them. They can be translated:

CHRYSOTHEMIS:
　　Then I'll be off, as you won't ever accept
　　The advice I offer nor I accept your way.
ELECTRA:
　　Very well, go in. I'll never follow you there,
　　However much you may want me to. Even
　　Pursuing an empty cause is the height of folly.

49. *Choral song* 2: In this textually difficult, though musically beautiful, ode, the Chorus returns to Electra's side in the theme of filial
devotion. They start with an image of the 'wisdom' shown by
birds in the mutual care and tenderness existing between parents
and young. The song then switches abruptly (1063) to the inevitability of punishment for the sinners (Clytemnestra and Aegisthus), before uttering 'reproaches' to the dead sons of Atreus
(Agamemnon and now, supposedly, Orestes) designed to rouse
them from the grave. The Chorus challenges them with the division in the house, manifested by the quarrel between the two
sisters, which has resulted in Electra's being left alone to struggle
against her father's murderers. In the second pair of strophes,
Electra is praised for the noble stance that has led her to champion 'the highest laws of heaven' through her *eusebeia* (see note
26). As in the *kommos* (823–70), the rhythm in the first pair of
strophes is mostly in a lilting 3/4 time, though it changes to 4/4
in lines 7–9 of each stanza, so marking the abrupt change of
thought at 1063. Similarly, the second pair has a more insistent
pulse, with heavy stresses on some adjacent syllables in the final
verse.

50. *birds*: Sophocles probably had storks in mind.

51. *Zeus ... Justice*: These deities are invoked as moral authorities
who punish the wicked.

52. *pair of Furies*: Clytemnestra and Aegisthus, seen as avenging
spirits in the murder of Agamemnon, the most recent stage in the
retaliatory sequence going back to Pelops and operating through
the generations in the house of Atreus.

53. *the highest laws / Of heaven*: Electra at this point is perceived as
like Sophocles' Antigone, who put the 'unwritten laws' of Zeus
before Creon's human decree prohibiting the burial of her
brother Polynices. She was punished for her disobedience by
immurement in a cave (see note 27) and left to die.

54. *Scene 5*: This powerful movement brings Orestes and Electra
together and builds towards the drama's climax. It falls into

three sections. In 1098–1231 (The Recognition), the Chorus'
'reproaches' (1069) seem to have been effective when Orestes and
Pylades arrive at last, with attendants bearing the urn supposedly
containing the prince's ashes. Orestes probably fails to identify
Electra at first, but must quickly do so, once she has asked to
take the urn in her hands and begins her famous lamentation.
The Urn Speech is one of the most moving in the whole of Greek
tragedy, and the property becomes an extraordinarily potent
symbol of Electra's sense of 'nothingness' (1166). At the end,
Orestes is allowed to show some feeling, and, in a gloriously
protracted and suspenseful passage of stichomythia, he gradually
reveals to Electra that her long-lost brother is alive and standing
before her. At the great climax the dialogue breaks into half-lines
as Electra's joy knows no bounds. In 1232–87, Electra expresses
her rapture in lyric mode, while in 1288–1383, the Old Slave
returns, and all prepare for the task ahead.

55.  *to attendants*: As Orestes uses the plural in the Greek imperative,
more than one attendant seems to be indicated.

56.  *O royal prince*: An extraordinary moment when Electra bursts
into song in agitated 'dochmiac' rhythms (see note 63). Her
ecstatic outpourings are characteristically punctuated by single
lines spoken by Orestes in sober dialogue mode and urging a
cautious silence at this critical moment.

57.  *Artemis*: Electra here invokes the goddess as the protectress of
young unmarried women.

58.  *Enough of words*: Orestes now tries to bring his enraptured sister
closer to earth.

59.  *You crazy fools*: The Old Slave's sudden re-entrance marks a
quickening of the pace.

60.  *Oh glorious day*: Electra's tone of hysterical rapture is maintained in her address to the Old Slave. He might be Agamemnon
returned!

61.  *our ancestral gods*: Apollo, no doubt, and probably Hermes
(1395–6).

62.  *O Lord Apollo*: Electra's prayer is as ugly in its implications as
Clytemnestra's earlier invocation of Apollo (637ff.), and one to
be fulfilled in a no less equivocal way (see note 34). An interesting
'mirror' effect.

63.  *Choral song 3*: As often in Greek tragedy before a crisis such as
a murder, the Chorus sings a brief song of tense anticipation,
which envisages the Furies, now in the form of Orestes and
Pylades, stalking through the palace. Note the striking imagery

as well as the taut, exciting rhythms. The opening phrase consists of two 5/8 bars in the form

♫ ♪ ♩ | ♫ ♪ ♩.

Thereafter the irregular 'dochmiac' (slanting) metre,

♪ ♩ ♩ ♪ ♩

or

♪ ♫ ♩ ♪ ♩

is used in contrast with phrases in steady iambic pulse.

64. *Closing scene*: The physical action, which has been so long suspended in the drama's concentration on Electra and her intense emotions, now follows thick and fast. As Clytemnestra's death cries ring out offstage, we hear Electra savagely call to Orestes to strike his mother a second time. The murderers emerge from the palace to report the deed done, only to withdraw again rapidly when Aegisthus' long-awaited return is announced. The moment when the odious bully of an usurper is confronted with his wife's corpse is a superlatively chilling *coup de théâtre*. No less horrible is Electra's demand that the villain's corpse should be thrown to the dogs and the birds. The victory has been won, but it has left her morally destroyed.

65. *destroyers*: The Greek word here, *apolluntôn*, could be an ironical pun on the name of Apollo.

66. *If Apollo prophesied well*: Sophocles is not implying any possible misgiving or revulsion on Orestes' part. On his lips, 'if' means 'as sure as'. But there may be some dramatic irony in the ambiguity.

67. *their way to her heart*: The deliberate irony here (as at 1457, 1464-5, 1471, 1474) is magnificent.

68. *Enter ... covered*: For the display of Clytemnestra's covered body see Preface p. 133. How the rest of the scene, including the removal of the corpse, was managed is a matter for further speculation.

69. *No gloating, though*: Aegisthus' triumph might provoke the wrath of the gods. Given his bullying characterization so far, his piety is almost certainly hypocritical.

70. *When a man's ... delay*: These two lines may be spurious. The dramatic pace is certainly better without them.

71. *dogs and birds*: The Greek text here says, 'Throw him out to the buriers it is appropriate for him to get.' The translation takes Electra to be asking for Aegisthus' body to be left exposed for

devouring by the dogs and birds, as Homer makes Nestor say Menelaus should have done if he had returned from Troy to find Aegisthus still alive (*Odyssey* 3.255–61). The echo of Sophocles' own *Antigone* is even more striking. If Electra was like Antigone in 1095–7 (see note 53), the Fury of vengeance she now embodies has turned her into a Creon. Her parting shot in these lines could not be more sinister or terrible.

72. *The curse of Pelops' house*: See notes 6, 33.

73. *Must there be more*: This is the only possible hint of an aftermath to the matricidal act as dramatized by Sophocles. When (in the Greek text) Aegisthus refers to 'future evils', he must certainly be thinking of his own imminent death. There might perhaps be an ironical reference to Orestes' subsequent pursuit by the Furies in the traditional myth, but Sophocles' tragedy of Electra is already complete. See note 75.

74. *No, I'd rather . . . so rife*: Orestes' final speech is extraordinarily unpleasant, loathsome as Aegisthus may have appeared. It typifies the ruthlessness of his character.

75. *O seed of Atreus . . . ending*: I take the Chorus' closing anapaests, perhaps spoken only by the Leader, to be addressed to Electra herself. If so, she remains briefly on stage after Orestes and Pylades have driven Aegisthus indoors, possibly while the *ekkyklêma* with her mother's corpse is withdrawn. In my view, these lines do not lend an unambivalently positive note to the play's conclusion, but are packed with irony. Electra is called 'the seed of Atreus', whose palace inherited from the cursed Pelops (511) was 'rich in blood' (10). After that, the emphasis falls on her suffering and on the strain of the process that has resulted in her 'freedom'. As for the 'ending', the consummation of revenge has been achieved, but it has also marked the end of Electra as a morally conscious human being.

# PHILOCTETES

1. *Scene 1*: Odysseus and Neoptolemus arrive on Lemnos, presented as a desert island. Odysseus outlines the background and purpose of their mission, which is to practise a deception on Philoctetes (see Preface p. 199). The action portrays Odysseus' moral seduction of Neoptolemus, whose inherited nature finds deception repugnant. Apart from the compelling interplay of personalities, the realistic details in the description of Philoctetes' cave and

presumed way of life on the island add to the atmosphere of caution, intrigue and expectancy.

2.  *offer sacrifice / Undisturbed*: Sacrifices and other rituals had to be performed in a reverent silence, or they would be ineffectual.

3.  *I can't tell from here*: Odysseus must be standing with his back to the cave, so as not to be seen or recognized by Philoctetes if he is inside.

4.  *most god-fearing*: This translates the Greek for 'pious'. Odysseus is asking Neoptolemus to subordinate 'piety' (here, his natural repugnancy to lying) to the end of capturing the bow. See notes 38, 52.

5.  *And may we ... Victory*: In his concluding prayer, Odysseus affirms his commitment to cunning as a means to an end, to the paramount needs of the Greek cause and to the importance of victory (compare 81, 1052). Hermes is invoked as the god of deceit and the 'escort' who guides men on their way. Athena was the patron goddess of the Athenian *polis*, and her temple of Victory can still be seen on the Acropolis, close to the Parthenon. She is closely associated with Odysseus in Homer's *Odyssey*.

6.  *Entry of the Chorus*: This movement takes the form of an exchange between the chorus (in lyric metres) and Neoptolemus (in anapaests). It would originally have entailed an alternation between sung and declamatory spoken delivery.

7.  *His dreadful ... to me*: An important speech. Neoptolemus announces that Philoctetes' afflictions are heaven-sent and proceed from cruel Chryse. The tradition went that Philoctetes intruded on the shrine of the minor goddess Chryse on the island that bore her name, and so received the wound in his foot from the bite of the snake that guarded the shrine. (The translation here is a little more specific than the Greek text.) We learn too that *the gods* are keeping Philoctetes on Lemnos till the appointed time has arrived for him to capture Troy with Heracles' bow and arrows. Philoctetes seems to be portrayed as an *innocent* victim rather than as guilty of the arrogance towards the gods which Ajax shows (*Ajax* 763–77).

8.  *Be silent, my son*: In the final pair of strophes, the metre becomes more agitated in response to the cry offstage, as the song builds up to Philoctetes' entrance. The cadences give a striking impression of the hero's approach, limping and struggling home to his cave.

9.  *Scene 2 ... Philoctetes*: This long sequence shows the development of Odysseus' plot, with Neoptolemus gaining Philoctetes'

confidence, and ends in Philoctetes preparing to go on board Neoptolemus' ship for the voyage to his home in Greece, as he believes, but in reality to Troy. It falls into three sections, punctuated by two short, metrically balanced, songs. In 219–390, Neoptolemus meets Philoctetes and they tell their respective stories; then 391–402 choral song (strophe). In 403–506, after a further exchange, Philoctetes supplicates Neoptolemus to take him home to Greece; then 507–18 choral song (antistrophe). In 519–675, the sailor disguised as a merchant, as promised by Odysseus to forward the plot (125–7), arrives and makes Philoctetes all the more eager to leave. Philoctetes allows Neoptolemus to handle his bow.

The awaited moment of Philoctetes' entrance inspires both pity and fear, the emotions that Aristotle specially associated with the experience of tragedy. Philoctetes' wild and ragged appearance, with his famous bow and bandaged foot, is a powerful piece of theatre; his opening speech, with its questions punctuated by silences, is extraordinarily poignant. His joy at hearing the *sound* of Greek (234–5) is not only moving in itself, but evidence that the ancient Greeks regarded their language as very special.

10. *the forceful Odysseus*: The Greek here follows a conventional formula for 'strong Odysseus', but its repetition at 321 and, later, at 592 may give a hint of the force or violence which Odysseus rejected at 103 but does resort to in his confrontation with Philoctetes after his next entrance at 974.

11. *Achilles must die*: Neoptolemus' mention of his father's death strikes a chord of sympathy in Philoctetes. The hero continually refers to the youth as 'boy' or 'son' almost from the outset of their relationship (236, 249, 260 and so on).

12. *They came for me*: In his own narration Neoptolemus is evidently entering into the spirit of Odysseus' plan, particularly in his portrayal of Odysseus himself (371–81). As with the Old Slave's account of Orestes' death in *Electra*, we are carried away by the vivid detail of the story, while knowing that it must be largely untrue.

13. *That's my story*: Three preceding lines (385–8) are omitted in the translation as a probable interpolation. They would read: 'I blame him less than I blame the men in charge. / An army, like a city, depends on its leaders. / Disorder is always due to bad instruction.' The last remark might be seen as an ironical comment reflecting on the 'instruction' that Neoptolemus himself has received from Odysseus, but the lines detract from the climax of

the speech in its pretended denunciation of Odysseus. See 65–6.

14. *O mountain goddess*: In this hymn-like lyric, the Chorus invokes the Earth Mother, Cybele, whose cult was centred at Sardis in Asia Minor and therefore appropriate to an incident alleged to have taken place at Troy. Besides helping to break up the long Scene 2, this short song gives an added lift to the effect of Neoptolemus' narration on Philoctetes.

15. *Pactolus' river, rich in gold*: Sardis was situated on the Pactolus, which was famous for its alluvial deposits of gold.

16. *Philoctetes*: Philoctetes' reaction to Neoptolemus' story is to accept it in good faith, but he goes on to question Neoptolemus further about the various heroes who might have been expected to help him against the generals. This sequence refers to the world, familiar from the *Iliad*, of the Greeks at Troy, to which Philoctetes must eventually be restored. It confirms the hero's disillusioned attitude and provides a lull in dramatic tension before the plot develops further. Neoptolemus' sentiment at 431–2 reflects ironically on his own moral situation.

17. *the greater Ajax*: The son of Telamon, as distinct from Ajax, the son of Oïleus. The story dramatized in *Ajax* that this Ajax expected Achilles' arms to go to him is suppressed by Neoptolemus for his own purposes.

18. *Sisyphus' / Spawn*: Odysseus, whose mother Anticlea (in one version of his ancestry) was pregnant by Sisyphus when Laertes, his recognized father, paid the marriage price for her.

19. *keeping crooks ... Hades*: Men such as Sisyphus (416), who managed to return from Hades as he had asked his wife to leave him unburied when he died and Persephone allowed him back to punish her – whereupon he stayed on earth.

20. *constantly changing*: The last three lines (504–6) of Philoctetes' speech are omitted as another probable interpolation (compare 385–8). They should read: 'If you're clear of trouble, you ought to beware of danger. / It's just when life goes well that you need to be / Most on the lookout. Death may suddenly strike.' The sentiments add nothing to the warning in 502–3 and are probably a quoted parallel from another play which became incorporated into the manuscript tradition.

21. *Show pity, royal sir*: In the balancing lyric to 391–402, the Chorus this time identifies with Philoctetes and, in supporting his plea, similarly gives an emotive lift to the preceding long speech.

22. *Enter ... sailor*: The function of the False Merchant scene has

been much discussed. From the plot angle it seems superfluous, as Odysseus' plan has already worked: Philoctetes has swallowed Neoptolemus' story and has asked to be taken on board. Theatrically, however, it is very effective. The Merchant's role-playing adds to the atmosphere of intrigue (note particularly the by-play at 573ff.). The theme of persuasion versus violence, articulated in Scene 1 (103), is repeated in 593–4. The statement of Helenus' prophecy (603ff.) ties in with Neoptolemus' earlier affirmation in the *parodos* (195–20) and so comes across as genuine, though we cannot be absolutely sure of that. The Merchant is essentially part of Odysseus' plot (indeed they are played by the same actor), but Sophocles can still use him to restate the theme of the divine will that Philoctetes *must*, by whatever means, be brought to Troy.

23. *Theseus' sons*: Acamas and Demophon.

24. *he and Diomedes*: A reference with a subtle allusion to earlier versions of the story. See Preface p. 194.

25. *his cheat of a father*: See note 19.

26. *the famous bow*: The long scene reaches its climax in an extraordinary piece of stage business. We watch spellbound as Philoctetes – in a gesture of gratitude, trust and friendship – allows Neoptolemus to take the sacred bow in his hands. Will the youth use this chance to steal it? No, he hands it back when asked. Neoptolemus has played the part assigned him by Odysseus to perfection, but has at the same time established a warm relationship with Philoctetes as a counterforce that will eventually wreck Odysseus' plan. In 671–3, his moving affirmation of friendship appears sincerely felt and could well be played by an actor as such.

27. *Choral song*: This is the only movement in which the Chorus is left by itself on stage. For an interpretation of its place in the dramatic continuum, and especially of the final stanza, see Preface p. 200.

28. *Ixion*: The myth went that Ixion treacherously murdered his father-in-law. He was purified of his crime by Zeus, but then attempted to seduce Zeus' consort, Hera. For this he was bound on a wheel of fire in the underworld. Ixion's suffering is quoted as a mythological parallel to Philoctetes', though the Chorus sees the latter as essentially innocent (684–5). There is also an implied contrast between Ixion's ingratitude to Zeus and Philoctetes' gratitude to Neoptolemus.

29. *the strong warrior / Heracles*: The famous hero of the twelve

Labours. The reference in 727–8 is to his apotheosis after immolation on Mt Oeta, an event implied in the ending of *Women of
Trachis*.

30. *Scene 3*: The next main movement of the drama brings the
plot to a crisis and holds the situation in suspense. It shows
Neoptolemus' change of heart on witnessing Philoctetes in a
paroxysm of agony, Odysseus' subsequent intervention and,
finally, Philoctetes facing the prospect of death on Lemnos after
being deprived of his bow. It is divided in the middle by a lyric
section for the Chorus, interrupted briefly by Neoptolemus.

31. *four groans*: These introduce a sequence of extraordinary dramatic power. It is often said that the Greek tragedians excluded
representations of violent horror on stage, but this one is deeply
disturbing in the theatre and a special challenge for the actor
playing Philoctetes. It is not, of course, horror for horror's sake.
The effect on Neoptolemus is as important as Philoctetes' agony.

32. *What can I do*: These or similar words are a constant refrain in
the text from now on and epitomize the moral dilemmas implicit
in the drama.

33. *Chorus*: See Preface pp. 200–201. At 833–8 Sophocles makes the
Chorus suggest to Neoptolemus that his task will be completed if
he steals the bow and they all escape while Philoctetes is asleep.
In 839–42 Neoptolemus interrupts the triadic lyric structure with
four lines of dactylic hexameters – the form associated with
heroic epic and also with oracles – to insist that Philoctetes
himself must come.

34. *His is the crown*: At this point, Neoptolemus still seems to be
going along with Odysseus' plan, so that the break-point at 895,
though prepared for earlier on, comes as more of a surprise.

35. *You coves and jutting headlands*: Philoctetes expresses his sense
of betrayal by calling on the only witnesses he can: the mountain
beasts and the inanimate features of the landscape who are his
'neighbours' on Lemnos.

36. *Traitor*: Odysseus' completely unexpected entrance in the middle
of a line is quite unparalleled in Greek tragedy and is something
of a *coup de théâtre*. We can only speculate as to how it was
managed in the ancient theatre (see *Ajax*, Preface note 7, and
notes 2, 69), but the actor must suddenly have seemed to emerge
from a hiding place. 1003 suggests that he was followed on by
two 'extras' in a visible show of the force that is a motif in the
following sequence.

37. *Odysseus*: Odysseus' sudden volte-face is another surprise. How

is it to be interpreted? Is he bluffing in the hope that Philoctetes, faced with the prospect of dying on Lemnos without his bow, will change his mind and come to Troy of his own accord? With the bow in Neoptolemus' hands, Odysseus could have forced Philoctetes to Troy, but he chooses not to. Certainly, in making Odysseus say, 'All right, we have your bow, we don't need *you*,' Sophocles is once again exploiting the uncertainty implicit in the Sleep chorus at 833–64 (and see Preface p. 199). The audience is kept guessing. Indeed, it is the unexpected turn of this speech that makes it dramatically effective. In any case, the poet needs to contrive an exit for Odysseus and Neoptolemus in such a way as to leave the acting area clear for the great lament that follows.

38. *my pious scruples*: Odysseus admits to these, but they take second place to his desire for victory (1052). See notes 4, 5.

39. *Lament*: This long, magnificent movement for Philoctetes and the Chorus shows the hero in the depths of despair in his helplessness and resentment of Odysseus. The style is very much akin to modern opera, as the actor playing Philoctetes in the ancient theatre would have sung his lines, and the effect would have been one of high emotional intensity. The Chorus is no longer used to sympathize but more as a foil, to suggest that Philoctetes can avoid death by going to Troy. In the epode there is an exciting change of tempo to a rapid interchange in a variety of more agitated metres and involving a lot of hasty movement. The sailors respond to Philoctetes' rejection of them by starting to move off, only to be called back, as Philoctetes (I think) faces another spasm of pain in his foot. At the climax, he demands a sword to kill himself, before staggering back inside his cave. There is nothing quite like this passage elsewhere in Sophocles.

40. *Scene 4 . . . followed by Odysseus*: The relationship between Philoctetes and Neoptolemus is restored when the bow is returned, but Neoptolemus is still unable to persuade Philoctetes to go to Troy. The unannounced re-entrance of the two men, apparently in the middle of an angry exchange, is another surprise effect which gives the action, now at an impasse, a fresh kick-start. Lines 1218–21 for the Chorus Leader are omitted in the translation as a certain interpolation: 'I by now would be back at my ship long since, / Philoctetes. However, I see Odysseus coming / Along with the son of Achilles towards us here.' Philoctetes must have gone back into his cave at 1217, in order to re-enter at 1263. The lines must have been added by someone

who was puzzled by the unannounced return of Odysseus and Neoptolemus.

41.  *I can't be bothered with you*: Another striking moment as Odysseus backs down again (see 1054). Discretion has proved the better part of valour.

42.  *Re-enter Odysseus*: Once again he bobs up out of hiding at a critical moment, but vanishes as fast, with some indignity, at 1302 – an astonishingly short appearance for a character in Greek tragedy.

43.  *a cheat like Sisyphus*: See notes 18, 19.

44.  *carefully take it to heart*: Neoptolemus now amplifies the prophecy of Helenus mentioned by the False Merchant (604–13) and confirms what he himself said at 192–200 and 839–42. The new details, which complete the picture, are that Philoctetes' wound will be healed and that Troy is destined to fall to his arrows during the present summer. The appointed time has come.

45.  *Chryse's watcher*: See note 7.

46.  *They'll never ... to Troy*: A crucial line. For Philoctetes' motivation in finally rejecting Neoptolemus' persuasion, see Preface p. 195.

47.  *Off at once, then*: Here the metre suddenly changes to a faster pace in long trochaic tetrameters, divided between the two speakers in antiphonal dialogue and building up to Heracles' entrance at the climax.

48.  *Walk ... shoulder*: Neoptolemus' taking of Philoctetes' weight recalls the earlier image (893–4) when he helped the hero to his feet, to lead him down to the ship. The action there was interrupted by the youth's agony of indecision; now it is on its way to fulfilment.

49.  *Closing scene*: For the significance of this scene in the play's design, see Preface pp. 197, 199.

50.  *Heracles appears above*: Sophocles' presentation of the deified Heracles as a deus ex machina to cut the Gordian knot is another surprise, though one prepared for by the references to the god at 262, 726–8. It also gives a new meaning to the Chorus' remark 'The god will provide for it' at 843. The actor might have been costumed in Heracles' traditional lionskin and carrying a club, perhaps also wearing some form of divine insignia like a wreath (1419). At all events, the sudden epiphany, almost certainly above the ancient stage building (however that was achieved), to arrest the departure of Philoctetes and Neoptolemus, must have been a visually striking and powerful theatrical

moment. It introduces a completely new atmosphere into the drama.

51. *Not yet . . . my commands*: The god opens his address in anapaestic metre, before changing to the normal iambic line at 1418.

52. *A second time*: Heracles refers to the earlier destruction of Troy in the time of King Laomedon.

53. *show piety . . . cannot perish*: Heracles' warning here has often been read as an ironical reference to the tradition that Neoptolemus, during the sack of Troy, committed sacrilege by killing King Priam while he was taking refuge at the altar in the palace shrine. If so, this reminder runs counter to Sophocles' characterization of Neoptolemus as a young man with a fundamental regard for human decencies. Irony here cannot be ruled out, as Sophocles evidently liked to hint at sequels in the tradition which lay outside the scope of his drama. See *Women of Trachis* 1270, *Electra* 1498. However, the emphasis on *eusebeia*, piety, as a supreme value, coming as it does as the climax to Heracles' speech, is surely wider in its significance (see p. 197). The lines were delivered in the ancient theatre by the actor who had also played Odysseus, and they may be linked and contrasted with the passages in Odysseus' role that involve the same concept (85, 1051).

54. *Come now, let me . . . land*: Philoctetes' final speech is in anapaests. For its tone and atmosphere see p. 197.

55. *Lycian Apollo's Fountain*: A curiously anomalous reference to a tradition that Apollo provided Philoctetes with fountains supplying wine and honey. For the title 'Lycian' (= Lycean), see *Electra* note 3.

# Appendix
# The Ancient Greek Theatre and the
# Tragic Poet's Task

To appreciate the great plays composed in Athens in the fifth century BC, it is helpful to know a little about the social context in which they were performed, the kind of theatre for which they were composed, the human resources that the dramatists had at their disposal and, finally, the form and conventions of their artistic genre.

The occasion for which Sophocles wrote his plays was the annual spring festival of Dionysus, the god of wine, ecstasy and impersonation. Three tragic poets were officially selected to compete with one another in composing and mounting three tragedies and a satyr-play in lighter vein for performance on a single day. The festival was a major civic and religious event, extending over five days and attended by a large proportion of the citizen population as well as by visitors from abroad, and the performances of tragedy and comedy excited the liveliest interest.

The plays were planned for performance in a large open space, with tiered seating, accommodating perhaps 15,000 spectators, in a semi-circular or horse-shoe shape round an *orchêstra*, or dancing-floor. This came to be backed in Sophocles' time by a wooden stage building, the *skênê*, which served as a dressing room for the actors and provided a central doorway for their entrances and exits. There are grounds for believing that this was mounted on a lowish platform, which afforded a raised acting area at a level above the *orchêstra*, but linked with it by a line of, perhaps, three or four steps. The action of most Greek plays is set against the background of a house or palace represented by this stage building. At either side, between the *orchêstra* and *skênê*-platform, were two long entrances known as *eisodoi*, indicating approaches from farther afield.

This basic setting could be supplemented by a few technical contrivances. Two of the plays in this volume required the *ekkyklêma*, a low platform wheeled out of the central doorway with tableaux displaying events supposed to have taken place inside the house. Secondly, it was possible for gods to appear above the *skênê*, either on the roof or hoisted up by a kind of crane. Two of our texts also seem to require painted wings in front of the *skênê*, which could allow entrances from the side other than down the longer approaches from the *eisodoi*.

The poet's human resources consisted of a chorus (fifteen in Sophocles' plays), three actors who divided all the solo speaking parts between them, 'mutes' for non-speaking characters, and various attendants as required. All performers were male. The origins of the Chorus can be traced to an earlier cultural form, consisting of hymns sung and danced by local groups in honour of gods and heroes to the accompaniment of a lyre. In Sophocles' day, there were several types of such choral performance, including the 'odes' of Greek tragedy, which were distinctively accompanied not by the lyre but by the *aulos*, a double-reed pipe. The role and art of the solo actor will have owed much to the public performances of Homer's epics, which were established at Athens in the sixth century BC and presented by the so-called 'rhapsodes'. These recitals included substantial speeches for the characters, which must have entailed some degree of impersonation, as well as passages of normal narration. The latter survives as an important element in tragedy, particularly in the 'messenger speech' convention, often used to describe the catastrophe in vivid detail and to guide the audience's response to its wider significance.

Multiple impersonation in the theatre was achieved through changes of costume and mask, which could be made in the *skênê* during the course of the play. Masked drama in a large open-air space no doubt required a bold style of physical movement and gesture, but strong and skilful declamation must have been paramount, and the demands on the actors must have been similar to those on an opera singer today.

Sophocles' extant plays all conform to a standard structural pattern, into which a tragic poet would mould the story he had chosen to dramatize. First came an opening scene for one or more of the solo actors, known as the *prologos*, meaning what was spoken *before* the entry of the Chorus and the performance of their opening, formally choreographed song, termed the *parodos*. The drama was then developed in a succession of scenes called *epeisodia* (literally 'insertions') for the main actors, punctuated by brief contributions from the Chorus Leader. These alternated with songs for the Chorus or movements for soloist and chorus together, known as *kommoi* (laments) or *amoibaia* (exchanges). The *exodos*, or closing scene, brought the tragedy to a conclusion in the exit of all actors and the

Chorus. Whereas the actors in their different roles could come and go, the chorus, once they had entered, normally remained in the *orchêstra* throughout the play.

The Chorus is the aspect of Greek tragedy that probably strikes us as most alien, but it was absolutely integral to the genre. Supported by the music of the *aulos* and choreographed movement, its songs would have been exciting high spots, not dull interruptions. Its function within the drama is very flexible. Sometimes it is actually involved in the plot, at others it adopts a more detached role; its utterances can express the viewpoint of the group it represents in the play or voice insights more appropriate to the poet himself. As a group, it stands for the community and is in that sense a link between the drama and the community of spectators. It could thus be used by the poet to guide the audience's sympathies or to hint at the universal truths that he wished to elicit. In Sophocles, the choral songs are never mere interludes, but part of the dramatic continuum. During the scenes for the solo actors when the Chorus (except for their leader) is silent, the poet could have used them to direct the audiences's attention by their concentration or, occasionally, by a collective reaction.

The tragic medium had another defining factor in the three distinctive 'modes of utterance', corresponding to three types of metre, each involving a different degree of emotional intensity. The whole play was in verse, with the bulk of the lines composed in iambic trimeters, a form closer to the rhythms of ordinary speech than the more artificial dactylic hexameter of the epic recitations. This mode is to be found in all the soloists' long speeches and in the characteristic line-for-line dialogue, known as *stichomythia*. By contrast, the choral 'numbers' and the *amoibaia* (in whole or in part) were composed to be *sung* in so-called 'lyric' metres, associated with dancing and entailing more complex syllabic patterns of rhythm. These were arranged in symmetrical structures of *strophes* ('turns', or choreographic sequences), built out of phrases of varying length called *cola* (limbs). A *strophe* would generally be followed by a metrically identical *antistrophe*, and the pair would sometimes be complemented by another stanza, known as an *epode*, to form a triad. Besides the iambic and lyric modes, there was a third, a kind of halfway house in intensity, composed in the anapaestic (ti-ti-túm, ti-ti-túm) metre. This was often used for the entry of the Chorus, almost always at the end of a play, and at some intermediate points. Delivery of this is sometimes described, rather unhelpfully, as recitative. In all probability it was nearer to speech than to singing (though it may have been accompanied, like the lyric movements, by the *aulos*), but the rhythm was pointed with stronger emphasis than in the more fluid iambic metre of the normal dialogue.

Apart from composing the text, the tragic poet was usually himself the *didaskalos*, the 'teacher' who taught the play to the performers. He was thus also responsible for the music and choreography for his plays, but very little evidence survives for either. As Sophocles must have depended on the skill of his speaking and singing actors, he is also likely to have relied on the artistry of the *aulêtês* – the professional musician who played the pipe in sight of the audience – and of the leading members of his Chorus. The music and dancing for his productions may thus have been the result of expert collaboration in the preparatory stages.

Whatever the uncertainties, it is clear that the plays in this volume are the product of an already well-developed and complex theatrical art, different in many ways from our own, but still accessible in the light of the knowledge that we possess.

# Glossary of Proper Names

The main purpose of this glossary is to serve as a guide to the accentuation and pronunciation of the names of people and places as has been assumed in the translation. This seems needed as practice in these respects varies considerably today, even among classical scholars, and many lines of the verse will sound rhythmically 'false' if the names are stressed in delivery otherwise than shown. Brief information is also supplied against the names to help the reader if required, but references to the texts have not been included. For further details, a classical dictionary or atlas will be best consulted.

The translation follows what was, until recent decades, the normal convention for pronouncing Greek and Latin names in English, and the assumed stressing is indicated by an acute accent on the relevant syllable. In names of two syllables, the stress always falls on the first, which is sometimes artificially lengthened in English (for example, Líchas, where the 'i' in Greek is short). In words of more than two syllables, the stress normally falls on the penultimate syllable where that is quantitatively long in the ancient languages (for example, Philoctétes, not Philóctetes), but on the antepenultimate if the penultimate is short (for example, Neoptólemus).

Rather confusingly, though, conventional English pronunciations do not always correspond to the actual vowel quantities in ancient Greek. For example, in the place-name Nemea, the second 'e' is short, but it is customarily treated as long. We speak of Heracles strangling the Neméan lion and Pindar's Neméan Odes, occasioned by the Neméan Games.

The following guide to the pronunciation of Greek vowel sounds and consonants in English may also be useful:

# VOWELS

| | |
|---|---|
| ae and oe | 'ee' as in 'Aegean', 'Boeotia' |
| ai and ei | 'eye' as in 'Maia', 'Poseidon' |
| au | 'or' as in 'Aulis' |
| eu | 'yoo' as in 'Atreus', 'Odysseus' |
| | (– eus is one syllable, rhyming with 'deuce') |
| y | rhymes with 'nib' when short, as in 'Cybele', |
| | 'eye' when long, as in 'Chryse' |

Vowels conventionally pronounced long in English are marked with a macron and rhyme with the words shown: *a* with 'fate', *e* with 'feet', *i* with 'eye', *o* with 'bone', *u* with 'sue', *y* as above.

A diaeresis printed on the second of two adjoining vowels indicates that these are to be pronounced separately and not as a diphthong – for example, Acheloüs, Deïanira, Spercheüs. 'e' at the end of a name should be sounded, as in 'Persephone', with the exception of 'Crete', a conventional English form like 'Athens' or 'Priam'.

# CONSONANTS

| | |
|---|---|
| c | is soft (like *s*) before *e, ae, oe,* i and *y*; hard like *k* before *a* and *o* |
| ch | is equivalent to a hard *c* |
| sc | is usually *sk* before any vowel |
| g | before *e* and *i* varies between soft, as in 'gentle' and 'giant', and hard, as in 'get' and 'gift' (see under individual names; before *a* and *o* it is always hard) |

**Acháea** a region in the northern Peloponnese
**Acháeans** one of the names for the Greeks at Troy
**Acheloüs** a river in Epirus (northern Greece) and its god
**Ácheron** a river in Hades
**Achílles** son of Peleus, the greatest of the Greek warriors at Troy
**Áeacus** a son of Zeus and king of Aegina; father of Telamon
**Aegéan Sea** [soft *g*] the sea between Greece and Asia Minor
**Aegísthus** [hard *g* perhaps more usual] son of Thyestes; with Clytemnestra, Agamemnon's murderer and ursuper of his throne
**Aénian** from a tribe in southern Thessaly (northern Greece)
**Aetólia** a region in northern Greece

**Agamémnon** son of Atreus and king of Mycenae

**Ájax/Aías** son of Telamon; the greatest Greek warrior at Troy after Achilles

**Alcména** the mother of Heracles by Zeus

**Amphiaráüs** an Argive seer

**Antílochus** a son of Nestor

**Aphrodíte** the goddess of sexual love

**Apóllo** son of Zeus and Leto; god of music, healing, prophecy and the Delphic oracle

**Áres** son of Zeus and Hera; the god of war

**Árgive(s)** [hard g] one of the names for the Greeks at Troy

**Árgos** a city in the Peloponnese, close to Mycenae

**Ártemis** daughter of Zeus and Leto; goddess of wildlife and fertility; a virgin huntress

**Asclépius** son of Apollo and a god of medicine; father of Machaon and Podalirius

**Athéna** (also called Pallas) daughter of Zeus; goddess of wisdom, war and domestic crafts; the patron goddess of Athens and the city-state

**Áthens** the chief city of Attica (northern Greece)

**Átreus** son of Pelops; king of Mycenae

**Atrídae** the sons of Atreus, Agamemnon and Menelaus

**Áulis** a port on the Greek mainland, opposite Euboea

**Boeótia** a region in northern Greece

**Bósporus** the Hellespont, the strait leading from near Troy into the Propontis (Sea of Marmara)

**Cálchas** a Greek prophet

**Calchódon** king of Euboea

**Cenáeum** a promontory in Euboea

**Chíron** a centaur with prophetic powers

**Chrýse** an island near Lemnos and its goddess

**Chrysóthemis** a daughter of Agamemnon and Clytemnestra; Electra's sister

**Clytemnéstra** Agamemnon's wife and murderess

**Créte** an island in the Mediterranean

**Crísa** a place near Delphi with a seaboard plain

**Cýbele** the mother-goddess of Phrygia, invoked as Mountain Mother and Earth; equated with Rhea, mother of Zeus

**Cylléne** a mountain in Arcadia; the birthplace of Pan

**Cýpris** a name for Aphrodite, from her birthplace in Cyprus

**Dánaans** one of the names for the Greeks at Troy

**Dëianíra** daughter of Oeneus and the wife of Heracles

**Délos** one of the Cyclades in the southern Aegean; Apollo's birthplace

**Délphi** a city in Phocis, where the temple and oracle of Apollo were situated

**Diomédes** son of Tydeus, one of the Greek heroes at Troy, close to Odysseus

**Dodóna** a place in Epirus (northern Greece) celebrated for its sacred oaks and oracle of Zeus

**Éléctra** a daughter of Agamemnon and Clytemnestra; sister of Orestes

**Eréchtheus** a mythical king of Athens, regarded as an ancestor of the Athenians

**Eriboéa** wife of Telamon and mother of Ajax

**Erymánthus** a mountain in Arcadia (Peloponnese) where Heracles killed a great boar

**Eubóea** an island off the east coast of Greece

**Eurýsaces** Ajax's young son by Tecmessa

**Eurýstheus** king of Tiryns who set Heracles to perform his twelve Labours

**Eúrytus** king of Oechalia

**Evénus** a river in Aetolia

**Hádes** the underworld and realm of the dead

**Héctor** a son of Priam; the bravest of the Trojan warriors

**Hélen** Menelaüs' wife, for whom the Trojan War was fought

**Hélenus** a son of Priam and a Trojan seer

**Hélios** the sun god

**Hephéastus** the god of fire and metal crafts

**Héra** wife of Zeus; the patron goddess of Argos

**Héracles** son of Zeus and Alcmena; performer of the twelve Labours and other exploits

**Hérmes** son of Zeus and Maia; the messenger of the gods; the god of cunning; escort of the dead to Hades

**Hýllus** a son of Heracles and Deïanira

**Icárian Sea** the sea between Delos and Asia Minor

**Ílium** the principal Greek name for Troy

**Ínachus** a river in Argos

**Íole** daughter of Eurytus, brought home by Heracles as his concubine

**Iphianássa** a daughter of Agamemnon and Clytemnestra

**Iphigenía** [soft *g*] a daughter of Agamemnon and Clytemnestra; sacrificed by her father at Aulis

**Íphitus** son of Eurytus; murdered by Heracles

**Ítys** son of Procne; murdered by his mother

**Ixíon** a treacherous king of Thessaly

**Laértes** father of Odysseus

**Laómedon** a king of Troy, father of Priam

Lémnos an island in the northern Aegean
Léto the goddess mother, by Zeus, of Apollo and Artemis
Líbya a region in North Africa
Líchas Heracles' servant
Lýcéan / Lýcian titles of Apollo
Lýcomédes Neoptolemus' maternal grandfather
Magnésia a region in Thessaly
Máia the goddess mother of Hermes
Mális a region in northern Greece, fronting the Malian gulf and includ-
  ing Trachis and Mt Oeta
Meneláüs son of Atreus; brother of Agamemnon; king of Sparta;
  husband of Helen
Mýcénae a city in the Peloponnese; home of the house of Atreus
Mýrtilus a charioteer, killed by Pelops
Neméa a city in Argolis (Peloponnese), where Heracles killed the
  Nemean lion
Némesis the spirit of revenge
Néssus a centaur, shot and killed by Heracles
Níobe a queen of Thebes, frozen to stone in Lydia (Asia Minor)
Nísa a mythical mountain of the god Dionysus
Odýsseus king of Ithaca; one of the leading Greeks at Troy, renowned
  for his cunning and resourcefulness
Oéneus king of Calydon and father of Deïanira
Oéta the highest mountain in Malis, where Heracles had his funeral
  pyre
Ómphale a queen of Lydia (Asia Minor)
Oréstes son of Agamemnon and Clytemnestra
Pactólus a river in Lydia, on which Sardis, the centre of the worship
  of Cybele, was situated; famous for its alluvial deposits of gold
Pállas another name for Athena
Pan the god of the countryside, the herds and of rustic dancing
Páris a son of Priam; the abductor of Helen
Patróclus a Greek at Troy, Achilles' closest friend
Pélops son of Tantalus and father of Atreus
Peparéthos an island in the Aegean
Perséphone daughter of Demeter and queen of the underworld
Phánoteus a Phocian, ally of Clytemnestra and Aegisthus
Philoctétes son of Poeas; commander of seven ships on the Greek
  expedition to Troy; abandoned on Lemnos
Phócis a region in northern Greece
Phóebus another name for Apollo, meaning 'bright' or 'pure'
Phóenix a Greek at Troy, Achilles' tutor

**Phrýgia** [soft *g*] the region in north-east Asia Minor where Troy was situated

**Pléuron** a town in Aetolia, Deïanira's original home

**Póeas** ruler of the coastal region of Malis; father of Philoctetes

**Póntus** the Black Sea

**Poséidon** the god of the sea and of horsemanship

**Príam** the king of Troy

**Pýlades** son of Strophius, king of Phocis; a close friend of Orestes

**Pýthian Games** the games held at Delphi in honour of Apollo

**Sálamis** an island off Attica, close to Athens; the home of Ajax and Teucer

**Scamánder** one of the rivers at Troy

**Scýros** an island in the Aegean; the home of Neoptolemus

**Sigéum** [hard *g*] a port in the Troad, close to Ilium

**Sísyphus** a legendary king of Corinth and a trickster; said by Odysseus' detractors to have been his father

**Spárta** a city in the southern Peloponnese

**Sperchéüs** a river rising in Mt Oeta and running into the Malian gulf

**Súnium** a promontory on the southern tip of Attica

**Tecméssa** a noble Trojan captive and Ajax's concubine

**Télamon** king of Salamis; father of Ajax and Teucer

**Teléutas** a Trojan, father of Tecmessa

**Téucer** son of Telamon and Ajax's half-brother; an outstanding bowman

**Thermópylae** a town on the Malian Gulf, famous for its hot springs

**Thersítes** a Greek at Troy, a subversive chatterbox

**Théseus** a king of Athens, one of the great Greek heroes

**Théssaly** a region in northern Greece, famous for breeding horses

**Tíryns** a city in the Argolid (Peloponnese), associated with the story of Heracles

**Tráchis** a city in Malis

**Troy** a city in north-west Asia Minor, otherwise known as Ilium

**Týdeus** father of Diomedes

**Zeus** the god of the sky and king of the gods; father of Heracles; ancestor of Ajax

# PENGUIN CLASSICS

## THE FROGS AND OTHER PLAYS
ARISTOPHANES

The Wasps/The Poet and the Women/The Frogs

'This is just a little fable, with a moral: not too highbrow for you, we hope,
but a bit more intelligent than the usual knockabout stuff'

The master of ancient Greek comic drama, Aristophanes combined slapstick,
humour and cheerful vulgarity with acute political observations. In *The Frogs*,
written during the Peloponnesian War, Dionysus descends to the Underworld to
bring back a poet who can help Athens in its darkest hour, and stages a great debate
to help him decide between the traditional wisdom of Aeschylus and the brilliant
modernity of Euripides. The clash of generations and values is also the object of
Aristophanes' satire in *The Wasps*, in which an old-fashioned father and his loose-
living son come to blows and end up in court. And in *The Poet and the Women*,
Euripides, accused of misogyny, persuades a relative to infiltrate an all-women
festival to find out whether revenge is being plotted against him.

David Barrett's introduction discusses the Athenian dramatic contests in which
these plays first appeared, and conventions of Greek comedy – from its poetic
language and the role of the Chorus to casting and costumes.

Translated with an introduction by David Barrett

# PENGUIN CLASSICS

**LYSISTRATA AND OTHER PLAYS**
ARISTOPHANES

Lysistrata/The Acharnians/The Clouds

> 'But he who would provoke me should remember
> That those who rifle wasps' nests will be stung!'

Writing at a time of political and social crisis in Athens, Aristophanes (*c.* 447–*c.* 385 BC) was an eloquent, yet bawdy, challenger to the demagogue and the sophist. In *Lysistrata* and *The Acharnians*, two pleas for an end to the long war between Athens and Sparta, a band of women and a lone peasant respectively defeat the political establishment. The darker comedy of *The Clouds* satirizes Athenian philosophers, Socrates in particular, and reflects the uncertainties of a generation in which all traditional religious and ethical beliefs were being challenged.

For this edition Alan H. Sommerstein has completely revised his translation of these three plays, bringing out the full nuances of Aristophanes' ribald humour and intricate word play, with a new introduction explaining the historical and cultural background to the plays.

Translated with an introduction by Alan H. Sommerstein

# PENGUIN CLASSICS

**HOMERIC HYMNS**

> 'It is of you the poet sings ...
> at the beginning and at the end
> it is always of you'

Written by unknown poets in the sixth and seventh centuries BC, the thirty-three *Homeric Hymns* were recited at festivals to honour the Olympian goddesses and gods and to pray for divine favour or for victory in singing contests. They stand now as works of great poetic force, full of grace and lyricism, and ranging in tone from irony to solemnity, ebullience to grandeur. Recounting significant episodes from mythology, such as the abduction of Persephone by Hades and Hermes' theft of Apollo's cattle, the *Hymns* also provide fascinating insights into cults, rituals and holy sanctuaries, giving us an intriguing view of the ancient Greek relationship between humans and the divine.

This translation of the *Homeric Hymns* is new to Penguin Classics, providing a key text for understanding ancient Greek mythology and religion. The introduction explores their authorship, performance, literary qualities and influence on later writers.

'The purest expressions of ancient Greek religion we possess ... Jules Cashford is attuned to the poetry of the Hymns' Nigel Spivey, University of Cambridge

A new translation by Jules Cashford with an introduction by Nicholas Richardson

# PENGUIN CLASSICS

---

**MEDEA AND OTHER PLAYS**
EURIPIDES

Medea/Alcestis/The Children of Heracles/Hippolytus

'That proud, impassioned soul,
so ungovernable now that she has felt the sting of injustice'

*Medea*, in which a spurned woman takes revenge upon her lover by killing her children, is one of the most shocking and horrific of all the Greek tragedies. Dominating the play is Medea herself, a towering and powerful figure who demonstrates Euripides' unusual willingness to give voice to a woman's case. *Alcestis*, a tragicomedy, is based on a magical myth in which Death is overcome, and *The Children of Heracles* examines the conflict between might and right, while *Hippolytus* deals with self-destructive integrity and moral dilemmas. These plays show Euripides transforming the awesome figures of Greek mythology into recognizable, fallible human beings.

John Davie's accessible prose translation is accompanied by a general introduction and individual prefaces to each play.

'John Davie's translations are outstanding ... the tone throughout is refreshingly modern yet dignified' William Allan, *Classical Review*

Previously published as *Alcestis and Other Plays*.

Translated by John Davie, with an introduction and notes by Richard Rutherford

read more

# PENGUIN CLASSICS

**THE LAST DAYS OF SOCRATES**
PLATO

Euthyphro/The Apology/Crito/Phaedo

'Nothing can harm a good man either in life or after death'

The trial and condemnation of Socrates on charges of heresy and corrupting young minds is a defining moment in the history of Classical Athens. In tracing these events through four dialogues, Plato also developed his own philosophy, based on Socrates' manifesto for a life guided by self-responsibility. *Euthyphro* finds Socrates outside the court-house, debating the nature of piety, while *The Apology* is his robust rebuttal of the charges of impiety and a defence of the philosopher's life. In the *Crito*, while awaiting execution in prison, Socrates counters the arguments of friends urging him to escape. Finally, in the *Phaedo*, he is shown calmly confident in the face of death, skilfully arguing the case for the immortality of the soul.

Hugh Tredennick's landmark 1954 translation has been revised by Harold Tarrant, reflecting changes in Platonic studies, with an introduction and expanded introductions to each of the four dialogues.

Translated by Hugh Tredennick and Harold Tarrant with an introduction and notes by Harold Tarrant

# PENGUIN CLASSICS

---

**THE HISTORY OF THE DECLINE & FALL OF THE ROMAN EMPIRE**
EDWARD GIBBON

> 'Instead of inquiring why the Roman empire was destroyed,
> we should rather be surprised that it had subsisted so long'

Edward Gibbon's *Decline and Fall of the Roman Empire* compresses thirteen
turbulent centuries into an epic narrative shot through with insight, irony and
incisive character analysis. Sceptical about Christianity, sympathetic to the
barbarian invaders and the Byzantine Empire, constantly aware of how political
leaders often achieve the exact opposite of what they intend, Gibbon was alert both
to the broad pattern of events and to significant revealing details. The first of its
six volumes, published in 1776, was attacked for its enlightened views on politics,
sexuality and religion, yet it was an immediate bestseller and widely acclaimed
for the elegance of its prose. Gripping, powerfully intelligent and wonderfully
entertaining, it is among the greatest works of history in the English language and
a literary masterpiece of its age.

This abridgement is based on David Womersley's definitive three-volume Penguin
Classics edition of *Decline and Fall of the Roman Empire*. Complete chapters
from each volume, linked by extended bridging passages, vividly capture the style,
argument and structure of the whole work.

Edited and abridged by David Womersley

---

# PENGUIN CLASSICS

**CITY OF GOD**
ST AUGUSTINE

> 'The Heavenly City outshines Rome, beyond comparison.
> There, instead of victory, is truth; instead of rank, holiness'

St Augustine, bishop of Hippo, was one of the central figures in the history of Christianity, and *City of God* is one of his greatest theological works. Written as an eloquent defence of the faith at a time when the Roman Empire was on the brink of collapse, it examines the ancient pagan religions of Rome, the arguments of the Greek philosophers and the revelations of the Bible. Pointing the way forward to a citizenship that transcends the best political experiences of the world and offers citizenship that will last for eternity, *City of God* is one of the most influential documents in the development of Christianity.

This edition contains a new introduction that examines the text in the light of contemporary Greek and Roman thought and political change, and demonstrates the religious and literary influences on St Augustine and his significance as a Christian thinker. There is also a chronology and bibliography.

Translated with notes by Henry Bettenson with an introduction by Gill Evans

# PENGUIN CLASSICS

## THE CAMPAIGNS OF ALEXANDER
### ARRIAN

'His passion was for glory only, and in that he was insatiable'

Although written over four hundred years after Alexander's death, Arrian's *Campaigns of Alexander* is the most reliable account of the man and his achievements we have. Arrian's own experience as a military commander gave him unique insights into the life of the world's greatest conqueror. He tells of Alexander's violent suppression of the Theban rebellion, his total defeat of Persia, and his campaigns through Egypt, India and Babylon – establishing new cities and destroying others in his path. While Alexander emerges from this record as an unparalleled and charismatic leader, Arrian succeeds brilliantly in creating an objective and fully rounded portrait of a man of boundless ambition, who was exposed to the temptations of power and worshipped as a god in his own lifetime.

Aubrey de Sélincourt's vivid translation is accompanied by J. R. Hamilton's introduction, which discusses Arrian's life and times, his synthesis of other classical sources and the composition of Alexander's army. This edition also includes maps, a list for further reading and a detailed index.

Translated by Aubrey de Sélincourt
Revised, with a new introduction and notes by J. R. Hamilton

# PENGUIN CLASSICS

## THE CONQUEST OF GAUL
### CAESAR

'The enemy were overpowered and took to flight.
The Romans pursued as far as their strength enabled them to run'

Between 58 and 50 BC Julius Caesar conquered most of the area now covered by
France, Belgium and Switzerland, and invaded Britain twice, and *The Conquest
of Gaul* is his record of these campaigns. Caesar's narrative offers insights into
his military strategy and paints a fascinating picture of his encounters with the
inhabitants of Gaul and Britain, as well as lively portraits of the rebel leader
Vercingetorix and other Gallic chieftains. *The Conquest of Gaul* can also be read
as a piece of political propaganda, as Caesar sets down his version of events for the
Roman public, knowing he faces civil war on his return to Rome.

Revised and updated by Jane Gardner, S. A. Handford's translation brings Caesar's
lucid and exciting account to life for modern readers. This volume includes a
glossary of persons and places, maps, appendices and suggestions for further reading.

Translated by S. A. Handford
Revised with a new introduction by Jane F. Gardner

# PENGUIN CLASSICS

---

## THE ANNALS OF IMPERIAL ROME
TACITUS

'Nero was already corrupted by every lust, natural and unnatural'

*The Annals of Imperial Rome* recount the major historical events from the years shortly before the death of Augustus to the death of Nero in AD 68. With clarity and vivid intensity Tacitus describes the reign of terror under the corrupt Tiberius, the great fire of Rome during the time of Nero and the wars, poisonings, scandals, conspiracies and murders that were part of imperial life. Despite his claim that the *Annals* were written objectively, Tacitus' account is sharply critical of the emperors' excesses and fearful for the future of imperial Rome, while also filled with a longing for its past glories.

Michael Grant's fine translation captures the moral tone, astringent wit and stylish vigour of the original. His introduction discusses the life and works of Tacitus and the historical context of the *Annals*. This edition also contains a key to place names and technical terms, maps, tables and suggestions for further reading.

Translated with an introduction by Michael Grant

# Penguin Classics

---

**THE AGRICOLA** *AND* **THE GERMANIA**
TACITUS

> 'Happy indeed were you, Agricola,
> not only in your glorious life but in your timely death'

*The Agricola* is both a portrait of Julius Agricola – the most famous governor of Roman Britain and Tacitus' well-loved and respected father-in-law – and the first detailed account of Britain that has come down to us. It offers fascinating descriptions of the geography, climate and peoples of the country, and a succinct account of the early stages of the Roman occupation, nearly fatally undermined by Boudicca's revolt in AD 61 but consolidated by campaigns that took Agricola as far as Anglesey and northern Scotland. The warlike German tribes are the focus of Tacitus' attention in *The Germania*, which, like *The Agricola*, often compares the behaviour of 'barbarian' peoples favourably with the decadence and corruption of Imperial Rome.

Harold Mattingly's translation brings Tacitus' extravagant imagination and incisive wit vividly to life. In his introduction, he examines Tacitus' life and literary career, the governorship of Agricola, and the political background of Rome's rapidly expanding Empire. This edition also includes a select bibliography, and maps of Roman Britain and Germany.

Translated with an introduction by H. Mattingly
Translation revised by S. A. Handford

---

# PENGUIN CLASSICS

**THE LETTERS OF THE YOUNGER PLINY**

> 'Of course these details are not important enough for history …
> you have only yourself to blame for asking for them'

A prominent lawyer and administrator, Pliny (*c.* AD 61–113) was also a prolific
letter-writer, who numbered among his correspondents such eminent figures as
Tacitus, Suetonius and the Emperor Trajan, as well as a wide circle of friends and
family. His lively and very personal letters address an astonishing range of topics,
from a deeply moving account of his uncle's death in the eruption that engulfed
Pompeii and observations on the early Christians – 'a desperate sort of cult carried
to extravagant lengths' – to descriptions of everyday life in Rome, with its scandals
and court cases, and of his own life in the country. Providing a series of fascinating
views of imperial Rome, his letters also offer one of the fullest self-portraits to
survive from classical times.

Betty Radice's definitive edition was the first complete modern translation
of Pliny's letters. In her introduction, she examines the shrewd, tolerant and
occasionally pompous man who emerges from these.

Translated with an introduction by Betty Radice

# THE STORY OF PENGUIN CLASSICS

**Before 1946** ... 'Classics' are mainly the domain of academics and students; readable editions for everyone else are almost unheard of. This all changes when a little-known classicist, E. V. Rieu, presents Penguin founder Allen Lane with the translation of Homer's *Odyssey* that he has been working on in his spare time.

**1946** Penguin Classics debuts with *The Odyssey*, which promptly sells three million copies. Suddenly, classics are no longer for the privileged few.

**1950s** Rieu, now series editor, turns to professional writers for the best modern, readable translations, including Dorothy L. Sayers's *Inferno* and Robert Graves's unexpurgated *Twelve Caesars*.

**1960s** The Classics are given the distinctive black covers that have remained a constant throughout the life of the series. Rieu retires in 1964, hailing the Penguin Classics list as 'the greatest educative force of the twentieth century.'

**1970s** A new generation of translators swells the Penguin Classics ranks, introducing readers of English to classics of world literature from more than twenty languages. The list grows to encompass more history, philosophy, science, religion and politics.

**1980s** The Penguin American Library launches with titles such as *Uncle Tom's Cabin*, and joins forces with Penguin Classics to provide the most comprehensive library of world literature available from any paperback publisher.

**1990s** The launch of Penguin Audiobooks brings the classics to a listening audience for the first time, and in 1999 the worldwide launch of the Penguin Classics website extends their reach to the global online community.

**The 21st Century** Penguin Classics are completely redesigned for the first time in nearly twenty years. This world-famous series now consists of more than 1300 titles, making the widest range of the best books ever written available to millions – and constantly redefining what makes a 'classic'.

The Odyssey continues ...

*The best books ever written*

PENGUIN 🐧 CLASSICS

SINCE 1946

Find out more at www.penguinclassics.com